+ for intro chapters — cf 4-5 — assumptions + justification
of method ((method here

Chicano Narrative

+ 5 + add
en ch
nrda

biblio - aaración in Fall cult crit + incl

235 chicano crit in a social context
230 mc kemre   229 Lmas
236 valenzuela
49 hist/surveys chicano lit
132 + cult studies?

+ 263 — 1145
marxist
refgs

+ de acuña
1981

223
↓
calderón
in NM
Romance
on X pt
Cde Bt

27 + for MTSI hybrid unblontk genre —
insist that genre develops as cultural artic/response
to political events

32 I disagree, in intro, w/ his assumption
@ nation forms

*+112 —
① e function of
curandera
ideol function
w/ respect to
Anglo audience —
suture of
class + race
conflict,
Hispano y
Indio
+ antidote to
<Anglo> MMA

+226 gramsci
for chapters 1 + 2

* 39 + critique S's suggestion chicana y mexicana lit

* 42 - + for workbook —
Suddivar in considering regard cult

** 72 the politicizing text —
historizes the private domain

*154 for
intro chapter —
cite + critique

* 165 + for mdunives —
(1) note that chicanos too may eulogize
la curandera as última

*155 - + use to
suggest om ① e
one subversive
writing - +
crit sugs from
foucault n xparkson
for htery-minded way
they foreclose
avenue for dissent —
cult vs one power?

Ramón Saldívar

Chicano Narrative
The Dialectics of Difference

The University of Wisconsin Press

The University of Wisconsin Press
114 North Murray Street
Madison, Wisconsin 53715

3 Henrietta Street
London WC2E 8LU, England

5   4   3   2   1

Printed in the United States of America

Library of Congress Cataloging-in-Publication Data
Saldívar, Ramón.
   Chicano narrative : the dialectics of difference / Ramón Saldívar.
   262 pp.   cm.—(The Wisconsin project on American writers)
   Includes bibliographical references.
   1. American literature—Mexican American authors—History and
criticism—Theory, etc.   2. American literature—Mexican American
authors—History and criticism.   3. Mexican Americans—Intellectual
life.   4. Mexican Americans in literature.   5. Narration (Rhetoric)
I. Title.   II. Series.
PS153.M4S24   1990
810.9'6872—dc20   89-40535
ISBN 0-299-12470-3   CIP
ISBN 0-299-12474-6 (pbk.)

To my beloved son, David

Contents

ILLUSTRATIONS / ix

ACKNOWLEDGMENTS / xi

INTRODUCTION / 3

1
Race, Class, and Gender in the Southwest: Foundations of an American Resistance Literature and Its Literary History / 10

2
The Folk Base of Chicano Narrative: Américo Paredes' *With His Pistol in His Hand* and the *Corrido* Tradition / 26

3
Paredes, Villarreal, and the Dialectics of History / 47

4
Beyond Good and Evil: Utopian Dialectics in Tomás Rivera and Oscar Zeta Acosta / 74

5
Romance, the Fantastic, and the Representation of History in Rudolfo A. Anaya and Ron Arias / 103

6
Rolando Hinojosa's *Korean Love Songs* and the *Klail City Death Trip*: A Border Ballad and Its Heroes / 132

7
Ideologies of the Self: Chicano Autobiography / 154

8
The Dialectics of Subjectivity: Gender and Difference in Isabella
Ríos, Sandra Cisneros, and Cherríe Moraga / 171

Conclusion: The Reconstruction of American Literary
History / 204

WORKS CITED / 221

INDEX / 239

Illustrations

1. Mexican American laborers and their children, 1915 / 43
2. Texas Rangers displaying Mexican American Insurrectionists killed during the raid on Las Norias, October 8, 1915 / 44
3. The Olmito train derailment, October 18, 1915 / 45
4. Chicano World War II veterans attending reburial services in Corpus Christi, Texas, April 1949 /46
5. Migrant farmworkers and hiring agents at an informal employment agency, April 1949 / 99
6. A farm laborer and his grandchild, May 1949 / 100
7. Migrant farm laboring families, May 1949 / 101
8. A sign enforcing the Jim Crow laws and segregation of "Mexicans" and "Spanish" in San Antonio, Texas, June 1949 / 102
9. Schematic map from *Estampas del valle* / 138
10. A Chicana worker at "La Malinche" tortilla factory in Corpus Christi, Texas, May 1949 / 148
11. A typical low-cost housing unit in Corpus Christi, Texas, May 1949 / 149
12. A Mexican American child in the courtyard of an urban working-class housing unit, May 1949 / 150
13. A Chicana schoolgirl in San Angelo, Texas, May 1949 / 151
14. A school-age boy in San Angelo, Texas, May 1949 / 152
15. Chicano laborer and his daughter in San Angelo, Texas, May 1949 / 153
16. The cover illustration of Ernesto Galarza's *Barrio Boy* / 166
17. Mother and newborn child beside a family shrine to the Virgin of Guadalupe in Corpus Christi, Texas, April 1949 / 200
18. Grandmother and child at a family shrine, April 1949 / 201
19. Wistful child of the Chicano urban working class, April 1949 / 202
20. Chicana photographed in Stockdale, Texas, June 1949 / 203

Acknowledgments

I wish to mention with gratitude the people who have read and helped me with various drafts of this book: Barbara Harlow and Gayatri Chakravorty Spivak, for their example of committed scholarship; José David Saldívar, Héctor Calderón, and Sonia Saldívar-Hull, for their many helpful criticisms and suggestions; Warwick Wadlington and Evan Carton for their insightful comments on early drafts. Members of the Ethnic & Third World Studies group of the Texas English Department provided a community of support. Students in my Fall 1988 graduate seminar on Chicano Narrative actively participated in the final construction of my thinking. Friends, colleagues, and students at Yale, UCLA, UC Davis, UC Santa Barbara, and Princeton, heard and commented helpfully on early versions of some of the chapters. Portions of some chapters appeared in *MELUS*, *Critical Exchange*, *Revista Chicano-Riqueña*, and *Diacritics*. I am grateful to all of these people for their support and to the editors and publishers concerned for permission to reprint this material.

The main part of the book was written in 1985–86, during a research leave of absence from The University of Texas at Austin. The John Simon Guggenheim Memorial Foundation and the University Research Institute of The University of Texas at Austin supported my research and writing with generous grants. Project Quest at the University of Texas provided computer equipment and advice. I extend my gratitude to these institutions and to William S. Livingston, Dean of the Graduate School, for their assistance.

The encouragement and love of friends and family allowed me to press on at times when, to paraphrase Bruce Springsteen, I was sick and tired of sitting here trying to write this book. Mitzi VanSant helped me research, select, and organize the illustrations and then came up with the idea for the jacket cover design. She has also shown me the meaning of what Cherríe Moraga writes: that we can find "familia among friends where blood ties are formed through suffering and celebration shared." I dedicate this book with love to my familia, especially, to my son, David.

Chicano Narrative

Introduction

In struggling for the retention of cultural integrity and an organic sense of unity, the Mexican American communities of the American Southwest in the nineteenth and twentieth centuries have produced a significant body of literary texts. This literature presents a serious challenge to the established ways of defining the canons of both the theory and the practice of literature and its criticism as these have developed in the Anglo-American world. *Chicano Narrative: The Dialectics of Difference* is an examination of representative aspects of Mexican American narrative forms, including the novel, short story, narrative verse, and autobiography, that have to date been largely excluded from the canon of North American literature, not only in traditional departments of literature (English, American Studies, Spanish), but even in the field of comparative literature, which claims to provide an opportunity for the study of cross-cultural and bilingual literary interactions.

The study seeks also to test the usefulness of new developments in literary theory such as structuralism, poststructuralism, deconstruction, psychoanalysis, Marxist criticism, feminist theory, and other nontraditional forms of literary analysis for analyzing the literary products of a segment of contemporary American society that in many respects continues to define itself in opposition and resistance to mainstream social, historical, economic, and cultural modalities. Is it possible to use deconstruction politically, for example, as Michael Ryan has claimed that we may, to understand the relationship between grammatological, sociopolitical, and cultural discursive structures in literary works that do not speak from within the dominant tradition? Can theories of mass culture developed by the Frankfurt School and extended by Stuart Hall and other scholars as "cultural studies" help us to understand the unvoiced, unread literature of Mexican American men and women in the United States?

3

Are the theoretical paradigms of European and American scholars working within the parameters of hegemonic cultural and aesthetic traditions appropriate for an understanding of the literary productions of a culture at the margin of both the Anglo-American and Latin American cultural worlds? Does Fredric Jameson's notion of a "political unconscious" functioning through socially symbolic acts have strategic value for understanding the oppositional work of Chicano texts?

As these questions suggest, we will be concerned with the social and ideological context of contemporary Chicano fiction, attempting to map out, on the basis of selected texts, its "imaginative geography" (Said 1979, 59), the symbolic features of its constructions of meaning. The social world represented in the writings of Chicano men and women is an emphatically political one. And yet, the very act of representation urges a distinctive kind of political consciousness upon us through a deliberately constructed set of imaginary and symbolic productions. We will be concerned here with understanding how these imaginary and symbolic productions serve both a unifying communal function as well as an oppositional and differentiating end. And we will see how Chicano narrative, like African American, feminist, lesbian, Third World, and other radical writings in general, takes for its point of departure, "the right of formerly un- or mis-represented human groups to speak for and represent themselves in domains defined politically and intellectually as normally excluding them" (Said 1979, 91).

From the perspective of the dominant culture, the peoples of the American West and Southwest, Native American and Mexican American alike, helped define Anglo America by serving as its contrasting personality, idea, and experience. Yet from the other perspective, this contrastive function has had, paradoxically, both debilitating and potentially liberating effects. It has been debilitating when as the contrastive other of the dominant culture, Chicano culture has become for Anglos subordinate in all respects. It has been potentially liberating when as the contrastive other Chicano culture has produced for Chicanos a consistent and highly articulated set of oppositions to the dominant cultural system surrounding it. Our concern with the imaginary and symbolic functions of narratives by Chicano men and women as they represent this contrastive situation is not merely aesthetic. I hope to show how these imaginary and symbolic functions are an integral part of *material* Chicano history and society.

Concerned with the practical understanding of unjustly ignored texts, with literary history, and with literary theory, the study uses narrative analysis, rhetoric, semiotics, and ideology as the basic co-ordinates of an interpretive model of contemporary Chicano narrative. Chicano literature today forms one of the most provocative but least-known segments of American literature. It is a corpus of texts that explicitly demands the interpretive framework I have fashioned because of its foregrounding of sociopolitical themes.

I argue that the assumed homology between narrative language and narrative representations is not one that we as readers of post-modern texts can accept. The language of narrative, especially that of Chicano narrative in its place of difference from and resistance to American cultural norms, can best be grasped as a strategy to enable readers to understand their real conditions of existence in postindustrial twentieth-century America.

This narrative strategy for demystifying the relations between minority cultures and the dominant culture is the process I term "the dialectics of difference" of Chicano literature. In the course of my discussion, I will show how the dialectical form of narratives by Chicano men and women is an authentic way of grappling with a reality that seems always to transcend representation, a reality into which the subject of the narrative's action seeks to enter, all the while learning the lesson of its own ideological closure, and of history's resistance to the symbolic structures in which subjectivity itself is formed. For Chicano narrative, *history* is the subtext that we must recover because history itself is the subject of its discourse. History cannot be conceived as the mere "background" or "context" for this literature; rather, history turns out to be the decisive determinant of the form and content of the literature.

In the decades since its contemporary renaissance, Chicano narrative has contributed to a general reassessment of the cultural and historical situation of Mexican Americans in the American West and Southwest. It has provided a mediated truth about a culturally determinate people in a historically determinate context. The truth of the real world that Chicanos experience has thus been made to inhabit literature. Readers and critics have assumed that to know this cultural truth one has simply to read the literature of that experience. In reading, we are supposed to be able to penetrate the superficialities that both separate us from the truth and keep us from bringing it to light. Contemporary Chicano narrative calls this assumption about the transparency of reading into question. In effect, it calls upon its readers to dissipate its external features and its formal patterns, to eradicate them in order that readers might perceive the substantial

ground on which ideological representations of truth are built. Its
function is thus different from what readers normally expect from
literary texts. Not content with mirroring a problematic real world of
social hardship and economic deprivation, Chicano narratives seek
systematically to uncover the underlying structures by which real
men and women may either perpetuate or reformulate that reality.

Today, three decades after the publication of Américo Paredes'
originary study of the Texas Mexican border ballad, *With His Pistol in His Hand* (1958), and of José Antonio Villarreal's novel *Pocho*
(1959), it is necessary to evaluate fully, for the first time, the course
of contemporary Chicano narrative. We can no longer continue to
ignore this body of works or to read it, when it has been read, as a
"regional" or a "marginal" literature. It is time to see Chicano narrative as something more than a simple mirror of the life and folklore
of a heretofore invisible segment of American society.

I argue that the narratives of Chicano men and women are predominantly critical and ideological. This does not mean that they
simply represent a given set of doctrines or dogmas. Rather, it means
that as oppositional ideological forms Chicano narratives signify the
imaginary ways in which historical men and women live out their
lives in a class society, and how the values, concepts, and ideas pur-
veyed by the mainstream, hegemonic American culture that tie them
to their social functions seek to prevent them from attaining a true
knowledge of society as a whole. My study shows how Chicano narratives, individually as texts and together as a genre, confront and
circumscribe the limiting ideologies imposed upon them (and sometimes created from within Mexican American culture itself) and how
they have in complex ways determined the horizons within which
their history has emerged.

The task of Chicano narrative is thus not simply to illustrate, represent, or translate a particular exotic reality, nor even a certain conception of reality—this epistemological theory of reflection is theo-
retically sterile. Instead, it serves to realize the agency of thematic
figures in the process of demystifying the old world and producing
a new one. The developments in literary form represented in the
works of such authors as Américo Paredes, José Antonio Villarreal,
Tomás Rivera, Oscar Zeta Acosta, Rudolfo Anaya, Rolando Hinojosa, Ernesto Galarza, Isabella Ríos, Sandra Cisneros, and Cherríe
Moraga show the various responses of Chicano writers to the collective ideological needs of the Mexican people of the United States
in their struggle for social and economic justice. As literature, these
narratives embody new ways of perceiving social reality and signifi-

cant changes in ideology. As resistant ideological forces in their own right, their function is to shape modes of perception in order to effect new ways of interpreting social reality and to produce in turn a general social, spiritual, and literary revaluation of values. Thematically, aesthetically, conceptually, and politically, the works of these women and men constitute no single literary *tradition* but they do manifest a common idea of the *function* of literature as a result of the specific historical, social, and economic experience that these authors have been obliged to share.

Rather than passively reproducing images of reality, the task of contemporary Chicano narrative is to deflect, deform, and thus transform reality by revealing the dialectical structures that form the base of human experience. In opting for open over closed forms, for conflict over resolution and synthesis, in proclaiming its very difference, the function of Chicano narrative is thus to produce creative structures of knowledge to allow its readers to see, to feel, and to understand their social reality.

Testing the value of recent critical work on the subject, my study outlines the possibility of a new way of viewing Chicano narrative structures. The book presents readings of the works of selected Chicano and Chicana writers to illuminate what an interdisciplinary, poststructuralist critical methodology guided by ideological analysis might teach us about the special features of Chicano narrative works. Those literary works, in turn, help us to understand the viability and the limitations of the literary theories that we use to read works of literature. The analysis shows how the thematics of the individual works themselves provide readers with heterogeneous frameworks by which the still-unwritten literary histories of Chicano literature might be elaborated. I argue that from such literary histories might emerge a truly "new literary history" and "new criticism" of American culture, in the form of rigorously self-critical theories of Chicano narrative forms in their American context.

The subversive edge of each of the texts I examine effects destruction. But this destruction always implies the reconstruction of what has been undone at the site of its former presence. This reconstruction is not simply the ordering of the chaos of reality. The ideology of difference of Chicano narrative emerges from a more complex unity of at least two formal elements: its paradoxical impulse toward revolutionary deconstruction and toward the production of meaning. Theories of Chicano narrative must be able to handle this duality. The general notion of "difference" I propose allows us to consider this dual tendency of Chicano narrative faithfully, for it uses a dialectical conception that determines the semantic space of Chicano literature as that intersection of the cultural-historical reality appropriated by the text to produce itself, and of the aesthetic reality produced by the text. Chicano narrative is thus not so much the expression of this ideology of difference as it is a production of that ideology.

To be true to the principles of the text and the world that conditions it, criticism must take the text's dialectical pattern as its analytical model. We must remember, moreover, that a true dialectic necessarily involves us in negation. In a relationship between opposed terms, one annuls the other and lifts it up into a higher sphere of existence: development through opposition and conflict—neither Mexican, nor American, nor yet a naive Mexican American, but something else. This something else is the difference of contemporary Chicano narrative, a difference not of kind, but of dialectical position; a difference that allows it to retain its special relation both to its Mexican and American contexts, while also letting it be marked by a relation to its own still-unconditioned future. I do not intend to reduce the differences among Chicano narratives. I do intend to outline various theoretical frameworks around which practical literary histories and criticisms of the difference of Chicano narrative, understood within its Anglo and Latin American contexts, might be articulated.

As genealogies of significant intertextual relationships, such histories would not provide a tool for revealing immediate and essential truths, for the texts tend to show that such truths are never unambiguously present. They would provide us rather with frameworks for analysis, which, while remaining alive to the social and historical forces present in the artistic word, would allow the word to free itself from the enslaving myth of absolute and universal truths that often turn out to be, as Nietzsche argued in *On the Genealogy of Morals*, institutionalized expressions of a will to power. They would place "truth" itself in brackets and consider analysis to be a dynamic process in historical time and cultural space, rather than a static event. And such revisionary theories would permit, perhaps for the first time, the development of an authentically reconstructed American literary history.

My study is to the best of my knowledge the first comprehensive analysis of contemporary Chicano narrative from a theoretical perspective. I show that the narrative writings of Chicano women and men must be understood as different from and in resistance to traditional American literature, yet must also be understood in their American context, for they take their oppositional stance deliberately, in order to offer readers a reformulation of historical reality and contemporary culture that is more consistent with the way reality and culture are actually experienced than do other representations. I show that Chicano narrative is not content with merely reproducing the world but also attempts to reveal the ideological structures by which we continue to create that world. In the process of thus defining Chicano narrative, I hope to offer also a way of understanding a truly American literature, one that includes the voices of Mexican American men and women as significant figures in the socioeconomic and cultural history of the Americas.

1
Race, Class, and Gender in the Southwest

Foundations of an American Resistance Literature and Its Literary History

Narrative analysis, dialectics, and ideology are the coordinates within which I would like to suggest an interpretive model for Chicano narrative. Chicano literature is today one of the most striking, ambiguous, and least-known bodies of fiction produced in the United States. It is also a corpus of texts that explicitly demands the interpretive framework outlined in the preceding chapter by its continual foregrounding of political, economic, and racial oppression and by its unique practice of style. Many of us trained in the American academy are not, however, in the habit of reading in the "margins" of American literature and since for better or worse it is to the margins that Chicano literature has been consigned, a general introduction to the cultural and historical context of this margin is in order before proceeding to a detailed examination of texts. Raymond Williams has argued that

at any time, forms of alternative or directly oppositional politics and culture exist as significant elements in the society. We [should] explore their conditions and their limits, but their active presence is decisive, not only because they have to be included in any historical . . . analysis, but as forms which have had significant effect on the hegemonic process itself. That is to say, alternative political and cultural emphases, and the many forms of opposition and struggle, are important not only in themselves but as indicative features of what the hegemonic process has in practice had to control. (1977, 113)

I begin by sketching a historical profile of Mexican Americans as an ethnic working-class minority and of their art as an example of one of the most independent cultural and literary "forms of opposition and struggle" that the dominant culture of the United States

10

has attempted to control, neutralize, and integrate. My concern here is not so much to justify the narratives of Chicano women and men as to locate those works in the history of which they speak and from which context they arise.

"The Mexico-Texan," a narrative poem written by Américo Paredes in 1935, tells in brief the history of the Chicano in the Southwest:

> The Mexico-Texan he's one fonny man
> Who leeves in the region that's north of the Gran',
> Of Mexican father he born in these part,
> And sometimes he rues it dip down in he's heart.
> For the Mexico-Texan he no gotta lan',
> He stomped on the neck on both sides of the Gran',
> The dam gringo lingo he no cannot spik,
> It twisters the tong and it make you fill sick.
> A cit'zen of Texas they say that he ees,
> But then, why they call him the Mexican Grease?
> Soft talk and hard action, he can't understan',
> The Mexico-Texan he no gotta lan'. . . .
>
> Except for a few with their cunning and craft
> He count just as much as a nought to the laft,
> And they say everywhere, "He's a burden and drag,
> He no gotta country, he no gotta flag."
> He no gotta voice, all he got is the han'
> To work like the burro; he no gotta lan'. . . .[1]

1. Américo Paredes, "The Mexico-Texan," from an unpublished manuscript, dated October 17, 1935. In the notes to the manuscript, Paredes explains that "a first version was done in Spring, 1934, when I was a senior in high school. Composed while walking the 21 blocks home from school one afternoon and written down—with revisions —shortly afterward. This second, written version became current in manuscript form in south Texas, was used in political campaigns, was reprinted a few times as anonymous, and entered oral tradition locally. Collected in Brownsville as 'folk poetry' in the 1960s by a student of one of my colleagues, Roger D. Abrahams. When it began to circulate in manuscript, writer Hart Stilwell criticized the language as sounding too much like the stage 'Italian' dialect of the time. I made revisions and it is this third version, done in 1935, that appears here." Quoted by permission of the author. In a conversation and a following letter of February 14–15, 1989, Paredes recounted to me the full history of the poem. Paredes' brother had circulated an early unattributed manuscript version of the poem at a political rally in Brownsville, Texas, in 1934. As Paredes notes, the poem quickly caught on as an anonymous folk expression of popular resistance. Two recent books quote "The Mexico-Texan" in that spirit: Guadalupe San Miguel, Jr., uses it as an epigraph for the first chapter of his *"Let All of Them Take Heed"* (1987). According to Paredes, this "is an altered version of the "Italian-

After the Mexican-American War of 1848, the United States added a vast territory to its possessions and an entire new people that, as Paredes describes it, were now without land, without a country, and without a voice, but who were put to work to create the Southwest and West. In addition to the various Native American groups that inhabited the region, the area contained many communities, some dating back to the early eighteenth century, of these former Mexican citizens who were ethnically part Native American, Spanish, and African (Barrera 1979, 1). Separated by vast distances as well as by internal class differences, these communities nevertheless shared a common language, Spanish, a common identity, as *mexicanos*, and a common fate of racial, political, and economic oppression within the new American civil framework.

Responding in different times and places to a variety of designations, the people of these communities have continued to express this historical differential unity. Mexican, Latin American, Spanish American, Mexican American, Hispano, Latino, and most recently, Chicano, are all terms that have been used to designate the group. Each of the terms has a different psychological, historical, and political connotation that sets it apart from the others: Mexicano, has been the preferred term in South Texas and along the border regions, for example; Hispano and Spanish American have been preferred in northern New Mexico and southern Colorado; while Chicano has

ate" original done in the Spring of 1934 and which was picked up and circulated fairly widely in ensuing years, verbally for the most part. . . . San Miguel reprints from the LULAC News, July 1937, where the piece appeared without my knowledge. In fact, I have never seen a copy of that issue of LULAC News. Apparently the author was listed as anonymous." David Montejano also uses parts of the 1934 version in his epigraph for Part Three of his *Anglos and Mexicans in the Making of Texas, 1839–1986* (1987), identifying the author as Américo Paredes Manzano. Paredes notes that Montejano "gives his source as the *First Year Book of the Latin American Population of Texas*, ed. J. Montiel Olvera, a Catholic priest. Montiel Olvera probably was copying from *La Prensa* of San Antonio, which printed the 1934 version in 1937. His *First Year Book* is dated 1939. During the half century plus since I composed the first version, I have seen other anonymous reprintings of that version, which apparently caught on because of the heated politics of South Texas during the 1930s. . . . I first met Rolando Hinojosa about nine years ago. He had known of me since he was young as the author of 'The Mexico-Texan.' So perhaps I can at least qualify as a folk poet." In its curious history, "The Mexico-Texan" is a perfect example of the ways in which cultural productions in both their popular oral and literary written forms interact in mutually determining ways in twentieth-century mass media culture. The 1935 version quoted here, according to Paredes, the one "I considered the definitive one," is included in Paredes' *Versos Varios*, poems written from 1930 to 1985, currently being prepared for publication by Arte Público Press.

been used by younger and more politically radical people "to identify an ethnic, nationalist individual or position, one opposed to accommodation and assimilation with United States culture and society."[2] Whatever the designation, however, this variety of self identifiers signals the special importance of the questions of group identity and group reference among Mexican Americans. It is a situation that grows out of the unique historical circumstances that have affected the creation of this social entity as an ethnic minority in a conquered homeland (McLemore and Romo 1985, 4).

An understanding of the nature of their historical genesis as an ethnic minority is vital to an understanding of contemporary Chicano narrative. Unlike many other ethnic immigrants to the United States, but like the Native Americans, Mexican Americans became an ethnic minority through the direct conquest of their homelands. Their internal differences, then, as pronounced as they may be, are counterpoised by their shared experiences as a "conquered minority" in a colonized land (G. Sánchez 1961–62, 123). Under these circumstances, where a new cultural life was forced upon them after 1848 while they attempted tenaciously to cling to their traditional way of life, Mexican Americans developed a decisive sense of opposition to Anglo-American forms and institutions. Thus thrown into a new political reality by force of the American imperial conquest of Mexico, Mexican American culture after 1848 developed in the social interstices between Mexican and American cultural spheres, making that new cultural life patently a product of both but also different in decisive ways from each.

Not the least factor determining the differential unity that characterizes the group is the fact that from their earliest appearance, the Mexican inhabitants of the eighteenth-century Southwest were a racially heterogeneous group (Barrera 1979, 8). Historian Ricardo Romo notes, for instance, that of the early Mexican colonists of the pueblo of Los Angeles "Mestizos made up the greater share" (1983, 17), although one could also find mulattoes, blacks, American Indians, as well as Spaniards. Similarly, the earliest settlers of the region that is now Texas included mestizos, blacks, Indians, and Sephardic Jews (Paredes 1958a, 7–15). Carey McWilliams and others have thus

2. Limón (1981, 200); see also, McLemore and Romo (1985, 4), J. García (1981), Nostrand (1973), and Villanueva (1980). Limón adds: "Almost immediately after . . . the public appearance [of the term *Chicano*] within the student movement [in the 1960s], the term set off controversy and debate within the larger U.S.-Mexican community. The general reaction ranged from indifference to outright rejection and hostility" (1981, 201).

discredited the romantic myth that the early settlers of the Southwest were pure-bred Castilian conquistadores (McWilliams 1973, 162). The descendants of these earliest "Spanish" settlers were instead racially no different from the people who made up the first major wave of immigrants to the United States after 1890 and were, like those later inhabitants of the region, the products of a Mexican, that is to say a *mestizo*, cultural entity.

The course of this early Spanish colonization of the Southwest followed a pattern similar to that of English colonization of the eastern seaboard.[3] In both cases a European-based cultural group sought to acquire land and natural resources and to convert the native inhabitants to Christianity, resulting in both cases in open conflict (McLemore and Romo 1985, 6). But the efforts of the Spanish to Christianize the native American groups were significantly more successful than those of the English colonists:

Even though the Spanish took an enormous toll in human lives, they followed a policy of bringing Christianized Indians into the colonial society that they were building. The "place" of the Indians in this society was at the very bottom; nevertheless, they were counted "in" rather than "out." This policy of the Spanish led to a much higher degree of intermarriage with the dominant Europeans than was true in the English colonies. As a result, by the time Mexico achieved independence in 1821, the culture and population of Mexico was much more 'Indianized' than was the culture and population of the United States. (McLemore and Romo 1985, 6)

As one indication of the fundamental ideological differences between the racial attitudes of the two colonizing groups and the two national states that emerged from the colonial period after the respective wars of independence, one historian has noted that "an Indian could not have been elected president of the United States as Don Benito Juarez was in Mexico. . . . The new society in the United States was . . . a great deal more homogeneous than in Mexico since it was fundamentally a European adaptation to the new land and not in any way a mixture of Indian and European elements" (Alvarez 1973, 35).

After the Louisiana Purchase of 1803, the Roman Catholic, mestizo society of Mexico and the Protestant, Anglo-American one of the United States came into direct and continuous contact, setting up the competition for the province of Texas which was to determine Mexi-

3. See Sacvan Bercovitch (1981) and Richard Slotkin (1973) for a summary of Puritan attitudes. James Duban offers a fine discussion of contemporary nineteenth-century critiques of American "self-reliant" values (1988).

can and American political history until at least the mid-nineteenth century. American design on the region was an open ambition as early as 1767 when Benjamin Franklin had marked Mexico and Cuba for future English colonial expansion, but by 1809 ambition was turning almost into national policy, as when Thomas Jefferson predicted that the Spanish border regions "are ours the first moment war is forced upon us" (in Acuña 1981, 3). The War of 1812 brought the United States and Spanish Mexico closer to the moment of actual conflict. As the easternmost region of these border territories, the province of Texas became the site of this coming clash of political and cultural ideologies and its history can serve as a model for an understanding of the American expansion into the Southwest and of the attitudes of the people which that clash determined.

The Adams-Onís Treaty of 1819 had ceded Spanish Florida to the United States and set the United States boundary with Spanish territory at the Sabine River, thus nullifying the United States claim to Texas. Yet, given the seeming inevitability of westward growth, this frontier could hardly be accepted as a permanent restriction. Inevitably, the border became not a fixed dividing line but merely a moveable outpost, "the outskirts of the advancing kingdom of God" (Bercovitch 1981, 23). By the time the treaty was ratified in 1821, Texas was part of Coahuila, a state in the independent republic of Mexico. Realizing the difficulty of holding the frontier region of Texas against both various Indian groups and the ever-westward-expanding Anglo-American settlers, the central Mexican government, in hopes of creating a buffer zone between it and the expansionist United States, agreed in 1823 to allow United States immigrants to settle in Texas. Perhaps too naively expecting to secure the loyalty of these immigrants, Mexico required them to become Mexican citizens and members of the Roman Catholic Church (Acuña 1981, 4–5; McLemore and Romo 1985, 7). The strategy failed. As the number of Anglo Americans in Texas increased, their economic advantage as slaveholders also grew. Coupled with the vastness of the territory and its distance from the central Mexican government, these factors allowed the new Anglo Texans to remain defiant.

By 1836 Texas had broken from Mexico to establish an independent republic. Although the revolt had been precipitated in no small part by the differences between the two rival cultural and racial groups, many native Texas Mexicans (*Tejanos*) had sided with the Anglo Texans in opposition to the central Mexican government and in support of what they saw as the legitimation of their traditional local provincial autonomy, an autonomy that had existed *de facto* if not *de jure* from the period of the founding of the original Tejano settlements by virtue of the distance between those communities and the central seat of government. "Initially at least, the rebellion appeared to be another provincial revolt of liberal federalists against the conservative constitutionalists led by Santa Anna" (Montejano 1987, 26). Thus, it was quite possible for Tejanos like José Antonio Navarro and Juan Seguín to think that they could be "both a proud Mexican and a loyal Tejano" (Montejano 1987, 26).

Conflict between Texas and Mexico continued during the period of the Texas Republic (1836–45) and as it did, relations between native Tejanos and Anglo Texans deteriorated:

Although the ethnic distinctions had been there from the first contacts, they had not always served as badges of superior or inferior social status, and the numerically smaller *Tejano* population was not cast in the role of a subordinated ethnic minority. The Anglos, however, increasingly failed to distinguish the *Tejanos* from the Mexican nationals with whom they were struggling; and, in the process, the ethnic boundary between the groups gradually was sharply drawn. (McLemore and Romo 1985, 7–8)

During the period of the Texas Republic the Texas Mexican populace was subjugated and suffered expulsion, forced marches, dispossession, and random violence at the hands of Anglo Texans (Montejano 1987, 26). By 1846 the desire among many Anglo Texans for United States statehood together with the continuing westward expansion and capitalist development of the United States led to the annexation of Texas. When U.S. troops entered the disputed border regions between the Nueces River and the Rio Grande in April 1846, war between the United States and Mexico ensued.

In the west, the experience of the native Tejanos was duplicated by that of the native Mexicans of California (*Californios*). From the period of statehood with Mexico through the mid-1840s, "*Californios* did not view Anglos as enemies and were not prepared for the conflicts that ultimately arose" (Acuña 1981, 95). As the Anglo population increased between 1821 and 1846, however, a new ruling group of Anglo settlers became prominent, replacing the original landgrant power elite. As the Mexican war neared, these Anglo Californians instigated a revolt against Mexican authority. With the discovery of gold in 1848, the Anglo population grew substantially in numbers and political power so that by the latter part of the century the Anglos had gained control of the economic and political machinery of the region as the traditional society of native Californios crumbled (Camarillo 1979, 51–52). A similar pattern of subjugation could be traced in the rest of the post war occupied territories of the Southwest over the remainder of the nineteenth century (Acuña 1981; Barrera 1979; Alvarez 1973; Rosenbaum 1981; McLemore and Romo 1985).

In sum, with the signing of the Treaty of Guadalupe Hidalgo in 1848, Mexico surrendered all claim to Texas and ceded to the United States the territories of California, New Mexico, Nevada, and parts of Colorado, Arizona, and Utah, thus fulfilling the "manifest destiny" of the United States to extend its political, economic, and ideological hegemony over the American continent in the very year of the great European revolutions. That ideology fused Protestantism and American patriotism, capitalist economics and Christian morality. "While bourgeois Europe faced social revolution [in 1848], America fulfilled in the Mexican War the Manifest Destiny initiated on Indian soil" (Rogin 1979, 20). Agricultural products grown by black slave labor and cheap Mexican wage labor on land expropriated from the Indians and Mexico thus paid for the growth of American agriculture and industry in the nineteenth century.

In the process of the ideological and political transformation of the Southwest, all Mexican nationals in the conquered borderlands were converted into an ethnic minority under the political control of the alien power of the United States of America. At this precise historical moment, "the Mexican American people were created *as a people:* Mexican by birth, language, and culture; United States citizens by the might of arms" (Alvarez 1973, 37). The metaphysics of the new American culture, at base homogeneously white, Anglo-Saxon, Protestant, and middle class, did allow for the possibility of an absorption into the broad American consensus, but at the cost of the opposing group's traditional culture. In addition, the "internal stresses" that by mid-century were beginning to tear the union apart were being felt in the Southwest with the expansion of slavery to the new territories, undoubtedly exacerbating the racial conflicts between Mexicans and Anglos as well (Rogin 1979, 102–3). The racial and class differences between the two groups plus the inability or unwillingness on the part of the former Mexican nationals to give up their traditional ways explain both the stance of resistance that Mexican American culture develops and its dialectical relationship to both of its original contexts, Mexico on the one hand and the United States on the other. Américo Paredes has argued that this sense of "an in-between existence" characterizes Mexican American border culture from the very first days of the establishment of the Nuevo Santander settlement by Escandón in 1749 and becomes greatly intensified after 1835 (Paredes 1978, 73). It also characterizes one aspect of the complex polarity of identity, both Mexican and American but neither one nor the other fully, that is so evident in contemporary Chicano narrative.

After 1848, those Mexican settlers, now United States citizens by the terms of the treaty of Guadalupe Hidalgo, who remained north of the new border "not only lost their family and communal lands but became subject to racial and political discrimination as well as cultural erosion. Their eventual second-class status set the pattern for later treatment of Mexican immigrants" (M. García 1981, 1). It is crucial to understand the racial distinctness of the post-1848 Mexican American from the Anglo settlers who were to follow them into the Southwest after its acquisition by the United States, for this difference remains one of the central barriers between the old and the new inhabitants of the region. It forms the base for other important differences that were to follow the growth of American industrial capitalism during the post–Civil War period with the arrival of thousands of new Mexican immigrants into the former Mexican territories that were now part of the United States.

These differences were by no means always passively felt by either Anglos or Mexicans in the region. Over the last half of the nineteenth century interethnic violence was common throughout the border areas but especially in Texas. It has been estimated that during the period 1850–1930 the number of Mexican Americans killed in incidents of racial violence in the Southwest was greater than the number of lynchings of black Americans during the same period in the South (Moquin and Van Doren 1971, 253). Often sanctioned by Anglo capitalist interests if not openly committed by state police forces like the Texas Rangers who protected those interests, these acts of violence produced bitter resentment and then retaliation which in turn often led to further rounds of violence.

The course of this border story of racial and economic conflict was recorded on the Mexican American side in the folk art form of *corridos* (ballads) and later becomes one of the subtexts for much of contemporary Chicano narrative. Américo Paredes has shown that the heroes of these corridos are compelling figures who stand for social justice even though they must do so outside the Anglo-American law and its official pieties. "The Mexicans on the left bank of the river were now legally citizens of the United States, with all the rights of citizenship. In actuality, they were not granted those rights. They were cheated out of their property by English-speaking newcomers and suffered all kinds of indignities from the new masters of the land. An oppressed minority had been created; protest on the part

of these newly created Mexican-Americans was early and violent" *corridos —* *socially symbolic acts of resistance*
(Paredes 1976, 22). As socially symbolic acts of resistance, these ballads chronicle the fact that while America may have escaped the historically rooted, feudal social inequality of Europe, American institutions did generate racial, caste, and class divisions that turned out to be just as explosive as European ones. In chapter 3, we will return to a fuller discussion of the role of the corrido as a socially symbolic act.

Aside from the open racial hostility that characterized the last half of the nineteenth and the early part of the twentieth centuries in the Southwest, the course for the industrialization of the American economy during that period also had a decided impact on the development of the region and its Mexican American working-class citizenry and the development of its narrative artforms. In the north, east, and midwest of the United States, the rise of the American industrial state produced an industrial working class. The south, southwest, and west, however, remained less developed; it served as the source of raw materials, industrial metals, and agricultural products, and required only an unskilled labor force. As Mario García puts it: "In this regional division of labor the Southwest became integrated into the American industrial system":

Limited in industrial production, the Southwest was in special need of unskilled railroad hands, farmworkers, mine and smelter laborers, and a variety of other forms of menial labor. Lacking a local labor market and finding it difficult to recruit European and Asian immigrants owing to geographic distance and racial prejudices, entrepreneurs soon discovered a profitable and acceptable labor supply south of the border. Together, industrialization, regional economic specialization, and Mexican immigrant labor launched an economic boom in the Southwest and in the process created new and enlarged Mexican communities within the United States. Mexican immigration, as such, is rooted in late nineteenth-century American economic developments associated with the growth and expansion of American capitalism. (1981, 2)

These new arrivals, together with the descendants of the earliest eighteenth-century colonists of California, Arizona, New Mexico, and Texas, were the forebears of the subjects of the literature at hand: the Mexican Americans and Chicanos of twentieth-century America. In Chicano narrative the history of these people is the subtext which must be recovered from the oblivion to which American social and literary history have consigned it. Our literary texts will show how aesthetic and cultural productions often turn out to be the ideological rewriting of that banished history.

One of the most problematic of issues that must be dealt with
in any attempt to rewrite the history of the status of the Mexican
American in the nineteenth and twentieth centuries is the question of gender. A rich body of historical materials on the role of
the Mexican American woman in the nineteenth century has begun to surface, although much research remains to be done on the
topic. This historical material shows that, given the nature of traditional family structures in Mexican society, Mexican American
women surely labored in the home throughout the nineteenth century (Barerra 1979, 53; M. García 1981, 200–201). But the new research also shows that the division of labor did not always correspond
to the traditional, rigid, sexual division of production—men laboring
outside the home, women working within it. Indeed, historian Vicki
Ruiz has shown that nineteenth-century Mexican American women
worked not only in the home, but also in the general labor market,
all the while caring for each other as their own physicians, attorneys,
and counselors as the need arose (1989).[4]

The entry of women into the labor market was required by the dire
economic conditions that Mexican American families faced. Rosaura
Sánchez argues that

the rise of cotton cultivation in Texas, the growth of agriculture in Colorado
and the rapid expansion of the citrus and vegetable industries in California
created enormous demands for a cheap labor force, men, women, and children. During this agricultural period the Mexican women, not allowed by
their culture to work outside the home as waitresses, maids or laundry help,
were nevertheless needed to work in the fields during the seasonal harvest
to which the families migrated. Here women were culturally "protected,"
and simultaneously exploited by the growers, as much as the male members
of their families.[5]

Thus by the 1880s entire families enter the migratory agricultural
labor market. Gradually, Chicanas begin to find employment in fruit
canneries and other food processing plants (Camarillo 1975; Ruiz
1987; Zavella 1987) and by the early twentieth century are employed

4. Vicki Ruiz (1987, 1989); see also Alfredo Mirandé and Evangelina Enríquez
(1979), Mario Barrera (1979), Margarita Melville (1980), Mario T. García (1980), Rosalinda M. González (1983), Richard Allan Griswold del Castillo (1984), Patricia Zavella
(1987), and Adelaida del Castillo (1988).

5. R. Sánchez (1977, 7). She adds that "the myth of 'family unity' among Chicanos
projects an image of families which, although poor, are willing to accept their divorced or separated daughters, as well as their grandchildren, back into the home. All
too often these divorced women are encouraged by their families to seek remarriage
rather than remain in their parents' home . . ." (1977, 6).

as domestic servants, in textile and light manufacturing, clerical work, and other service industries (Mirandé and Enríquez 1982, 333; M. García 1981, 4; R. Sánchez 1977, 3–15). They also participate in early union organizing among cannery and agricultural workers in California and pecan shellers in Texas (Mirandé and Enríquez, 333–37). Feminist groups such as "Luz y vida" of Los Angeles and "Grupo Práxedis G. Guerrero" of San Antonio participated in these early labor struggles as did La Liga Femenil Mexicanista, formed at the meeting of the Primer Congreso Mexicanista in September 1911.[6]

The entry of women into the labor market outside the home could not but help produce major cultural changes within the traditional Mexican American family: "Besides acquiring some new material and cultural tastes that they introduced into the home, by the 1920s young Mexican working women appear to have begun to exhibit a desire for greater independence from strict family practices. . . . The economic necessity for Mexican women to find jobs . . . appears to have challenged to a degree the traditional male-dominated Mexican family structure" (M. García 1981, 200–201). This economic necessity, however, did not automatically give women greater authority or autonomy within the male-dominated family. As women entered the workforce, they raised important questions concerning the traditional division of labor in the home; they demanded a greater role in the economic decision-making within the family; and they desired a different status in relation to the family elders, fathers- and mothers-in-law, who required that their sons' wives be subordinate, submissive, and decorously respectful.

Socialist feminist scholarship has shown how under capitalist patriarchy "the control of wage labor by capital and men's control over women's labor power and sexuality in the home are connected. In the labor market, job segregation is the primary mechanism maintaining the domination of men over women, for example, in enforcing lower wages for women. Women's labor-market activities are restricted through the bearing and rearing of children and men's efforts to control home life" (Zavella 1987, 3). The relationship of women to men must be understood in both the labor market and families with the result that the family becomes a primary site of political struggle.

While capitalism and patriarchy relate in contradictory fashion,

6. Acuña (1981, 192–95). On Chicana historiography, see especially, Judith Sweeney, "Chicana History: A Review of the Literature" (1977, 99–123), and Richard Allan Griswold del Castillo (1975, 41–58); on La Liga Femenil Mexicanista and El Primer Congreso Mexicanista, see Acuña (1981, 306–7), and Limón (1974, 85–117). For additional references to Chicana feminism, see notes to chapter 8.

capitalists and husbands or fathers having competing interests in women's labor (Zavella 1987, 3), ideological forms exist to cover over the contradictions. Of primary importance in disguising the contradictions is the ideology of woman's "proper place"—"the notion that women are moral guardians of the home and therefore should not enter the labor force" because of their family responsibilities, including "housework, child care, consumption, and emotional nurturance" (Zavella 1987, 4). When viewed from the perspective of socialist feminism, however, far from being a natural, transcendently legitimized relation, the concept of family becomes a way that men socialize women to defer to them. The concept of family is "a socially necessary illusion which simultaneously expresses and masks recruitment to relationships of production, reproduction, and consumption" (Zavella 1987, 5). As feminists have argued, the ideology of "maternal thinking" is supported by a variety of institutions, including schools, churches, mass media, unions, all of which rationalize the subordination of women (Barrett 1985, 65).

In Chicano families, no less than in Anglo families, societal contradictions bring conflict as women struggle to resist their subordination. Yet, as we have seen, while the ideology of socially constructed "sex-gender" roles may adequately describe a white middle-class situation, it does not entirely describe that of the Chicano working class, where from the late-nineteenth-century Chicanas needed to enter the labor market to help support their families. Cultural values and family ideology have not fully determined women's labor-force participation (Zavella 1987, 11). In working-class families, traditional Mexican patriarchal values defining a complete segregation of roles within the family have more often than not been breached rather than honored. Nonetheless, even though the reality of Chicano family life has placed women in opposition to the traditional cultural values, the ideology of traditional roles retains a powerful influence and source of conflict. Economic conditions and racism have thus combined to create a culturally specific version of family ideology, responding both to traditional Mexican and American social gender role constructions (Zavella 1987, 5).

In the light of these changing social and economic factors, Mexican American women and men sought, sometimes painfully, to forge new ideologies to supplement or replace those of the dominant patriarchy now put into question by the force of new social conditions. These conditions make concrete the contradictions involved concerning the relations between questions of class and race on one hand and gender on the other. These contradictions initiate an issue that remains problematic to this day and, as we will see in subsequent chapters, animate the writings of many contemporary Chicana authors.

By 1900 patterns of cultural, economic, racial, and sexual subordination of the Mexican American throughout the Southwest are in place. With the continuing growth of American industrial capital and its need for cheap labor in the Southwest, almost one million Mexicans entered the United States between 1880 and the Great Depression (M. García 1981, 4). Class, racial, and labor relationships between Mexicans and Anglos already having been determined by preceding generations, these new Mexican American workers began to enculturate to their new society according to the established patterns, traditional at base but not entirely immune to the Americanizing influences of the schools, churches, and the legal and political systems, as well as new material and recreational interests, creating thus a unique border culture.

While the labor system drew these new immigrants initially to rural areas, industrial development of cities brought drastic changes in the lives of rural Mexican American workers. As opportunities increased in the cities these workers moved to acquire urban occupations, often still of the menial type. Nevertheless, the changing pattern of the American labor market by the time of the Great Depression changed Mexican American labor patterns so that the majority—contrary to the stereotype—now lived in urban communities (McLemore and Romo 1985, 15–16). And despite their high rate of enlistment in both World War II and the Korean War, the Mexican American working class continued to experience discrimination and segregation during the prosperity following the war years and beyond. In this expansion Mexican American working men and women represented, despite exploitation and discrimination, an indispensable factor in the development of industrial and commercial agricultural capital in the United States.

Despite its long-standing cultural presence, Mexican American heritage has either been excluded from or relegated to the margins of American political, social, and literary history. Paraphrasing Frantz Fanon, we might say that the dominant Anglo-American culture did not simply alter the material conditions of the Southwest after 1848. In rewriting history, it distorted and disfigured its future (Fanon 1982, 169). This work of devaluing history continues and takes on dialectical significance today.

Contemporary Chicano writers are attempting to remedy this ex-

clusion and marginalization by depicting their own bicultural experience in the context of the broad historical events that have formed
our times. Their work in dramatic, poetic, and narrative forms are as
heterogeneous formally and thematically as are the people who refer to themselves as Mexican American. But certain large historical
issues continue to be the focus of their writings: the settlement of the
American Southwest, the Mexican Revolution of 1910 and the concomitant northward migration, the Great Depression, World War II,
the Korean War, the social and political upheavals of the sixties and
seventies, including especially the struggles of women, and perhaps
most inclusively, the consolidation of a postmodern, postindustrial
consumer society in the United States.

Together, the body of texts that have been produced in response
to this history constitute the Chicano resistance to the cultural
hegemony of dominant Anglo-American civil society. As Antonio
Gramsci has argued, society is made up of voluntary affiliations, like
schools, unions, churches, and families that are noncoercive in their
attempt to create a social whole, and of state institutions, like the
police force, armies, and central bureaucracies, whose role is direct
domination (1971, 257–63). The literary texts that we deal with here
position themselves against both the overt and the indirect components of social power. This distribution of domination into overt
and indirect forms has meant that the response of Chicano texts to
domination has occurred both thematically and formally. It allows
us justifiably to think of Chicano narrative as a "resistance literature" (Harlow 1987, xvii) and, thus a coparticipant in the broader
struggles of national liberation and resistance movements in Africa,
Latin America, and the Middle East.

As part of American literature, narratives by Chicano women
and men offer significant representations of the historical drama of
nineteenth- and twentieth-century American life, especially as that
life intersects, consciously or not, with the interests of what has
sometimes been referred to as the Third World. Moreover, as our historical sketch shows, the relationship between politics and culture
for the Mexican American community, positioned between the competing interests of a developed and a developing world, is an organic
one. Politics and art did not develop in isolation. Especially with the
beginning of Chicano social activism in the 1960s, narrative could
root itself in the concrete social interests of historical and contemporary events. In symbolic response to the events of our times, then,
the Chicano narratives to which we now turn take on critical, politi-

cal functions and appropriate the historical space of the southwestern borderlands as their imaginative universe. Positioned between
cultures, living on borderlines, Chicanos and their narratives have assumed a unique borderland quality, reflecting in no uncertain terms
the forms and styles of their folk-base origins.

2
The Folk Base of Chicano Narrative

Américo Paredes' *With His Pistol in His Hand* and the *Corrido* Tradition

It is not surprising that Tomás Rivera and Rolando Hinojosa, two of the major figures in the development of Chicano prose fiction in the 1970s, both mention the decisive influence on their literary careers caused by their first reading of Américo Paredes' *With His Pistol in His Hand* (1958).[1] Rivera and Hinojosa simply make explicit an influence that is implicitly felt by all of the major developers of Chicano fiction. With impeccable scholarship and imaginative subtlety, Paredes' study of the border ballads, that concern the historical figure of Gregorio Cortez and his solitary armed resistance to the injustices Mexicans faced in Anglo Texas, may be said to have invented the very possibility of a narrative community, a complete and legitimate Mexican American *persona*, whose life of struggle and discord was worthy of being told. Certainly other writers before Paredes had indicated how the Mexican American experience could be transformed into illuminating narrative texts. Jorge Ulica's *Crónicas diabólicas*, journalistic vignettes about Mexican American life in late-nineteenth- and early-twentieth-century California, comes to mind.[2] But Paredes' *With His Pistol in His Hand* became the primary

1. See, for example, Hinojosa's comments in "This Writer's Sense of Place" (1983). Hinojosa has acknowledged this influence in various personal conversations with the present writer. Rivera explicitly names Paredes as a major influence: "[Paredes' book] indicated to me that it was possible to talk about a Chicano as a complete figure. . . . *With His Pistol in His Hand* indicated . . . a whole imaginative possibility for us to explore" (Bruce-Novoa 1980, 150). The title of this chapter echoes Paredes' important essay, "The Folk Base of Chicano Literature," (1979, 4–17). See also the excellent biographical note by José E. Limón, "Américo Paredes: A Man from the Border" (1980, 1–5).

2. The essays compiled by Juan Rodríguez under the title of *Crónicas Diabólicas (1916–1926)* (1982) were written under the pen name "Jorge Ulica" by Julio G. Arce

imaginative seeding ground for later works because it offered both the stuff of history and of art and the key to an understanding of their decisive interrelationship for Mexican American writers. Paredes' study is crucial in historical, aesthetic, and theoretical terms for the contemporary development of Chicano prose fiction because it stands as the primary formulation of the expressive reproductions of the sociocultural order imposed on and resisted by the Mexican American community in the twentieth century.

Cultivated throughout most of Greater Mexico, including the Mexican communities in the United States, the corrido "is usually an anonymous folk song narrative composed in octosyllabic quatrains and sung to a tune typically in ternary rhythm and in ¾ or ⁶⁄₈ meter. The quatrains are usually structured in an a b c b rhyme pattern and the entire narrative may be framed with formulaic openings and closings" (Limón 1984, 11–12; see also McDowell 1981, 56–57; Paredes 1958b, 95; Mendoza 1954). Thematically, the corrido typically relates significant events, such as social conflicts, natural disasters, political issues, or individual crises. Formally, the corrido is related to the tradition of the *romance* (a ballad in octosyllabic meter with alternate assonants) and the *romance corrido* —that is, the *romance* sung straight through, rapidly and simply— brought to Mexico by the Spanish conquistadores (Paredes 1958b, 95). It does not crystallize as a distinctive genre, however, until the last half of the nineteenth century, and it does so apparently not in Mexico proper but in the area of the former northern border province of Nuevo Santander, the present Texas-Mexico border area (Paredes 1958b, 103–4). Additionally, the rise of the corrido genre seems to coincide with the increasing contact and the resulting clashes between Anglos and Mexicans in Texas after 1848.

In his now-classic study of the corrido, Paredes argues that before Texas Mexican border balladry entered its decadent period in the 1930s it was working toward a single type: "toward one form,

---

(1870–1926). Arce, a Mexican journalist who settled in San Francisco in 1915, wrote weekly columns of witty, sometimes scathing, satire for various Spanish language newspapers from Texas to California and in Mexico. His satirical jabs especially after 1920 are aimed at both Anglo-Americans and the new "Mexican-Americans," "their assimilation into the Anglo world, the loss of Spanish, and the disintegration of family life" (69). Rodríguez also mentions another such journalist, "Kascabel" (Rattlesnake), but notes that this type of writing did not develop beyond the Depression years (69). Francisco A. Lomelí argues that the New Mexican writer, Eusebio Chacón, author of *El hijo de la tempestad* and *Tras la tormenta la calma* (both 1892), should be considered the first Chicano novelist of the nineteenth century (1980a). See also Lomelí (1985b).

the *corrido;* toward one theme, border conflict; toward one concept of the hero, the man fighting for his right with his pistol in his hand" (1958a, 149). The older ballad forms of the early eighteenth and nineteenth centuries dealing primarily with everyday life lose their interest and relevance during the period of border conflict (roughly 1848–1930) and are superseded by folksongs about individual and organized resistance (1958b, 94).

Of these corridos of border conflict, "El Corrido de Gregorio Cortez" is probably the most widely known. Versions of it have been sung not only in Chicano communities along the entire Texas Mexican border but throughout the Southwest, California, and even the Midwest. However, it is certainly not the earliest expression of social protest. Among the oldest of these songs of cultural resistance that have survived from the first phases of border conflict is "El General Cortina." The corridos about Juan Nepomuceno Cortina, who in 1859 shot U.S. Marshal Bob Shears in Brownsville, Texas, in retaliation for various injustices and who published a manifesto outlining his grievances, date back to the late 1850s and the early 1860s. Forced into open conflict with American authority, Cortina and his men briefly occupied Brownsville before giving way to superior force (Paredes 1958a, 134; Acuña 1981, 33–37; Montejano 1987, 32–33). Cortina's proclamation to the Mexicans of Texas issued from his Rancho del Carmen in Cameron County on November 23, 1859, read in part:

Mexicans! When the State of Texas began to receive the new organization which its sovereignty required as part of the United States, flocks of vampires, in the guise of men, came and scattered themselves in the settlements, without any capital except the corrupt heart and the most perverse intentions. . . . Many of you have been robbed of your property, incarcerated, chased, murdered, and hunted like wild beasts, because your labor was fruitful, and because your industry excited the vile avarice which led them. (Montejano 1987, 32)

Cortina's rebellion and his subsequent defeat by the U.S. Army "set a pattern for other Texas-Mexicans who were forced into violent protest against exploitation and injustice" (Paredes 1976, 22–23). The corridos about Cortina's War helped establish a tradition of socially symbolic artforms in the Mexican American communities of the Southwest, and, more specifically, they are the model for a series of songs such as "El corrido de Kiansis," "Rito García," "Los pronunciados," and "Los sediciosos" (Paredes 1976, 1979).

"El corrido de Kiansis," versions of which Paredes reports as having been sung in the 1860s, expresses intercultural conflict "in professional rivalries rather than in violence" (1976, 26) between Texas-Mexican and Anglo-Texan *vaqueros* (cowboys) on the long cattle drives from South Texas to Kansas. In songs such as this one, overt resistance is sublimated into an aggressive competition over the vaquero's working skills:

Five hundred steers there were	Quinientos novillas eran,
All big and quick;	todos grandes y livianos,
Thirty American cowboys	y entre treinta americanos
Could not keep them bunched up.	no los podían embalar.
The five Mexicans arrive,	Llegan cinco mexicanos,
All of them wearing good chaps;	todos bien enchivarrados,
And in less than a quarter-hour,	y en menos de un cuarto de hora
They had the steers penned up.	los tenían encerrados.

(Paredes 1976, 55)

Armed conflict is, however, the theme of "Rito García," which relates events occurring twenty-five years after Cortina's raid on Brownsville. Reacting violently to "unwarranted search of his home accompanied by violence to members of his family" (Paredes 1976, 27), Margarito (Rito) García fought back against the law and then rode across the river into Tamaulipas, Mexico:

The Mexican-American in the Southwest felt that he was living in a part of Mexico occupied by a foreign country. He could "defend his right" with force of arms, or he could appeal to the Mexican government to take action in his favor through the Mexican consulates in the United States. . . . But such methods were not available to Rito García, so he uses his rifle to protest Anglo injustice. The officers he shoots happen to have Spanish names, but they are representatives of "Gringo law" as far as he is concerned. (Paredes 1976, 28)

With García's arrest and return to American authorities by the governor of Tamaulipas, the corrido in his honor counsels in rueful tone in 1885: "Nunca vayan a pedir a México protección (Never go ask for Mexico's protection)" (Paredes 1976, 27). The message is clear: the Mexican communities on the United States side of the border will find neither aid from nor refuge in Porfirio Díaz's Mexico but must instead fend for themselves.

In one such daring attempt to fend for themselves, a force of about a hundred men led by Catarino E. Garza, a Texas-Mexican who lived on a ranch near the border settlement of San Diego, Texas, crossed the Rio Grande on December 20, 1891, to overthrow the government of Porfirio Díaz. Garza, a newspaper editor who had been criticizing the Díaz regime for several years, had the support of influential men on both sides of the border (Pierce 1917; McNeil 1946; Acuña 1981; Paredes 1976; G. Saldívar 1943). "His proclamation of rebellion against Díaz demanded free elections, civilian rather than military rule in Mexico, individual freedoms, land for the peasants, and the restoration of the Constitution of 1857—the same goals that the men of the Revolution would espouse twenty years later" (Paredes 1976, 29). When Garza returned to Texas to regroup his forces, he was met on the Texas side of the border by U.S. Cavalry and Texas Rangers. His small group was quickly overcome and individuals were hunted down and turned over to Díaz firing squads across the river (Paredes 1976, 29).

Following what by the late nineteenth century is thus a traditional pattern, the corrido entitled "Los pronunciados" ("The Insurgents") is about the Garza rebellion and its defeat by American armed forces. Eric J. Hobsbawm has shown how the social "bandit" represents "a primitive form of organized social protest" (1965, 13). The rebellious actions of men like Cortina and Garza against the oligarchy of Anglo-American controlled wealth and racially based class distinctions represent a higher form of protest. Despite their eventual defeat, they resisted in organized form and under the guidance of a definite ideology.

Paredes also makes it clear that not all Border men who shot it out with the law were innocent and oppressed individuals, defending their rights. "But so keen was the Mexican sense of injustice against Anglo domination, so vivid the pattern of intercultural conflict in the *corrido*, that sometimes an outlaw with no conscience of social or political justice was elevated into a hero of Border conflict" (1976, 30). Such was the case of the train robbery, the first in South Texas, perpetrated by José Mosqueda in 1891. Mosqueda and his men stole several thousand dollars worth of Mexican silver, owned as it turned out primarily by Spaniards, Mexicans, and Texas-Mexicans. Mosqueda and one of his men went to prison for the crime, but most of the money was never recovered. Nevertheless, "El Corrido de José Mosqueda" is sung as though, like other songs of its genre, it were a corrido about cultural conflict: "The patterns of folk literature and the stresses of intercultural conflict triumph over historical fact in 'José Mosqueda.' Some minor historical data (a train robbery) are superseded by an overriding historical fact (the clash of cultures)" (Paredes 1976, 30).

The 1915 uprising set in movement by the "Plan de San Diego"

is commemorated in the córrido "Los sediciosos" ("The Sedition-
ists"). Written by a group of Mexicans held prisoner in Monterrey,
Mexico, in January 1915 and issued in final form from San Diego,
Texas, by Luis de la Rosa, the "Plan de San Diego" called for a union
of Mexicans with Indians, blacks, and orientals and the creation of
a Spanish-speaking Republic of the Southwest (Paredes 1976, 32–
34; 1978, 75–76; Acuña 1981, 308–9; R. Flores 1987, 3). Bands of
Texas Mexicans led by Luis de la Rosa and Aniceto Pizaña raided as
far north as the King Ranch and throughout the South Texas Border region, fighting the Anglo power structure as they went, burning
ranches, attacking U.S. Army detachments, and on October 18, 1915,
derailing a train in Olmito, Texas: "iban a tumbar el tren / a ese dipo
del Olmito" (they went to derail the train at the station of Olmito).
Finally, faced with overwhelming opposition from U.S. Cavalry and
Texas Rangers, Pizaña escaped to Mexico, where he was arrested and
confined by Mexican officials. Texas Rangers and sheriff's deputies,
frustrated at not having captured Pizaña, slaughtered many Texas
Mexicans, including 102 who were systematically executed following a raid on Norias, Texas (R. Flores 1987, 10). The corrido praises
Pizaña's rebellion but mourns the victims of the bloody Texas Ranger
(*rinche*) terror that followed his act of resistance (Paredes 1976, 33):

In nineteen hundred fifteen,	En mil novecientos quince,
Oh, but the days were hot!	¡qué días tan calurosos!
. . .	. . .
In that well-known place called Norias,	En ese punto de Norias
It really got hot for them;	ya merito les ardía,
A great many bullets rained down	a esos rinches desgraciados
On those cursed *rinches*.	muchas balas les llovía.
Now the fuse is lit	Ya la mecha está encendida
By the true-born Mexicans,	por los puros mexicanos,
And it will be the Texas-Mexicans	y los que van a pagarla
Who will have to pay the price.	son los mexicotejanos.
	(Paredes 1976, 71–73)

As quickly as *mexicotejanos* fled to Mexico to escape the repression,
Anglo developers seized their land. Between 1890 and 1930, with
the accelerated movement into South Texas of Anglo-American agricultural entrepreneurs who, in league with the elite Mexican upper
class, begin a pattern of class and racial oppression that is still in
place today, the necessity for overt and symbolic forms of resistance

on the part of the Mexican American community becomes all the more pronounced (Limón 1983c, 203; Montejano 1979).

Because the corrido is *"narrative, reflexive,* and propositional in semantic intent and *poetic* in technique" (McDowell 1981, 45), it lends itself readily to use as an instrument of ideological analysis. By the end of the nineteenth century, it has thus emerged as the dominant socially symbolic act of the Mexican American community. Not typically a form of personal narrative, a reproduction of idiosyncratic experiences, the corrido instead tends to take a transpersonal, third-person point of view representing the political and existential values of the community as a whole. Since its narrated events are historical in nature, the corrido focuses on those events of immediate significance to the corrido community that are capable of producing a heightened, reflexive awareness of the mutual values and orientations of the collective. It poetically selects "events for narration which have instrumental and symbolic value in the *corrido* community" (McDowell 1981, 46). It does not generally convey news as such. Rather, like classical epic, it takes a body of symbolically charged, iconically powerful experiences and plunges the audience *in medias res* to an examination of those events (McDowell 1981, 47). As an instrument suited to ideological analysis, the purpose of the corrido is thus "to interpret, celebrate, and ultimately dignify events already thoroughly familiar to the *corrido* audience" (McDowell 1981, 47).

By the late nineteenth century, therefore, many corridos functioning as elements of social resistance have preceded "El Corrido de Gregorio Cortez," but this particular song now comes to epitomize the genre of heroic epic ballads about a man who defends his rights "with his pistol in his hand." With the skills of a historian, Paredes first analyzes the sociocultural milieu of early-twentieth-century Texas to explain the genesis both of the song and the events that the song chronicles. With the sensibility of a novelist, he then recreates the style and substance of the heroic legends and songs surrounding the figure of Cortez. Finally, with the insight of a biographer he movingly narrates the actual events of Cortez's simple life of struggle, pointing out as he does so the very ground for future Chicano narrative fiction.

As Paredes recounts the events memorialized in the song, on the afternoon of June 12, 1901, Sheriff W. T. (Brack) Morris of Karnes County in south central Texas, who was hunting a horse thief, appeared at the farmhouse of the Texas Mexican brothers, Gregorio and Romaldo Cortez. Morris spoke no Spanish and the Cortez brothers spoke little English. Boone Choate, a deputy whom Morris had brought along as interpreter, mistakenly translates the Cortez's response to Morris's questions, causing Morris to think that the brothers are the horse thieves he seeks.[3] The first error in translation is apparently compounded by a second when the translator takes Gregorio's words that he cannot be arrested for a crime he has not committed to say that "no white man can arrest" him (Paredes 1958a, 62). Taking these words as a challenge to his authority and as an indication that Cortez is resisting arrest, Morris instantly draws his revolver, shoots Romaldo, and shoots at but misses Gregorio. Gregorio then shoots and kills the sheriff.[4] Cortez flees, "knowing that the only justice available to him in Karnes County would be at the end of a rope":

> In his flight toward the Rio Grande, Cortez walked more than 100 miles and rode at least 400, eluding hundreds of men who were trying to capture him. On the way he killed another Texas sheriff, Robert Glover of Gonzales County; and he was also accused in the death of Constable Henry Schnabel. (Paredes 1976, 31)

After this heroic flight of near-epic proportions and on the verge of making good his escape to Mexico, Cortez surrendered to American authorities near Laredo, Texas, when he learned that his family and all who had aided him had become the targets of American reprisals. His case united Mexican Americans in the cause of his defense. Armed resistance became a legal battle that lasted three years. In the course of several trials and appeals, Cortez was acquitted of murder in the deaths of Sheriff Morris and Constable Schnabel but was sentenced to life imprisonment for the death of Sheriff Glover. In 1913, Governor O. B. Colquitt pardoned Gregorio Cortez. Both the acquittals and the pardon were significant legal victories in the Mexican Americans' fight for civil rights in Texas and the Southwest, and, in the rarity of the justice received by the Mexican American defendant, they were part of the reason for the elevation of Cortez to the status of folk hero. "Gregorio Cortez and the *corrido* about him are a milestone in the Mexican-American's emerging group consciousness" (Paredes 1976, 31).

The events of history almost immediately become artform, as by

3. The original court records of both the trial and the appeals offer these details of the incident and its aftermath. These reports are stirring narratives in their own right. See "Cortez v. State" Court of Criminal Appeals of Texas, January 15, 1902 (66 SW 453) 1902; and "Cortez v. State" Court of Criminal Appeals of Texas, June 15, 1904 (83 SW 812) 1904. I owe these citations to Paulette Barwinkel Saldívar.

4. *Cortez v. State* (66 SW 453–60) and *Cortez v. State* (83 SW 812–16).

1901, both legendary tales and folk songs embellishing Cortez's real-
life historical deeds, his exceptional horsemanship, his use of the
pistol, and his undeniable courage, had transformed an incident of
heroic resistance into a folk hero's tale of almost mythic proportions
(Paredes 1958a, 109). In the years since the events, the ballad recount-
ing his deeds has retained a remarkably uniform stability. Paredes
cites eleven major variants of the song, but offers the following version, variant G, as "one of the best variants of the Cortez *corrido* that
one can find" (Paredes, 1958a: 198):

El Corrido de Gregorio Cortez

In the county of El Carmen
A great misfortune befell;
The Major Sheriff is dead;
Who killed him no one can tell.

En el condado del Carmen
tal desgracia sucedió
murió el Cherife Mayor,
no saben quién lo mató.

At two in the afternoon,
In half an hour or less,
They knew that the man who
    killed him
Had been Gregorio Cortez.

Serían las dos de la tarde,
como media hora después,
supieron que el malhechor

era Gregorio Cortez.

They let loose the bloodhound
    dogs;
They followed him from afar.
But trying to catch Cortez
Was like following a star.

Soltaron los perros jaunes

pa' que siguieran la juella
pero alcanzar a Cortez
era seguir a una estrella.

All the rangers of the county
Were flying, they rode so hard;
What they wanted was to get
The thousand-dollar reward.

Esos rinches del condado
iban que casi volaban
porque se querían ganar
tres mil pesos que les daban.

And in the county of Kansas
They cornered him after all;
Though they were more than
    three hundred
He leaped out of their corral.

En el condado de Kiancer
lo llegaron a alcanzar,
a poco más de trescientos

y allí les brincó el corral.

Then the Major Sheriff said,
As if he was going to cry,
"Cortez, hand over your weapons;
We want to take you alive."

Decía el Cherife Mayor
como queriendo llorar:
—Cortez, entrega tus armas,
no te vamos a matar.

Then said Gregorio Cortez,
With his pistol in his hand,
"Ah, so many mounted Rangers
Against one lone Mexican!"

Decía Gregorio Cortez
con su pistola en la mano:
—¡Ah, cuánto rinche montado
para un solo mexicano!

Now with this I say farewell	Ya con ésta me despido
In the shade of a cypress tree,	a la sombra de un ciprés
This is the end of the ballad	aquí se acaba el corrido
Of Don Gregorio Cortez.	de don Gregorio Cortez.

(Paredes 1958: frontispiece and variant G)

The several variants of the song offer a selection of different narrative techniques: from the journalistic broadside, to episodic or scenic representation, to dramatic dialogues, to straightforward narrative. Variant G of "Gregorio Cortez" follows the traditional corrido pattern of narration through a series of shifting scenes, dialogue, and action, and helps establish a thematic tradition: "The hero is always the peaceful man, finally goaded into violence by the *rinches* and rising in his wrath to kill great numbers of his enemy. His defeat is assured; at the best he can escape across the border, and often he is killed or captured. But whatever his fate, he has stood up for his right" (Paredes 1958a, 149). The heroic type of the corrido is thus created in opposition to Anglo-American characters and institutions, which serve as "reacting agents" (Paredes 1958a, 247) against which individual and cultural identity may be forged. Ten years before the Mexican Revolution, the interracial and class struggles that will become the focus of literary and everyday reality of South Texas are evident "already in full vigor in *El corrido de Gregorio Cortez*" (Paredes 1958a, 247).

As we have seen, the typical corrido situation posits a common, peaceful working man put into an uncommon situation by the power of cultural and historical forces beyond his control. The corrido hero is forced to give up his natural way of life by his attempts to defend his home, his family, his very community. In the process of this attempt to win social justice, his concern for his own personal life and his own solitary fate must be put aside for the good of the collective life of his social group. Composed for a predominantly rural folk and focused on a specific geographical locale, the unity of the corrido is culturally, temporally, and spatially specific; the corrido makes no effort to be "literary" or "universal." Its point of view is cultural rather than national (Paredes 1958a, 183–84). And since its principal aim is narrative, the corrido concentrates on the actions of the hero. "Though it avoids for the most part comments from the narrator and all unnecessary detail, the corrido gives a fairly complete account of the facts. . . . [T]he narrative style is swift and compact; it is composed into scenes; there is a liberal amount of dialogue (Paredes 1958a, 188).

Because of the narrative objectivity of the corrido's transpersonal point of view, only the narrative product, not the poetic producer, appears. Hegel's account in his *Aesthetics* (1835) of the narrative stance of classical epic appropriately describes that of the corrido as well:

Because the epic presents not the poet's own inner world but the objective events, the subjective side of the production must be put into the background precisely as the poet completely immerses himself in the world which he unfolds before our eyes. (1975, 2:1048–49)

Our subject is not epic but ballad; however, the analogy holds. In the corrido, the narrator is anonymous, as is the author. The distinction between reliable and unreliable narrators is totally inapplicable in the corrido context. Moreover, what has been said of the "authority" of epic is equally true of the corrido: "the connection between authorship and authority had not yet been made because it was not necessary; it was not necessary because there was no place or need for the idiosyncratic view to stand outside the communal concern" (Bernstein 1984, 51). Corresponding to the "subjectlessness" of the corrido at the level of author and narrator, one finds a curious lack of "individuality" on the part of the hero. Georg Lukács argues that "the epic hero is, strictly speaking, never an individual. It is traditionally thought that one of the essential characteristics of the epic is the fact that its theme is not a personal destiny but the destiny of the community" (1971, 66). In the same way, in the corrido, a product of an integrated community sharing a working-class world view and values, there is no place for the idiosyncratic, for an individual perspective that stands totally outside of communal concerns. No individual life, even that of the hero, may be regarded as uniquely different from the fate of the community as a whole. Gregorio Cortez stands, consequently, not as an individual but as an epic construction of the society that constitutes him. His fate cannot be disconnected from communal fate.

Compared to other variants of the song, variant G begins tersely, all extraneous characters and actions having been pared down to the central moment of Cortez's flight after the gunfight.[5] With the third quatrain begins the narrative core of the song, using a cycle of "flight-pursuit-encirclement-fight" (Paredes 1958a, 198). Swiftly, the song moves to the main point in the penultimate quatrain, that is, the image of the hero, tragically defiant, going down against great odds:

Then said Gregorio Cortez   Decía Gregorio Cortez
With his pistol in his hand   con su pistola en la mano:

5. See *With His Pistol in His Hand* (151–74) for variants of "Gregorio Cortez."

"Ah, how many mounted rangers   —¡Ah, cuánto rinche montado
Against one lone Mexican!"   para un solo mexicano!

All the details of the original fight, the ride to the border, the capture of the hero, and his subsequent legal battles have been eliminated in favor of the hero's brief words illuminating him as "the projection of the ballad people who created him." "Everything that is left is told in a plain sober style . . . , which was to the hearers of the ballad symbolic of themselves" (Paredes 1958a, 198–99). Deeds do not have clearly distinct public and private reasons, motivations, or consequences, but only a collectively symbolic dimension. In style and form, the epic heroic Border corrido is the product of the political imagination of a community whose environment was border conflict and that saw itself menaced in social, political, and cultural terms by a people more numerous and more powerful than itself: "cuánto rinche montado / para un solo mexicano."

Only against the background of the later bifurcation of time and plot in Chicano narrative fiction can we get a sense of the immanent unity of the corrido's forms and themes. The hero's individual life-sequences have not yet become totally distinct from those of his community; the private sphere of interior consciousness has not yet become the concern of the balladeer; the private quality of life has not yet coalesced into a central, independent identity that is distinct from the identity of the community. Life is one and it is "historicized" to the extent that all existential factors are not merely aspects of a personal life but are a common affair, as M. M. Bakhtin has argued concerning the nature of folk art in general (1981, 209). On the Texas-Mexican border, the corrido drew its vitality from the fact that the relationship between balladeer and audience, that is to say, between aesthetic producer and consumer, was still that of "precapitalist" modes of aesthetic production, "a social institution and a concrete social and interpersonal relationship with its own validation and specificity" (Jameson 1979, 136).

Like the aesthetic production of the corrido, its performance is decidedly a socially symbolic event, actualizing all of the possibilities and strategies of an oppositional symbolic discourse, a social discourse with its own validity and specificity. Paredes has identified two principal singing situations for the corrido: "organized audience" situations, involving either the family group or some all-male group setting, and "casual audience" situations, involving perhaps only the singer himself (1976, xx). Of these two, by far the most prevalent performance situation is the organized audience form. Compared to all-male group performance situations, a family group performance would be subdued in tone, in keeping with the decorum of respect that was obligated within the family. It would also be supplemented by commentary on the events in the song (McDowell 1981, 70). In the case of intimate family gatherings, all members of the family might perform songs, ditties, or riddles (Paredes 1976, xxi). The father, however, served as the primary "oral historian" in the family, achieving through song and narrative the ideological socialization of the children.

Although women might on occasion sing in these intimate family performances, the corrido is chiefly a male performance genre, and in extended family gatherings or in formal ceremonies "men were the performers, while the women and children participated only as audience" (Paredes 1976, xxi). In these special gatherings only the "oldest and wisest men had the privilege" of narrating and singing the corrido tales (Paredes 1976, xxii). In the more raucous male-only settings, such as in a cantina, the "propositional content [of the corrido] drawn from the heroic world view" is strikingly apparent and "reflects the large-scale allocation of men and women to separate material and symbolic spheres maintained within this community" (McDowell 1981, 71). Thus, while women were important in the transmission of ideological values through other kinds of song, they were not supposed to sing " 'men's songs' such as corridos and rarely did so in public" (Paredes 1976, xviii). The virtues and ideals maintained as oppositional forces in the corrido are consequently certain to be male ones.[6] As a result, while the corrido serves an indispensable function in the struggle on the part of the patriarchal Mexican American communities to retain their traditional culture in the face of the advancing Anglo-American hegemony, its symbolic value is decisively affected both in terms of performance and content by gender roles and specifically male values.

6. Paredes points out that while women did sing at public occasions such as weddings, most of the singing of Border women was related to their role as mother. And yet, Border society was not so rigid, according to Paredes, that exceptions to the rule did not arise. "There were women who became well known as [corrido] singers without losing their status as respected housewives, though they were likely to be viewed as somewhat unconventional." Paredes names three exceptions: Doña Petra Longoria de Flores of Brownsville, Texas, Jovita Cantú of El Tule, Tamaulipas (1976, xix), and Raquel Ocáñez de Guerrero also of Brownsville, Texas (1958a, 179). An excellent discussion of how "Greater Mexican folksong and folk poetry has been overwhelmingly created and performed by males and how . . . this tradition has legitimized violence against women," is Liliana Valenzuela's essay, " 'Nomás tres tiros le dió': Towards an analysis of women's images in Greater Mexican Folksong and Folk Poetry" (1986). See also, Renato Rosaldo, "Politics, Patriarchs, and Laughter" (1987), for a critique of the mythic patriarchal figure of the corrido.

Later, when Mexican American artists turn to other genres of symbolic action, the male-oriented system of values cultivated during the period of open conflict and transmitted through the corrido will initially be replicated by male authors. Only later still, with the emergence of narrative texts by women authors in the late 1970s and early 1980s, will the patriarchal virtues promulgated by the corrido and narrative texts be modified and indeed resisted by women authors as they too seek to employ the tools of symbolic action.[7] The link between the corrido and Chicano narrative forms helps explain the widely recognized male-centered themes and values of many of the Chicano novels, short stories, and autobiographies of the 1950s, 1960s, and 1970s.

In the struggle for control of the Southwest between 1848 and 1930, Mexican American men and women used the techniques of both overt and symbolic action. José E. Limón has shown how

> organized resistive efforts achieve maximum pragmatic and symbolic elaboration in 1911 with the [Texas] gathering of some 300 Mexican-Americans to seek peaceful political redress for the grievances and in 1915–16 with the armed uprising of Mexican-American seditionists in southern Texas, an uprising indiscriminately and violently suppressed by the Texas Rangers and the United States Cavalry. Amidst all of this resistive activity we should note the appearance of radical labor union activity among Mexican-Americans, activity which continues into the 1930s. (1984, 11)

In the symbolic sphere, the corrido became the preeminent form of action and resistance against the ever-increasing political and cultural hegemony of Anglo-American society, a living example of Jameson's force "with its own validation and specificity," representing a protonarrative about "a kind of ultimate class fantasy about the 'collective characters' which are the classes in opposition" (1981, 87).

Ideology functions best when the network of ideas through which the culture justifies itself is internalized rather than imposed, when it is embraced by society at large as a system of belief, a pattern of self-evident truths. This is the process that Gramsci has called "hegemony" (1971, 1985). It constitutes the very sense of reality in political and cultural terms for most members of a society. This sense

---

7. A discussion of this resistance to the male hegemony by women singers such as Lydia Mendoza from the 1930s to the present is beyond the scope of this discussion. See, however, Peña (1985, 7, 47–49, and 128–30). An interesting extension to contemporary Chicano rock-and-roll of the argument concerning the role of music as an act of cultural resistance is George Lipsitz's essay, "Cruising Around the Historical Bloc —Postmodernism and Popular Music in East Los Angeles" (1987).

of reality as a lived system of meanings and values is both constituted by and constituting of the experienced practices of the culture.
It dialectically affirms and is affirmed by the accepted, which is to
say dominant, mode of life.

Raymond Williams argues, however, that "a lived hegemony is
always a process." Hegemonic control is never simply singular in
form, never totally dominant in scope, nor passive in force. "It has
continually to be renewed, recreated, defended, challenged by pressures not at all its own" (Williams 1977, 112). In this manner, Williams argues, counterhegemonic factors arise which are also real and
persistent elements of practice. "At any time, forms of alternative
or directly oppositional politics and culture exist as significant elements in the society" (1977, 113). These counterhegemonic elements
are important not only in themselves but also for an understanding of what the hegemonic process has had to control. Moreover, it
is also important to note, according to Williams, that these oppositional forms are in practice inherently linked to the hegemonic. The
hegemonic "at once produces and limits its own forms of counterculture" (1977, 114).

In contrast to the "dominant" hegemonic cultural order and even
its determined forms of countercultural opposition, Williams also
points out the possibility of "residual" and "emergent" pockets of
culture that have resisted the encroachment of the dominant order:

> The residual, by definition, has been effectively formed in the past, but it is
> still active in the cultural process, not only and often not at all as an ele-
> ment of the past, but as an effective element of the present. Thus certain
> experiences, meanings, and values which cannot be expressed or substan-
> tially verified in terms of the dominant culture, are nevertheless lived and
> practised on the basis of the residue—cultural as well as social—of some
> previous social and cultural institution or formation. (1977, 122)

The sources of these residual counterhegemonic forces are difficult
to define. For Gramsci, an alternative hegemony can spring from the
working class. With its reflexive, poetic, and narrative techniques,
the epic heroic tradition of the socially engaged corrido functions as
one such active "residual" force prior to 1930. Its roots are determined by a confluence of powerful factors, including those of class
and race, and by omission, of gender, as well. These special concerns of the corrido serve it as defenses against incorporation into
the dominant culture's music industry. When after 1930 the corrido
enters a long period of decline due, as Limón demonstrates, to an "advanced capitalist cultural re-organization in the Southwest" (1984,

14) during which the region passes from one mode of production to another, it does not disappear altogether but continues to function in a "residual" manner for the Mexican American community.

As a folk art product of the isolated, self-sufficient, patriarchal Mexican American communities of the nineteenth century whose economic structure could well be termed "precapitalist," the corrido is decisively linked to the heroic past of cultural resistance. In the face of the dominant culture's different traditions, the corrido continues through the first three decades of the twentieth century to voice "experiences, meanings, and values which cannot be expressed or substantially verified in terms of the dominant culture." With the "fall" of the corrido and the diminution of its former potent function of symbolic resistance, other expressive forms, in song, drama, lyric, and narrative begin to be appropriated by Chicano artists. Residing as a repressed element of the political unconscious, thereafter the corrido exerts symbolic force in the spheres of alternative narrative arts.

For instance, in *The Texas-Mexican Conjunto: History of a Working-Class Music,* Manuel Peña has shown how in the 1930s a popular type of accordion music, commonly known as *conjunto,* began to appear, raising the serious issues of race, class, gender, ideology, and cultural hegemony in a new musical form. According to recent theories in the area of cultural studies, expressions of popular culture and "musical discourse" can document profound changes in the "social discourse" (Hall 1977a; Williams 1981). Using related analytical methods, Peña thus argues that the development of modern conjunto music from its first commercial recordings in 1935 to its full stylization in the 1950s "coincided with shifts in language usage, folklore, dress, and such social diacritics as educational and occupational mobility" (1985, 3). As in the corrido form before it, in conjunto music "stylistic developments went hand in hand with the complex movements taking place at the infrastructural base of Texas-Mexican society. . . . Conjunto music and musicians were expressing the multiple relations that exist between social means and social meaning" (Peña 1985, 4). All aspects of culture possess a semiotic value and can function as signs to be deciphered and interrogated. Inevitably, the forms and styles that these coded bits of culture take represent and validate given social relations and processes (Hebdige 1979, 13–14). The change in musical forms and styles from corrido to conjunto parallels a corresponding change in the use of high literary forms over the previously predominating expressive forms. Both developments occur in response to changing sociohistorical circum-

stances of the Mexican American people after the turn of the century and represent the changing ways by which they appropriated
or resisted the particular sets of social relations in which they now
lived.

By the time of the Great Depression and the World War II era, the
annexation of old Mexican settlements, the displacement of the traditional socioeconomic order by Anglo-American merchants, landowners, and businessmen, and the formation of major real estate
and agricultural companies throughout the West and Southwest are
complete. An agricultural revolution had occurred in this transition from subsistence cultivation to market production, displacing
a traditional family patrimony by a market economy of commercial
capital. The economic shift in the late nineteenth and early twentieth centuries from a cattle-raising, *rancho*-based economy to large-
scale industrial farming and ranching in South Texas created a need
for a cheap, dependable labor force. Tied to the land through violence, coercion, and law, Mexican American workers experienced
this economic revolution as race exploitation, separation, and exclusion (Montejano 1979, 132–33; 1987, 50–51). The class and racial-
cultural stratification that remains in place today emerged from the
Anglo-American establishment of political and economic hegemony
over the native population (Limón 1983, 216).

With Lukács, we might thus argue that contemporary Chicano
narratives and other forms of novelistic discourse are to problematic
mid-twentieth-century society what the epic heroic corrido was to
the integrated world of the late nineteenth and early twentieth centuries: self-consciously crafted acts of social resistance. These acts of
social resistance, like Chicano narrative in general, are crucial representations of what Lukács calls the reification or fragmentation of
modern life (1971, 56). Moreover, the shift from one symbolic form
to another is a convenient and effective marker for the end of one
historical experience and the beginning of another historical stage.
An understanding of the corrido as a vital item of Chicano cultural
politics and as a substantial part of the folk base of Chicano narrative
will help us in establishing the historical specificity of that narrative
and its work of resistance to the conditions of advanced postmodern
American capitalism. The transfiguration of the corrido's residual
cultural force in other forms of residual and emergent resistive value
with the rise of autobiography, prose fiction, and other narrative discourses in the field of Chicano literary practices during the 1930s,
1940s, and 1950s forms the next phase of our discussion.

1. Mexican American laborers and their children along the northern bank of the Rio Grande at Brownsville, Texas, posed for an excursion group of investors from the Midwest interested in land and the availability of cheap labor, c. 1915. The jacket illustration is also drawn from this same panoramic photograph. (Robert Runyon Collection, courtesy of the Eugene C. Barker Texas History Center, University of Texas at Austin)

2. Texas Rangers displaying Mexican American Insurrectionists killed during the raid on Las Norias, October 8, 1915, an incident from the "border troubles." On other negative plates of this photograph, Runyon identifies the dead men as "Mexican bandits." (Robert Runyon Collection, courtesy of the Eugene C. Barker Texas History Center, University of Texas at Austin)

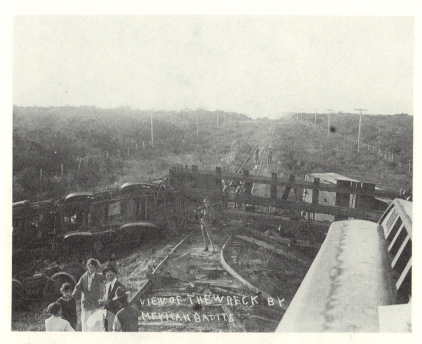

3. The Olmito train derailment. Action by Mexican American Insurrectionists near Brownsville, Texas, October 18, 1915. Runyon's caption on the negative plate of this photograph reads: "View of the wreck by Mexican badits (sic)." (Robert Runyon Collection, courtesy of the Eugene C. Barker Texas History Center, University of Texas at Austin)

4. World War II veterans, charter members of the American G.I. Forum, one of the first Chicano civil rights organizations, attending reburial services, Corpus Christi, Texas, April 1949. (Russell Lee Collection, courtesy of the Eugene C. Barker Texas History Center, University of Texas at Austin)

3
Paredes, Villarreal, and the Dialectics of History

In the preceding chapter I have argued that the corrido can be construed as a residual cultural form that continues to underwrite contemporary Chicano narrative. Decisive in this relationship of prefiguration between ballad and narrative is Américo Paredes' *With His Pistol in His Hand* in its presentation of literary and historical paradigms for the production of a shared narrative community. Our concern has been to establish the validity of that relationship not in empirical, point-by-point correspondences between the corrido as a folk artform and narrative as a high literary genre. At issue, rather, is to articulate the historical positioning of Chicano narrative, beginning with Paredes' short stories and Villarreal's novel *Pocho*, poised as it is between an integrated but distant heroic past and a fragmented and all-too-present reality.

I do not take either the corrido or contemporary Chicano narrative as unproblematic empirical terms that may be illuminated through simple contrast. The corrido does not in any homogeneous manner serve as the real or fictive "origin" of Chicano narrative nor as a "narrative paradise to be regained" (Bernstein 1984, 48). Certainly, the background to my argument is Lukács's attempt to place epic as an oral form against the novel as a written form. To the extent that many Chicano narratives opt for what Bakhtin has called "novelistic discourse" (1981, 41–83), Lukács's argument about the relation of novel to epic is pertinent, at least analogically. But my focus here is narrative as it relates to a particular ballad genre. As Bakhtin has also suggested, the two sets of relational terms (epic/novel, ballad/narrative) are not mutually exclusive (3–40). Similarly, I do not attempt to establish a single, originary source for all Chicano narrative. Against such an essentialist and ahistorical view, I show how the corrido has

47

served as much to incite narratives differing from its ideological base as it has informed narratives conforming to its world view.

Both corrido and epic mark the bounds of a historical reflection by which Chicano novelistic genres can be brought into consciousness in "historical specificity and antinomic complexity" (Bernstein 1984, 48). Bound as the corrido is by its formal quality as song, its oral quality prohibits it from being the isomorphic original upon which narratives as high literary forms are based. The very orality of the corrido serves instead as a boundary to a tradition of *writing*. Within these boundaries, the nineteenth- and early-twentieth-century corrido served the symbolic function of providing alternative interpretations of empirical events (functioning as a substitute for history writing) and of creating counterfactual worlds of lived experience (functioning as a substitute for fiction writing). As if in response to the encroaching force of the dominant American hegemony and the decline of the corrido as an organic culturally symbolic act, after 1930 other narrative forms emerge to provide those alternative interpretations of the historical world.[1]

Américo Paredes' "The Hammon and the Beans" and "Over the Waves Is Out"

Instrumental in the development of Chicano narrative in the post-corrido period are two short stories by Américo Paredes, "The Hammon and the Beans" (c. 1939) and "Over the Waves Is Out" (c. 1948).[2]

1. As our discussion in chapter 2 maintains, World War II and the Korean War served as thresholds in the social, cultural, and economic transformation of the Mexican American community. Paradoxically, the advanced Americanization of the community and increasing economic and educational opportunities for veterans and their children in the postwar years of the 1940s and 1950s provided the beginning of access to English-language publication outlets that, even if only in attenuated form, now took over the role of symbolic resistance formerly held by Spanish-language song, legend, folklore, and journalism.

2. Both stories have interesting publication histories, exemplifying the difficulties that Mexican American writers have had in securing access to mainstream American publications. "The Hammon and the Beans," while written c. 1939, was not published until 1963; "Over the Waves Is Out" was written c. 1948 but did not appear until 1953. From personal conversations with the author in Austin, Texas, on April 30, 1986, and in Colorado Springs, Colorado, on July 6, 1986. Recently, the author has graciously shown me the manuscript of an unpublished novel, entitled *George Washington Gómez* (in five parts, 451 typescript pages), written contemporaneously with these two stories and sharing with them the setting of "Jonesville-on-the-Grande" and the time period of the mid-1910s to the mid-1930s. Having had to set the novel aside because of the pressures of other commitments, Paredes is currently preparing the novel for publication (Houston: Arte-Público Press, 1990).

Certainly, one can find earlier writings that could be used as originary points for Chicano narrative, but these two stories exhibit in accomplished form virtually all of the formal and thematic features that will characterize the major products of the boom in Chicano writing that occurs after the mid-1960s.[3] In addition, both stories anticipate the artistic integrity and oppositional intensity of Paredes' own later scholarly-artistic recreation of the life of "Gregorio Cortez." More important, however, these stories already indicate the ironic revision of the nineteenth- and early-twentieth-century values of the Mexican American community represented, celebrated, and dignified in the corridos we have discussed. This revisionary move, made necessary by radical changes in the socioeconomic and cultural condition of Mexican Americans in the Depression and post–World War II eras, hereafter becomes one of the hallmarks of contemporary Chicano narrative.

In the South Texas border region, the center of both overt political and symbolic resistance, the effects of capitalist agribusiness were to initiate the dissolution and fragmentation of formerly unified Mexican American communities by way of the commodification of labor and the encroachment of the market system. By the mid-1930s, many of what had once been small family-owned or family-tenanted farms and ranches held and worked in common had been taken over by large corporate agribusiness interests organizing production for a competitive world market (Montejano 1979, 133). In the process of this takeover, Mexican Americans were increasingly displaced onto smaller and smaller parcels of land worked primarily through contract sharecropping, thus "ensuring the availability of cheap resident

3. The purported "awakening" of Chicano letters in the 1960s was not an absolute beginning. Various studies have shown recently the extent and quality of works by Mexican American authors prior to the flowering that did take place in the early 1960s. See, for example, Paredes' essay, "The Folk Base of Chicano Literature" (1979, 4–17). Good general introductions to the "prehistory" of Chicano literature are provided by Luis Leal, "Mexican American Literature: A Historical Perspective" (1979); Juan Rodríguez, "Notes on the Evolution of Chicano Prose Fiction" (1979b); Luis Leal and Pepe Barrón, "Chicano Literature: An Overview" (1982); Raymund A. Paredes, "The Evolution of Chicano Literature" (1982); Charles Tatum (1982). See also, Tomás Rivera's discussion of the importance of Mexican American newspapers of the nineteenth century as early sources of Chicano literature, "Into the Labyrinth: The Chicano in Literature" (1971). A complete bibliography of critical studies is Ernestina Eger (1982). An excellent reference guide is provided by Julio A. Martínez and Francisco A. Lomelí, who argue that Chicano literature should be "regarded as the literary output of Mexican Americans since 1848, with backgrounds and traditions as far back as the sixteenth century" (1985, xi). Additionally, a whole body of nineteenth- and early-twentieth-century writings by Chicanas is also presently being studied. See references to these texts in chapter 8. On the question of "origins," see Edward Said (1975).

labor throughout the year" (Montejano 1979, 138). Sharecroppers "were basically laborers who were compensated by payments in kind in lieu of cash wages. Under a halves agreement, the sharecropper furnished only his labor (and that of his family), for which he could keep one-half of the cotton cultivated on the acreage assigned him by the landlord" (Montejano 1979, 136). By the late 1920s, however, even sharecropping had become economically unfeasible for white landowners, as they could make more money by hiring Mexicans as wage laborers than by leasing to them. Especially at harvest times, agricultural work now came to be handled by a migratory workforce that was itself controlled by various economic and legal means (i.e., wage-fixing, mobility restrictions, vagrancy laws, etc.). These labor controls amounted to a program of labor repression.

Coupled with the commercialization of popular music by both the Mexican and the American music industries after the early 1930s, the need for alternative symbolic forms to express resistance to this social reality becomes all the greater (Peña 1985). The revisionary move on the part of contemporary Chicano narrative in the face of a quite different social reality from that of the older forms of the nineteenth and early twentieth centuries is hence all-encompassing. It takes as its object the mainstays of traditional culture, ranging from the nature of family and community interactions, to the process of individual subject-formation itself. Patterns of belief and behavior that go unquestioned in the corrido because they served as the grounds of personal and group identity now begin to be put at stake in narrative. Twenty years before the first full-length elaboration of these cultural dynamics in Villarreal's novel *Pocho* (1959), and thirty years before the full flowering of Chicano fiction in the late 1960s, Américo Paredes' stories and novel pose and confront those same issues that will remain the central concerns of later Chicano writers.

The first of these stories, "The Hammon and the Beans,"[4] is set in the midst of the region of the most intense border conflict, the Lower Rio Grande Valley of South Texas. Paredes' first-person narrator retrospectively recreates the mood of life on the border in the first two decades of the twentieth century, a historical moment when the heroic resistance of men like Gregorio Cortez, Catarino García, and Aniceto Pizaña is already fading into the hazy past. Brownsville, Texas, the site of García's rebellion and the focus of other incidents

4. Américo Paredes, "The Hammon and the Beans," *The Texas Observer*, April 18, 1963; rpt. in *The Chicano: From Caricature to Self-Portrait*, ed. Edward Simmen (New York: Mentor Books, New American Library, 1971): 274–78. I cite the text of the Simmen reprint.

of cultural resistance, is depicted in the story as "Jonesville-on-the-Grande," a place of diminished heroic quality and with all the feel of a town occupied by a conquering alien army. And indeed, the focus of life in the story is an army base, "Fort Jones," situated at the edge of town but dominating the entire community by virtue of its presence. "We told off our days by the routine on the post," says the narrator:

> Jonesville-on-the-Grande woke to the cannon's roar, as if to battle, and the day began. . . . At eight the whistle from the post laundry sent us children off to school. The whole town stopped for lunch with the noon whistle. . . . The post was the town's clock . . . or like some insistent older person who was always there to tell you it was time. (274)

As the temporal regulator of town life, the army post is like a testy parent or grandparent, ordering the schedules of its errant children. And lest we forget what serious function the army post really serves, the narrator reminds us that "it was because of the border troubles, ten years or so before, that the soldiers had come back to Fort Jones" (275).

The story thus specifically sets itself in the aftermath of the last great armed uprising by Mexican Americans seeking justice with pistols in hand, memorialized in the corrido "Los sediciosos." The rapid increase of the Mexican population throughout the Southwest during the first two decades of the twentieth century had triggered a period of particularly violent confrontations between Anglos and Mexican Americans. These "border troubles" peaked in intensity between 1915–17 and led to especially violent repression in South Texas.[5] As noted earlier, in July 1915 Mexicans led by Aniceto Pizaña had made a series of raids on Anglo ranches in retaliation for the murder in Brownsville of a Mexican man. "The raids provided an excuse for reprisals by Rangers and Anglo authorities" (Acuña 1981,

---

5. See Acuña (1981, 299–349), Rosenbaum (1981, 48–56), and Montejano (1987, 106–55) for a full account of the history of this "Repression and Resistance" in the early twentieth century. In differentiating between the corrido of Greater Mexico and the Texas-Mexican Border corrido, Paredes points out that "the outlaws against the Díaz regime were the first important *corrido* heroes of Greater Mexico. But since these men symbolized a struggle between classes rather than cultural strife or civil war, the ballads about them were of a proletarian cast: the ballad heroes rob the rich to give to the poor and the ballad style is definitely sentimental. Many of the Greater Mexico outlaw *corridos* were sung on the Border, and some of their commonplaces were borrowed for the heroic Border *corrido*. What was not borrowed was the concept of the *corrido* hero. The Border *corridos* make a very definite distinction between the hero of border conflict and the mere outlaw" (1958a: 143). Paredes' fiction reexamines ironically the figure of the heroic corrido, "the peaceful man who defends his right" with pistol in hand (150).

308). These reprisals were so indiscriminate and brutal that by 1917 35,000 United States soldiers were stationed on the border to help keep the peace. George Marvin, describing the atmosphere along the border for the magazine *World's Work* in January 1917, writes:

The killing of Mexicans ... along the border in these last four years is almost incredible. ... Some Rangers have degenerated into common mankillers. There is no penalty for killing, no jury along the border would ever convict a white man for shooting a Mexican. ... Reading over Secret Service records makes you feel as though there was an open gun season on Mexicans along the border.[6]

In the wake of these calamities, "Fort Jones" serves as both a metaphor for the paternal presence of the occupying army, and as a literal reminder of the force behind that presence. The "high wire fence that divided the post from the town" (274–75) is only a physical manifestation of the political and cultural distance that separates the occupying army from the Mexican American citizens of Jonesville-on-the-Grande. "Sometimes we joined in the ceremony, standing at salute until the sound of the cannon made us jump," continues the narrator. "But at other times we stuck out our tongues and jeered at the soldiers. Perhaps the night before we had hung at the edges of a group of old men and listened to tales about Aniceto Pizaña and the 'border troubles'" (275). The stories told by the old men must compete for the children's allegiance, however, with other stories of revolutionary resistance that the children are learning in their American schools: stories "about George Washington ... [and] about Marion the Fox and the British cavalry that chased him up and down the broad Santee" (275).

In ideological terms, what the scene of everyday life offers the child narrator is an ongoing dramatization of the conflicts between the residual elements of the child's traditional community and the forces of the new dominant culture, a conflict being fought for the hearts and minds of the Mexican American children. The power of American ideology is made concrete in the opening scene of the story by the physical presence of the army fort and by the spiritual influence of the American school. That ideological power struggle, as seen through the eyes of the child narrator and the outcome of which is already painfully obvious, is precisely what the story is about: "And so we lived, we and the post, side by side with the wire fence between us" (275).

6. Cited in Acuña (1981, 308).

As it turns out, however, the separation between the two is not as inviolable as the initial scenes of the story lead us to believe. While "none of us ever went to Fort Jones," there is one child who does, Chonita, "a scrawny girl of about nine" (276), who every evening would enter the forbidden grounds "to the mess halls and [press] her nose against the screens and [watch] the soldiers eat" (275). The daughter of impoverished working-class parents, who live in a one-room shack provided to them at no cost by the narrator's parents, Chonita is not only more daring than her playmates, she "was a poet too" (276). Every evening she would return from her forays into the fort with the left-overs from the soldiers' meals for her family and with imitations of the soldiers "calling to each other through food-stuffed mouths" for her friends' amusement: " 'Give me the hammon and the beans!' she yelled. 'Give me the hammon and the beans!' " (276).

Chonita, who probably does not attend the American school, speaks no English, but mimics with creditable accuracy the sounds of the soldiers' calls across their food-laden tables. (In Spanish, "ham" is "jamón," close enough for Chonita's purposes.)[7] Her mimicry and her daring are the instruments of her poetry. The other children—the narrator's friends, middle-class children who learn English at the American school—egg her on by pretending that Chonita "could talk English better than the teachers at the grammar school" (276). The narrator finds it a very bad joke to tease the little girl, but loses track of her and her escapades when he is suddenly taken ill.

One evening the local doctor appears at the narrator's home, very distraught with the news that Chonita has died. Of what? "Pneumonia, flu, malnutrition, worms, the evil eye. . . . What the hell difference does it make?" (277). Dr. Zapata angrily describes the scene of Chonita's death: "They're like animals. . . . Do you know what that brute of a father was doing when I left? He was laughing! Drinking and laughing with his friends" (277). The man is unconcerned apparently because he is not Chonita's real father. Her real father had been "shot and hanged from a mesquite limb. He was working too close to the tracks the day the Olmito train was derailed," according to the doctor. His reference to the derailment of the Olmito train identifies Chonita's real father as one of the victims of the Texas Ranger terror following Pizaña's sedition. The doctor continues:

7. Paredes has noted that "the American taste for ham plays a big part in border folklore, and now and then one hears the term *gringo jamonero*" (1978, 82) as a derisive term for Americans.

In classical times they did things better. Take Troy, for instance. After they stormed the city they grabbed the babies by the heels and dashed them against the wall. That was more humane. (278)

In contrast to the fate of a conquered people today—that is, the prolonged starvation of their children—the ritual infanticide by the victorious conquerors of classical times seems benevolent. Moreover, the catastrophic defeat of Troy at least did not dehumanize the vanquished into unfeeling "brutes," as this defeat has. The narrator's father picks up on Dr. Zapata's mood of despondency and teases him that he is beginning to sound as "radical" as his namesake and "relative down there in Morelos" (278), a reference to the Mexican revolutionary leader Emiliano Zapata. In the midst of an ensuing stirring political discussion about "radicals," "bandits," "outlaws," and "leaders of the people," the narrator is ignominiously sent to bed by his mother.

In bed, away from the adult conversations that he has been overhearing, the boy drowsily muses over what he has heard and only half understood concerning the heroic acts of men who lived and died before he was born. He begins metaphorically to confuse the heroes of the American revolution ("Marion the Fox") and those of the Mexican revolution ("Villa," "Zapata") by conjoining what he has learned at school, "The Song of Marion's Men," with the stories and legends he hears at home. The weirdly mixed song that combines his Mexican heritage and his American enculturation comes out like this: "Emiliano Zapata's cavalry charged down to the broad Santee, where there were grave men with hoary hairs." As his mind drifts among thoughts about these contradictory figures, all of a sudden he hears "the cold voice of the [post] bugle [that] went gliding in and out of the dark like something that couldn't find its way back to wherever it had been" (278). The stark loneliness of the bugle's homeless notes now remind him of poor Chonita, who according to his mother is "happy . . . in Heaven" (277):

I thought of Chonita in Heaven, and I saw her in her torn and dirty dress, with a pair of bright wings attached, flying round and round like a butterfly shouting, "Give me the hammon and the beans!" (278)

His mother's comforting words and the humorous vision of the little girl with wings really hold no comfort. As he has already admitted: "In later years I thought of [Chonita] a lot, especially during the thirties when I was growing up. Those years would have been just made for her. Many's the time I have seen her in my mind's eye, in the picket lines demanding not bread, not cake, but the hammon and the beans" (277). In another age the fragile, malnourished "butterfly" might have found life not in a deferred vision of a plentiful afterlife, nor by begging scraps from the army kitchens, but in radical politics or collective action, demanding social justice in the picket lines with her oppressed sisters and brothers. Her poetry might have been real rather than mimicry. "But it didn't work out that way" (277), he admits. The heroic age of resistance "with pistols in hand" seems as distant from present reality as are the deeds of the armies at Troy, and as tragic. There can thus be no falsely victorious ending to this story, as the narrator in later life fully realizes. But his night of mourning for Chonita ("I cried. And whether it was . . . Chonita or what, to this day I do not know"—278) is the source of his memorial to her: the story of her brief life of poverty. That written monument is one that might initiate the conditions for a reawakening of the spirit of symbolic action of a prior age and that might eliminate the possibility of other little girls having to suffer Chonita's fate. The text of the story thus becomes, as in the corridos the narrator overhears, an occasion for the expression of a symbolic solution to the determinate contradictions of history.

The decline of the heroic corrido age and the men it celebrates is also the subject of Paredes' second story, "Over the Waves Is Out."[8] But while in "The Hammon and the Beans" the narrator's recognition of that decline is linked to a child's tragic death, in "Over the Waves Is Out" the recognition of the end of the historical moment when men heroically defended their rights with their pistols in hand is not tragic but comic and almost bathetic. As in the first story, the insight to the reduced nature of present reality comes indirectly, from the discrepancies between what the narrator describes, what he hears, and what he later comes to understand. But also as in the first story, the understanding that comes with that view of the past does not preclude the possibility of future victories in the conflict between oppressors and oppressed; it does, however, admit to the necessity of its deferral to other times and other methods.

"Over the Waves Is Out" is also focused on the experiences of a young boy. The major conflict this time is not cultural, between Anglos and Mexican Americans but generational, between fathers and sons, in this case, a father who had ridden with Villa's revolutionary armies, and a son who "had always wanted to be a musician."

8. Américo Paredes, "Over the Waves Is Out," *New Mexico Review* 23, no. 2 (Summer 1953): 177–87. All citations refer to this publication.

The father, now a deputy sheriff, will not allow his son to become a musician because the father had once known the man who composed the song "Over the Waves." This composer had "succumbed to drink and women, which led him to a tragic end" (177).[9]

The boy "would often lie on the grass of afternoons and dream he was a minstrel in the court of El Cid Campeador" (177). The father "knew about the evils of drink and women, having investigated them in his youth" and also knew that his son was "a delicate boy" whose girlish face "wouldn't go well in a brothel. And that was the place for musicians" (177). Moreover, in his own youth the father "had liked the guitar" (177), but his father, the boy's grandfather, caught him playing it at a funeral and "broke the guitar on his head" (177). This incident had unceremoniously ended the father's guitar playing as well as his own relationship with his father. And its repercussions were still being felt, for it had made it difficult for the father to sympathize with his boy's romantic wish to be a musician.

But the boy was persistent. He would approach his father cautiously,

whenever he found him seated close to a window on his days off, reading *The Life and Times of Pancho Villa*, or *God, Grand Architect of the Universe*. His father would sit there reading in his shirt sleeves, the cowboy hat and the heavy pistol in the cartridge belt lying on the table beside him, the linen coat hanging on the back of a chair. (177–78)

The scene is thus set for the unexpected reconciliation that is about to commence between the dreamy boy with troubador ambitions and the father, who still lives his youth as a revolutionary soldier. At this point, however, a reconciliation seems anything but likely, as the generational difference between the two is made even wider by the clash of their proclivities, made present by the boy's wishes for a piano ("he would lie awake in the dark, imagining he was a pianist with wild hair and evening clothes, and that he was playing, playing, playing"—178) and by the father's obvious relish for the implements and duties of his position as an officer of the law.

One evening, miraculously, the boy begins to hear music welling

9. The waltz, "Sobre las olas" ("Over the Waves"), composed by Juventino Rosas, to which the story's title refers was immensely popular during the 1890s and the waning years of the Porfirio Díaz regime. It continues to be a singularly identifiable melody to this day. It is probably the best-known work by a Mexican composer, even though under its various titles audiences often assume that the waltz is a Tchaikovsky or a Chopin composition. Paredes reports that his own father knew the composer Rosas, who died an alcoholic in Cuba. From a personal conversation, July 6, 1986.

as if from inside of him: "He was lifted up in a sea of piano music which continued to pour out of him, churning and eddying about him in glowing spirals, slowly burying him in a glittering shower until he fell asleep" (179). The sonorous cascades of liquid sound disappear with the light, but not entirely, for the next morning "it was there, in some cranny of his mind, where he could just barely touch it" (179). The "rich warm secret" (179) that he carries down to breakfast is evident to all, even if its source is not.

The next evening, the boy impatiently waits for the music to flow again from the springs of his growing imagination. In languorous metaphors appropriate to the portrait of the artist as a young man he is painting, the narrator describes the musical climax:

He lay in bed waiting for the house to be dark and still so the music would come again. And finally it came, faintly at first, then more distinctly, though never loud, splashing and whirling about, twisting in intricate eddies of chords and bright waterfalls of melody, or falling in separate notes into the night like drops of quicksilver, rolling, glimmering. (180)

In the watery medium of his dreams, the music rolls over the waves of his sensual and spiritual desires. And it makes the dreamy boy seem even more dreamy the next morning, when he admits his mystical experience to his mother and sister.

Alarmed at the boy's insistence that the music he hears comes preternaturally from within him, the mother asks the boy's father to speak to him about it. The father's reaction is predictable; he attempts to force the child to deny that he is hearing music. Looking at his father who stands in judgment of him "with his memories of Pancho Villa and the man who composed 'Over the Waves,'" the boy "knew he could never make him understand about the music, how it came from inside him, how beautiful it was, and how it made everything else beautiful" (181). The boy thus denies to his father the sensibilities that once caused him to play the guitar at a funeral, while the father in turn distrusts his son's capacity to tame the impulses manifested by the music he hears. Music may indeed, as Theodor Adorno has argued, stir up "the dance of the Maenads and sounds from Pan's bewitching flute," but it also "rings out from the Orphic lyre, around which the visions of violence range themselves, pacified" ([1938] 1982, 270). The father and son's dissonant views of one another, like the conflicting aspects of music itself, begin to appear as the very conditions for their possible reconciliation. But not yet.

The next evening, the music begins again, as we find the boy again "floating about on the beautiful sounds" (182). This time, however, the music is interrupted by the sound of a gunshot down the street at the neighborhood bakery. The boy follows his father, "who was hurrying along, buckling on his cartridge belt" (183). He notices that his father's voice as he runs toward the sound of gunfire is "brisk and eager, strangely unlike his father's voice" (183). At the bakery, someone has shot at a radio, scared the baker, and escaped across the river into Mexico, leaving the boy's father no opportunity for the glory of former days. On hearing the story of the boy's musical hallucinations and after considering the possibility that the boy has experienced no Apollonian or Dionysian mystery but has only been hearing the radio in the bakery (which has apparently affected at least one other listener), the sheriff gives the boy a player piano, over his father's objections.

Returning home, the father "took out his gun as he walked, cocked it, and uncocked it, sighted along the barrel, twirled it around and put it back in its holster" (186). When he begins to tell his son again of other midnight chases and is corrected by the boy concerning details of the story, the father admits that "it's hard to remember [the details] at times, it's been so long ago. So long, long ago" (187). The boy himself is back in his musical dream floating harmonically over the waves, blissfully unaware that the player piano he has just been promised is not the piano of his dreams. Neither father nor son is present to the other as each lives a past and future world. But the boy is now jarred back to the present. The shock that follows his realization that "you don't have to practice with that kind of piano. You just pump the pedals" (187) is followed by another: the son's realization of the father's anticipated pleasure in pumping the pedals himself as he listens to "Over the Waves." Stopped in his tracks by the dual revelations, the boy watches his father "disappear into the night. He felt very sad and very old and very much alone" (187).

The degeneration from the heroic past of the corrido world view is here subtly allayed. The high rhetoric of the corrido hero's tragic defiance is modulated by Deputy De la Garza's declining age and by his son's intoxication with the sensuality of music. In both cases one senses a certain diminishing of the potential for heroic behavior; and yet, the narrator's gentle irony serves not so much to undercut the protagonists as to express their ambiguous position between two ages and two cultures. Their partial illusions as well as their partial insights about each other serve as critiques of their self-assured visions of themselves and the other. For the father, his rediscovery of his past musical consciousness opens the possibility of a reconciliation with the self that his own father denied him and with the son whom he has perhaps misapprised. For the boy, the seductive power of music survives only while the force of his illusions is strongest, hence his feelings of sadness, age, and solitude at the story's end. But these feelings might also allow him to participate in his father's history, viewing it now not as the irrelevant songs and tales of nostalgic old men, but as the substance of his own fate.

While this alternative melody serves to harmonize the discord between father and son, it also carries with it a contrapuntal line: the countervailing absence of women's song. Nowhere in the pattern of Chicano narratives informed by the corrido are the contradictions inherent in the ideological force of patriarchal value more clear than here in Paredes' short fiction. The boy's allegiance to music and the arts initially separates him from his father's masculine values. As it turns out, however, even Deputy De la Garza is capable of feeling what the child feels as he remembers his own father's denial of his affectivity. Significantly absent from this male interchange are all of the women of the family. And yet, in depicting the contradictory truths of patriarchal consciousness, Paredes' story offers unconsciously an image, albeit as a negative truth, of feminist consciousness. The consolidation of male solidarity, with the acceptance of the heterogeneity of male affective response, seems necessarily to entail driving to the margins of narrative any women's presence. Tania Modleski writes: "Psychoanalysis has shown that the process by which the male child comes to set the mother at a distance is of very uncertain outcome, which helps to explain why it is continually necessary for man to face the threat woman poses and to work to subdue that threat both in life and art" (1988, 4). Paredes' story shows how oppositional Chicano narrative attains hegemonic patriarchal force precisely by repressing the threat of its feminist consciousness.

With Deputy De la Garza and his son, we are now far removed from the collective concerns of the corrido and its heroes. We cannot but imagine that the music that now wells up and becomes the instrument allowing father and son to express an underworld of emotion that assists their opposition to being excluded from history and culture is for both a far cry from the reified and fetish-character music that by the 1930s had begun to dominate the Mexican American music industry.[10] In the wake of this decline of the heroic Border co-

10. For a discussion of the dramatic changes that occurred in the music of the Mexican American community after 1930, see Peña (1985) and Limón (1984). Adorno's essay, "On the Fetish-Character in Music and the Regression of Listening" ([1938] 1982, 270–99), offers a useful, even if limited, theoretical model for the understanding of the relationship between musical and sociopolitical concepts.

rrido and its patriarchal ideology, and with the impetus of Paredes'
works of fiction and scholarship, other literary figures appear to help
stave off the dominant hegemonic powers that were beginning to
liquidate a normative Mexican American individuality that was perhaps past saving. Representing individuals capable of enacting the
aims of collectivity, even if the nature of that collectivity continues
to be one cast by a masculine vision, these new figures open the next
stage of Chicano narrative. We turn now to one such instance, with
the first widely known Chicano novel.

Pocho and the Dialectics of History

In the second chapter of José Antonio Villarreal's seminal novel,
Pocho (1959), Juan Rubio—paradigmatic hero, patriarch, and warrior,
a virtual model of the stereotyped, sentimental, and reified hero of
the very different Greater Mexican corrido tradition, having participated in the Revolution of 1910—finds that he must flee in defeat
from Mexico to the United States. For Mexican Americans, Juan
Rubio's flight dramatizes an equally important historical event: it
marks the significant point in the rapid growth of Mexican communities in the American Southwest. And it is not accidental that here,
at the "beginning" of the Chicano novel, we find the events of fiction firmly rooted in the events of history. The novel, more so than
any other literary genre, insists on this tie to the real. In respecting
the necessity of this tie, Villarreal offers us not so much a slice of
reality as he does a representation of the cultural rules and conventions by which the fictional character Juan Rubio, and real men like
him, dealt with that reality.

For all of its sociohistorical significance, the Revolution is mainly
important in this novel for the tremendous personal meaning Rubio
has attributed to it: as a result of its shattering events, the world
of his values has been radically polarized. The rules of ethical con-
duct personified in his character sharply specify that one must live
and die with dignity, with pistol in hand if necessary, or else existence has no value at all. Juan Rubio is therefore represented in the
novel as being linked in fundamental ways to traditional sources of
independent and autonomous absolute value, which value he will
hold even against life itself. But already from the beginning of the
novel, when confronted with perversions of this value—first in the
person of a pimping *gachupín* (Spaniard), whom he cold-bloodedly
kills, and next in the figure of an old friend who has betrayed the
principles of the Revolution to become a general in the army of

the "institutionalized revolution," whom he unmercifully mocks—
Rubio begins to suspect that the passing of the revolutionary glory
days will mean more than political defeat. He realizes that with the
deaths of Pancho Villa and Emiliano Zapata, primary symbols of the
Revolution, the grand dream of social justice and individual dignity
has been subverted.

From this subversion has emerged a new class of men like René
Soto, a political intriguer, whom Juan sees as worthless: "He was
nothing," Rubio says to one of these, "and . . . you are *nothing*."[11]
Throughout the remainder of the novel, this will be Juan's vision of
the world: one is either something, dignified and real, or one is nothing. In this formulation, Villarreal seems less concerned with por-
traying what one critic has called "abstract stereotypes drawn from
the popular Mexican collective unconscious" (S. Sánchez 1978, 3)
than with representing the thematics of the patriarchal will to power
within the collective political unconscious. What is to be willed here
is the power of absolute value over and against any other formulation concerning human action. From the perspective of narrative
stratagem, not only is Villarreal's tactic of playing with stereotypes
effective, it is absolutely essential for the intended analysis of value
that is now to follow. Life, as action, manifests itself in Juan's view in
a continuing resistance to whatever forces would negate it. For Juan
there can be no middle ground, no reconciliation between the poles
of being and nothing, for these have become ethical and political as
well as ontological terms. In the certainty of his actions, he thus lives
out the stereotype of the corrido hero, one man alone, certain of his
moral ascendency. Yet, one result of this irreconcilability between
being and nothing is, as various readers have observed, a narrative
about "the menace of chaotic discontinuity."[12] What has not been
observed is the dramatic effect of this discontinuity in Juan's life.

But the novel is not primarily about Juan Rubio. It is about his
son, Richard, the eponymous *pocho* (a pejorative Mexican term for
an "Americanized" Chicano), born in a melon field in the Imperial
Valley of southern California. In the course of the novel, Richard
will freely accept the derogatory term *pocho* and transform it into a
sign of his ambiguous status as a child of two cultures—Mexican and
American—yet claimed by neither. His story is that of a sensitive
young child struggling to create an acceptable identity for himself

11. José Antonio Villarreal, *Pocho* (1959; rpt. New York: Anchor, 1970), 19. I cite
this edition of the novel throughout my discussion.

12. Juan Bruce-Novoa, "The Space of Chicano Literature," *De Colores* 1 (1975):
22–42.

from the clash of these two cultures. In successive chapters we are offered another portrait of the artist as a young man. We see Richard first working to understand the doctrinal answers that his Roman Catholic faith offers him about the nature of existence and then his attempts to correlate these answers to the historical reality of life as a child of agricultural workers in and around Santa Clara, California, in 1931. We follow him through union halls, strikes, and hunger marches as the boy receives a first-hand education in political action, repressive violence, and death. And we see him as an adolescent learning about sexual desires and the problems of interracial love and homosexual relationships. All the while as the young Richard matures, learns to live in an English-speaking American world, and realizes that he wishes to become a writer, we also see the gradual disintegration of his traditional Mexican family.

Thus, after the first chapter, the cataclysmic events of the Mexican Revolution have frozen into a past of intractable and alien value. If the hallmark of the corrido is the hero's unwavering commitment to his communal identity, the construction of identity as such is precisely the issue of contemporary Chicano narrative. In the corrido individual goals and communal concerns are one and the same. The dispositions of novelistic heroes, in contrast, are complex, ambiguous, and entirely problematic. In the case of the decidedly unheroic Richard Rubio, the United States is not his father's Mexico, and the old values that bolstered identity do not seem to apply. This does not mean that the novel idealizes the remote past of the Mexican Revolution in order to explain the increasing fragmentation of twentieth-century Chicano cultural life. Nor does it mean that the novel offers the conventions of Anglo-American culture as positive models, even though we continually see Richard at the point of being assimilated into the dominant culture. Instead, it offers us a difference. Among the various options of absolute value to be posed in the course of the novel for Richard Rubio by Anglo-American culture, by the Roman Catholic Church, by his father's demands, by his mother's wishes, and by his own sexual identity, Richard will consistently choose *not* to choose. Herein lies Richard's generic difference.

The sensitive young Richard reasons that since, as the Church teaches, only good and evil exist in the world, and that since the differences between good and evil are inherently ambiguous, then it is possible that these differences cannot be known. "He was frightened," the narrator tells us, "because he could not know" the differences and because "somehow God was in the middle of the whole thing. To do 'bad' things had something to do with being alive, but really what were bad things?" (37). This naive conflation of "life" and "bad things" is later expressed in more exact terms: "I was scared," says Richard, "because if He willed it so, I knew that the earth would *+ Rivera* open and it would swallow me up because I dared to demand explanations from Him. . . . Then, one day, I knew that . . . if He could do the best thing in the world, He could also do the most evil thing in the world" (65). If after this recognition the two concepts of good and evil are still to be differentiated, then the difference must be based on a perception of something other than a pure meaning or transcendental idea to serve as the substance of good or evil. Richard's question of the nature of good and evil is posed, therefore, not to eliminate their opposition, but to show that the terms appear as the *difference* [13] of the other: in Richard's view, "good" constitutes itself by its very relation to what it absolutely is not. Good is *not* evil; but it *is* evil that has not yet happened, and vice versa. The significance of the young Richard's elementary intuition into the differential structure of moral codes is that it removes value, and therefore meaning, from

13. In formulating my case for a theory of the "differential structure" of Chicano narrative, I draw on the now well-known sources of poststructuralist analysis, including especially, Paul de Man's "The Rhetoric of Blindness: Jacques Derrida's Reading of Rousseau" (1971, 102–41), Jacques Derrida's discussion of *differance* in "Differance," *Speech and Phenomena* (1973), and *Of Grammatology* (1976). "We shall designate the term *differance*," writes Derrida, "the movement by which language, or any code, any system of reference becomes 'historically' constituted as a fabric of differences. . . . Difference is what makes the movement of signification possible only if each element that is said to be 'present,' appearing on the stage of presence, is related to something other than itself but retains the mark of a past element and already lets itself be hollowed out by the mark of its relation to a future element" (141, 142). From Derrida's concept I would retain the two ideas of differance as a *differing* (in kind) and as a *defering* (in time). I would also emphasize that "differance" is the way that discourse is √ *historically* constituted.

See also Jameson, *The Prison-House of Language* (1972, 173–86); and his discussion of "ethnopoetics," "Collective Art in the Age of Cultural Imperialism," in ✳ *Alcheringa* 2, no. 2 (1976): 108–12. On deconstruction and Marxism, see especially, Jameson, *The Political Unconscious* (1981, 281–99). See also my discussion in *Figural Language in the Novel* (1984, 3–24 passim), as well as Michael Ryan's in *Marxism and Deconstruction* (1982, 1–81).

Of especial interest are the following essays: Spivak, "Marx after Derrida" (1984, 227–46), and Eagleton, "Marxism, Structuralism, and Poststructuralism" (1985); Gates, "Introduction: Writing, 'Race' and the Difference It Makes" (1985), Said, "An Ideology of Difference" (1985, 38–58), JanMohamed, "The Economy of Manichean ✳ Allegory: The Function of Racial Difference in Colonialist Literature" (1985), Barbara Johnson, "Thresholds of Difference: Structures of Address in Zora Neal Hurston" (1985), Derrida, "Racism's Last Word" (1985), and Baker, "Caliban's Triple Play" (1985). A related argument on "difference" and identity is made in R. Radhakrishnan, "Ethnic Identity and Post-Structuralist Differance" (1987).

the realm of a static, transcendent sphere and places it instead within the active domains of history and culture. As Jacques Derrida points out, however, "if the word 'history' did not carry with it the theme of a final repression of differance, we could say that differences alone could be 'historical' through and through from the start" (1973, 141). The story of Richard's life is precisely that of his attempt to repress the difference that history has imposed on him.

By the same token, his recognition of the differential structure of moral codes leads to Richard's later rejection of all "codes of honor," insofar as they are founded upon falsely absolute standards: "he thought of himself, and starkly, without knowledge of the words that would describe it, he saw the demands of tradition, of culture, of the social structure on an individual . . . and was resolved that he would rise above it" (95). The boy rejects his father's Mexican values and his mother's Catholic ones because he senses that moral codes, as cultural artifacts, are contingent upon time, and therefore not to be arrested into static presences by human knowledge. This inability to know absolutely characterizes the development of Richard's character and culminates in his portentous response to his mother's insistence that he be *something* when he grows up: "I do not want to be something; I *am*" (64).

The melodrama of adolescence aside, Richard's affirmation of being indicates that for him the world is not a source of value as it is for his parents. Thinking of his mother, "it occurred to him that his mother always followed rules and never asked the why of them" (62). As for his father and his unwavering allegiance to the old traditions, "he was angry that traditions could take a body and a soul . . . and mold it to fit a pattern." (63). Richard wishes rather to appropriate the world to himself, and to subjugate it by shaping it with his understanding, in the commanding mode of divine self-reference, "I *am*." The real world is thus not to be seen as a determinant of action, but more accurately, as the scene of action. A political option exists, represented by the work of the union organizers and communist activists depicted early in the narrative: "Comrades," says one at a labor meeting Richard attends with his father, "the time has come for us to show the instruments of our capitalist government that we are tired of being stepped upon" (49). Unable to lose the individualist habits of mind that have characterized him up to now, Richard does not choose the politics of trade-unionism. Instead, resisting the imposition of cultural and political norms, both traditional Mexican ones as well as new American ones, Richard wishes to devalue reality on metaphysical terms: "Everything does not have to be real," he claims (65).

If everything is not real, then what is it? Richard Rubio, at the source of contemporary Chicano narrative, addresses the un-real, the nothing, that his father rejects. But at this point, as his mother realizes when she says to him, "I have really lost you, my son!" (66), Richard is indeed no longer with us. It will be instructive to find out where he is.

Pocho has always been somewhat of an embarrassment to Chicanos. Even the preface to the Anchor paperback edition attempts to apologize for the novel. Richard's rejection of his father's values ("who the hell were his people?" [162]), his statements that "codes of honor are stupid" (108), his rejection of the Catholic faith (" 'I no longer believe in God,' he said . . . and at last he was free" [172]), and, finally, his departure at the novel's end to join the United States armed forces in the months after Pearl Harbor are seen as assimilationist tendencies, indicating an uncritical acceptance of "melting pot" theories of American immigration. But given the fact that Richard has always been besieged by an apparently monolithic apparatus of social, religious, sexual, and moral ideologies that leave no room for resistance, and given the fact that he sees the coming war as an event spawned by wrong and bound to create only further wrong, Richard's decision to enlist can be seen either as a supreme contradiction, or as a preliminary step in a dialectic of developing protopolitical understanding.

As an indication that we may pursue this second option, it should be noted that at the conclusion of the novel Richard is in fact closer in spirit to his father than he has been at any other time in their relationship. He realizes that within that other world of value, "Father had won his battle" because he "had never been unaware of what his fight was" (187). "What about me?" asks Richard, for he enters a battleground where definitive distinctions between right and wrong are not as apparent as he imagines that they must have been for his father. Richard's decision to fight for his country is made with the clear recognition that his is a country that refuses him his own measure of social justice, that imprisons his friends simply because they are Mexican Americans, and that assigns his family to subsistence labor. As soldiers and men, Juan and Richard thus symmetrically oppose and reflect one another, with history serving as the mirror of their reflection.

For both men, life constitutes itself on the basis of concerted

human action. Life does not happen to men and women; they happen
to life. The first and foremost moment of this constituted life is that
which is presently in action against anything that would restrict it.
But the dialectics between fathers and sons are such that while for
Juan it is the "nothing" that would restrict life, for Richard it is the
codification of life that would destroy it. In dramatic terms, Juan's
and Richard's opposed lives and values might thus be seen as Villarreal's artistic intuition of the differential structure of human values
as revealed by a Marxist transformational criticism.[14] Juan projects
personal, heroic power into separate spheres—codes of honor and
traditions of action—that determine his actions. Richard's desire for
an authentic existence within a different historical reality—a reality
not that of the epic corrido—requires him to turn his father's values
around, making codes of honor valid only as they arise from the
actual movement of *personal* history: "I can be a part of everything,"
thinks Richard at one crucial point in his struggle between his Mexican and American enculturations, "because I am the only one capable
of controlling my destiny. . . . Never—no, never—will I allow myself to become a part of a group—to become classified, to lose my
individuality" (152).

The narrator breaks in, however, to dispel any notions one might
have to grant the finality of Richard's presumed independence from
either his Mexican or American value system or the privileging of
liberal-democratic notions of rugged individualism: "He thought this
and other things, because the young are like that, and for them nothing is impossible; no, nothing is impossible, and this truism gives
impetus to the impulse to laugh at abstract bonds" (153). Nonetheless, the interaction between these two ways of perceiving the value
of human action creates the novel's complex dialectical force. Since
this dialectic of values is inherent in the reality the novelist describes, it makes little difference whether the novelist intends to
reveal it or not; the economy of opposed forces that he dramatizes
reveals it for him.

When at the novel's end, preparing to depart for a Navy training
station in San Francisco, Richard claims that for him "there would
be no coming back," we cannot be certain that his earlier confrontations with death, "the infinite nonentity" (180), have not been foreshadowings of his own real death in combat, or that his escape to war

14. See Robert C. Tucker's "Introduction" to *The Marx-Engels Reader* (xix–xxxviii),
for a discussion of Marx's development of a "transformational criticism" from Hegel's
theory of history.

does not mask a repressed death wish. But even if Richard does not here embrace a literal death, he welcomes a figural one: the death of the child he was, at the mercy of random historical forces and of determinant social codes. Now he begins to seem capable of overcoming the opposition between the real and the unreal, between the options of absolute value and the nothing, by plunging directly into the dynamics of history. He does so not so much to validate either the world or the self in isolation, as to validate the actions of the self in the world. Richard's acceptance of the unreal allows him to transform his father's idealist concept of history as the realization of Value through Man, into the materialist concept of history as the self-realization of men and women, through the detour of alienation in the spheres of society and culture.[15] As Marx points out in the eleventh thesis on Feuerbach, the necessary logical step after this *interpretation* of the world is to *change* the world.[16] That Richard may turn to the politics of change is suggested by the fact that the book that he has always hoped to write *is* written, as semiautobiographical fiction, in the form of the novel *Pocho*.

In contrast to the imposed world of cultural and ethical law, the "traditions which could take a body and a soul . . . and mold it to fit a pattern," Richard sees the possibility of figuring his own world, in the difference between the absolute value and the nothing, a world which might serve as the foundation for a revitalized personal and cultural identity. But the price of this emancipation is the security of the known, lamentable present reality in favor of "the unknown" (144). In effect, *Pocho* might well be thought of as the narrative equivalent of that earlier declaration of independence, "I don't want to be something; I *am*." The force of both his singular utterance and of the novel itself is such that it brings about an alteration in Richard's subjective condition, solely by virtue of the fact that the declaration and the novel have been symbolically performed. His words, embodied as narrative, testify to the power of language to constitute a state of subjective integrity, even if it is an integrity founded upon an initial act of renunciation and delimited by the horizon of ideological forces beyond the subject's control.

Juan Rubio expresses himself entirely in words and acts and is thus

15. Tucker, "Introduction" (xxiii–xxv), makes this distinction between idealist and materialist views of history. See also Marx, *The German Ideology*, part 1, "Feuerbach: Opposition of the Materialist and Idealist Outlook" (147–48).

16. Marx, "Theses on Feuerbach," published in 1888 as an appendix to *Ludwig Feuerbach and the End of Classical German Philosophy* (145).

a knowable quantity to himself and to those around him. He has no motives other than the ones he lives; his life is like one of J. L. Austin's performative speech acts: he says and does what he means.[17] Faced with the imminent disintegration of his family from the social, cultural, and economic pressures of their new American lives, Juan cannot understand that disintegration in sociological or psychological terms: "To him life was to be lived, and if in its course things went badly—why that was life, and he must act to make it as good as possible. . . . as for temporal life, it was enough that he maintain his dignity as a man, that he be true to himself, that he satisfy his body of his needs" (135). This continuity between intention and action, speech and deed in his own life effectively separate him from his son for whom that continuity does not exist. In contrast to his father, who is for the most part unproblematically at one with his own history, even if it is not the history he would have, Richard is always at best only an uneasy, volatile synthesis of his intentions and actions. This temporary synthesis is one that he must continually remake with each of his actions. And the novel gives us no indication that for Richard a return to the state of affairs of his father's heroic world of epic action is either possible or desirable. The necessity of Richard's reflexive situation, wherein he must abide on the borderline *between* the absolute value of his father's former world and the instability of the present world, figured by the metamorphosis of the Rubio family's daily life as agricultural workers in Depression-era California, is not historically reversible. Assuming that the option between "something" and "nothing" had been conceivable and attainable for Juan and men like him in prerevolutionary Mexico, the option is decisively unavailable to Richard as a *pocho* in the pre–World War II United States. Instead, Richard acquires a shadowy, in-between identity that is formed by individualist ideologies of which he is only dimly aware. As Louis Althusser has argued, these ideologies have no other function than of " *'constituting' concrete individuals as subjects"* (1969, 171). The process by which Richard constitutes himself and thus becomes the proper subject of his own narrative is a classic example of what Althusser has termed the *"interpellation"* of the subject by the determining forces of class and race (174). According to Althusser, the individual:

is interpellated as a (free) subject in order that he shall submit freely to the commandments of the Subject, i.e. in order that he shall (freely) accept

17. J. L. Austin, "Performative Utterances," (1961), and "Performative-Constative" (1958); and my discussion (1984, 110–55).

his subjection, i.e. in order that he shall make the gestures and actions of his subjection 'all by himself'. *There are no subjects except by and for their subjection.* (182)

Juan's nostalgic desire for a past world in which the individual was free from subjection is not now with Richard simply projected into the future. Earlier in the novel, with American enculturation well under way, Juan had dreamed of returning to Mexico and the mere "reference to their life in Mexico brought on nostalgia and regret, and a mood of slight depression" (121). This was to forget that for the past twenty years Juan had planned that *"next year we will have enough money and we will return to our country.* But deep within he knew that he was one of the lost ones" (31). For Richard no simple utopian vision arises from the past or the future to substitute for his father's exhausted dream. At novel's end, that utopian vision is not being denied so much as it is being indefinitely postponed as a historical possibility for Richard. The novel is the art form that is wholly of this suspended temporality between an alien past of self-evident form and an intractable future of open-ended formlessness. Whereas the corrido served as the genre appropriate to the historical stability of *a priori* value, the Chicano novel emerges as an artform responding to the fragmentation of traditional social relations under the pressure of twentieth-century American cultural hegemony in the Southwest.

In contrast to Juan's existential nostalgia and the metaphysical tone of Richard's anguished resolution of cultural conflict, the novel, with its generic ties to the real, hints at a decidedly more material solution to the plight of the *pocho.* Early in the story, Richard and his father had attended a meeting of a local "unemployed council," where "a professional organizer" was to speak about the nature of work and power: "The wall behind the table was bedecked with bunting, of which a red flag with hammer and sickle was the centerpiece" (48). Later, Richard finds himself watching "from a detached point of view" (51) a labor demonstration at the county courthouse in San Jose that becomes a violent clash between progressive and reactionary social forces.

The author draws these scenes from historical events. In the spring of 1931, a demonstration at St. James Park in San Jose called by the Cannery and Agricultural Workers Industrial Union (CAWIU) in support of job actions protesting wage cuts by fruit growers in the Santa Clara Valley turned into a battle when the pro-union workers clashed with anti-union people and police. At the time, the CAWIU was not chartered by the American Federation of Labor because its workers were only seasonal employees and because the broad social aims of the union were said to be "utopian" and "communist" (Zavella 1987, 40). The union's own charter called for the "unity of all agricultural workers—field workers and fruit and vegetable cannery workers" without regard to race or sex, unlike the AFL unions that segregated by race and sex (Zavella 1987, 41). Ultimately unsuccessful in its organizing attempts, the CAWIU nonetheless set the stage for later more successful labor organizing efforts. Richard's fate is set in the context of powerful events drawn from the early stages of Mexican American labor struggles. Caught in his own private affairs, however, he can only watch "from a detached point of view" the rise of collective political action. Richard accedes singlemindedly to the ideological demands interpellating his own private subjectivity, even to the extent of denying the call of the public domain and of repressing the full burden of history that his precritical intuition of "difference" has called into view.

Still, the writing of Richard's story does instantiate a significant literary historical moment. Together with Paredes' *With His Pistol in His Hand*, *Pocho* changes the world of literature in general and American literature in particular by opening a place for Chicano literature, a place from which future Chicano authors might open up the vistas of the genre of the novel and of other narrative forms to their own significant culture. From the perspective of literary history, therefore, the historical phenomenon of cultural consciousness expressed by later Chicano writers can become a reality only after Richard Rubio postulates his own identity as a new and different source of personal, cultural, and political consciousness. At least this recognition is due Villarreal's first novel.

The preceding description of Villarreal's novel attempts to emphasize that Richard's story is an operation of rectification, an attempted ontological restitution of values that have ceased to be effective in a new cultural, historical, and ideological space. The narrator thus claims that "what was done [the damage to the traditional values] was beyond repair. To be just, no one could be blamed, for the transition from the culture of the old world to that of the new should never have been attempted in one generation" (135). It is certainly significant that what occasions this observation is the growing independence of the Rubio women, mother and daughters:

Richard's mother was a different person altogether now, and constantly interfered when her husband was in the act of disciplining a child. . . .
Although he loved his mother, Richard realized that a family could not

survive when the woman desired to command. . . . Consuelo [his mother],
who had always been proud of her talents for housekeeping, now took the
dirty house as a symbol of her emancipation. (134–35)

In a later scene, Richard returns home from a date "early one morning" to find that his sister Luz, who has also just returned, is being
"disciplined" by Juan. Housekeeping is not now the issue—the sexuality of Juan's daughter is, and the violence implicit in the corrido
hero's character comes brutally to the fore:

Juan Rubio hit her with the back of his hand, and she bounced off the
wall but she did not fall. Again she screamed to Consuelo, and Consuelo,
given courage by the utterance of that which she had been lately telling her
daughters, lost her head and stepped forward, screeching, "Do not dare to
touch her again, you brute!" She took hold of his arm, and he spun toward
her, the force of his movement knocking her off balance, so she stumbled
crazily through the door and landed on her face in the kitchen.
Richard stood on the opposite side, transfixed. . . .
His sister brought him out of shock. "Stand there! Just stand there, you
weak bastard, and watch this son of a bitch hit your mother!" She leaped at
Juan Rubio's face with her hands, and very deliberately he hit her in the face
with his fist. She did not get up. (166)

Although the novel's focus is on the question of the boy's identity
as it undergoes transculturation, it cannot entirely marginalize the
fact that male identity is not formed in a vacuum but in correla-
tion with and response to the changing identities of the women
around him. Neither the heroic corrido stereotype, now no longer
engaged in armed resistance against overwhelming odds but abusing
his daughters and threatening his wife, nor his half-assimilated son,
who cannot intervene on behalf of his battered mother, can face the
reality of women's lives. As has been the case in the corrido and
Paredes' fiction, Villarreal's novel represents by omission another
history of oppression. That untold story, present in all the interstices of Richard's narrative, is the substance of Chicana writings
in the 1970s and 1980s. As Renato Rosaldo observes, "Ultimately,
it is against a reading of these recent feminist texts that the warrior heroes of pioneering Chicano writers must be discussed" (1987,
86). In the reified form that Villarreal presents him, the stereotype
of the corrido hero will serve as the negative counterpoint, itself to
be negated, of an alternative presentation of the relations between
Chicano men and women.
Our discussion emphasizes the novel's own operation of interpretation as it moves in narrative time from Juan's to Richard's life; and

within Richard's story, from belief to doubt and back again, as he attempts to pass from a surface to an underlying reality and finds a measure of certainty only in the opposition of their difference. That Richard has failed to locate that reality absolutely in either personal, cultural, or political terms by the novel's end does not negate the procedure. The failure simply indicates that the closure of interpretation, by characters within fiction or by readers outside of it, cannot be established in this or perhaps any text until what are seen initially as private, individual questions are understood to be the internalized instances of transpersonal history.

Short of that historicizing of the private domain, what a text can do is activate the components of our concrete social life—words, ideas, desires, intentions—by revaluing them (as did the master texts of a former era, the corridos of border conflict), or even when necessary by *de*valuing them (as will the writings of Chicanas in the 1970s and 1980s). This foregrounding of value can neither create a meaning that was not already present in the words of the text, nor can it cause the end of interpretation. But *Pocho* succeeds as a novel, and more significantly as a paradigmatic Chicano narrative, precisely because in bringing to the fore the question of value it both violates and subverts our received ideas of value, and forces us to define in real historical terms what has not been defined within the text.

Given the strength of the model texts, it should not be surprising that subsequent Chicano novels and other narrative forms have looked, consciously or not, to Paredes' work on the corrido, to his short fiction, and to Villarreal's novel *Pocho* for inspiration. Paredes keeps alive the form and spirit of the corrido in his own poetry and fiction after the period of its decline. His anthropological work functions as a socially symbolic narrative act as well. This work identifies him as one of the key literary intellectuals of our time, the kind of organic intellectual

whose radical work of transformation, whose fight against repression is carried on at the specific institutional site where he finds himself and on the terms of his own expertise, on the terms inherent to his own functioning as an intellectual. (Lentricchia 1983, 6; cited in Limón 1986, 31)

As José E. Limón has argued, in the 1950s Américo Paredes "continued to be this kind of intellectual, doing so by drawing creatively on his own cultural background and bringing it to bear in critical dialogue" (1986, 31) with traditional hegemonic distortions of the history of the western United States. His writings represent a transformation of the corrido in the service of the Mexican American community and as a model for the emergence of antirepressive movements at large.

Like the folk base text, the Border corrido, Chicano narrative after Paredes' work and after *Pocho* will continue to emphasize in no uncertain terms the importance of cultural conflict in its formation, even when, as in the case of the works by subsequent women writers, the forms and objects of cultural conflict change or are to be rejected altogether. I am not here making a case for a Chicano "anxiety of influence,"[18] however appropriate for understanding the literature such a schema may be, but I am suggesting that in their isolation of the differential structure of meaning, of the dialectic between history and art, and of the roles played by these issues in the protagonist's creation of a new cultural, personal, and political consciousness, Paredes' and Villarreal's early work are originary Chicano narrative texts.

In following chapters, I will both sketch a history of the influence of these works on the major texts of contemporary Chicano narrative and trace out the deviations from their imposed patterns. I do not presume to offer a full account of contemporary Chicano narrative. Instead, I offer here a provisional model of a possible Chicano literary history. While certain major historical patterns determine the course of Chicano narratives and cultural productions in general, no single, comprehensive tradition of Chicano narrative emerges from those patterns. The differential structure that I have described leads us rather to the heterogeneity of the forms representing the Chicano experience, a heterogeneity structured by a dialectic that takes us beyond static, unhistorical notions of good and evil.

18. The phrase is Harold Bloom's in *The Anxiety of Influence* (1973); it refers to the intertextual debts incurred and remissed by "weak" and "strong" poets. For excellent applications and critiques of Bloom's theory as it applies to Chicano poetry, see Limón, "The Greater Mexican *Corrido* and Don Américo Paredes as Poet: Oral Tradition, Poetic Influence, and Cultural History" (1983b), and "Mexican Ballads, Chicano Epic: History, Influence and Self in Mexican-American Social Poetics" (1984).

4

Beyond Good and Evil

Utopian Dialectics in Tomás Rivera and Oscar Zeta Acosta

The magisterial work of Tomás Rivera (1935–84), . . . *Y no se lo tragó la tierra / And the Earth Did Not Part* (1971), takes to their limits the formal, thematic, and ideological issues raised by Paredes' and Villarreal's works. *Tierra* represents the first milestone in Mexican American literary history after the turbulent events of the 1960s and sets itself explicitly within the political and social contexts of the post–World War II agricultural worker's life. Winner in 1970 of the first Quinto Sol Prize for literature, the most prestigious literary award in the early years of Mexican American literature, Rivera's novel immediately established itself as a major document of Chicano social and literary history.

Oscar Zeta Acosta's *The Autobiography of a Brown Buffalo* (1972) and *The Revolt of the Cockroach People* (1973), while differing formally and thematically from Rivera's work, represent with *Tierra* a shared desire, itself related to the historical moment of the late 1960s and early 1970s, to fashion out of the instability and fragmentation of social life a utopian vision of collective action. The works of both authors should be read within their common historical horizon of the politicization of Chicano labor struggles and the emergence of a broad-based Chicano movement. Each presents, in different ways, the Chicano response to the conditions and circumstances of existence of the late sixties.

. . . *Y no se lo tragó la tierra* / *And the Earth Did Not Part*

In the original South Texas Spanish, Rivera's prose is tight and lean, the vocabulary and syntax rigorously controlled and held deliber-

74

ately within the world of the Chicano migrant farmworker.[1] Like Faulkner's *Go Down, Moses* and *As I Lay Dying*, or Juan Rulfo's *El Llano en llamas* and *Pedro Páramo*, Rivera's narrative is not expository; in documenting the life of the farmworker in the immediate post–World War II era and trying to keep its significance alive, *Tierra* does not give us historical depiction in the mode of more traditional realisms so much as a complex narrative of subjective impressions where strict chronological presentation, orderly compositional development, and linear plot progression have broken down. The twelve sections of Rivera's novel, preceded and concluded by a frame story, follow a stream-of-consciousness thread, bereft of traditional narrative causality, relating the seasonal events of an allegorical year in the life of an unnamed migrant child. The narrator-protagonist is not actually present as a main character in all of the sections of the novel but rather serves as what Bakhtin has termed a chronotopic point—a figural intersection of time and space (1981, 84)—around which the collective subjective experiences of Rivera's Texas-Mexican farmworkers coalesce, forming a communal oral history. Only in the very last section of the novel, where we find a child under a house reminiscing about the events that have formed the core of the story we have just read, do we begin to sense the novel's coherence. As Juan Bruce-Novoa has pointed out, however, what we have read is not the stream-of-consciousness itself in its amorphous flow (1980, 137). Even though the texture of the narrative is not at all that of an interior monologue but of the carefully crafted written word, *Tierra* retains a distinctly oral quality, as Rivera is able to capture the cadence and flow of his native people's speech.

In writing about the marginal people of the Texas-Mexican border, Rivera turns to a narrative form that shuns easy synthesis and easy unity, that shuns exactly those features of narrative that arbiters of narrative style from Aristotle to Wayne Booth have prescribed. Why should this be the case? What did real life in South Texas have to do with narrative experimentation and the violation of traditional narrative strictures? In dealing with the "real life" of the West and Southwest, Anglo-American writers have tended to favor a traditional, tough-minded style that one might call "realism." Larry McMurtry's novels, *Horseman, Pass By* and *Lonesome Dove*, for instance, offer

1. Bruce-Novoa, "Tomás Rivera" (1980, 137), discusses aspects of Rivera's style; see also, Ralph Grajeda, "Tomás Rivera's Appropriation of the Chicano Past" (1979), Daniel P. Testa, "Narrative Technique and Human Experience in Tomás Rivera" (1979), and Joseph Sommers, "Interpreting Tomás Rivera" (1979).

good examples of this preference. The idea of "realism," however, is a complex one. As an antidote to the romantic style and sentimental impulses that Western fiction has generally cultivated in its invention of the American West as a province of an exclusively white, male, individualist imagination, realism has its advantages. More powerfully, Lukács has argued that the literature of realism, "aiming at a truthful reflection of reality," can demonstrate "both the concrete and abstract potentialities of human beings" ([1955] 1972, 478). But what Rivera's novel attempts to remind us is that "realism" is not a style that gives us an undistorted reflection of the world. It simply represents the ideologically dominant way of conceiving and expressing our relationship to the natural and social worlds around us.

"Realism" functions ideologically: it offers itself as a neutral reflection of the world when it is but one way of *imagining* a world (Althusser 1969, 162–63). Echoing Lukács, what we might call "the ideology of realism" disguises the fact that what is natural in viewing the world tends to be defined by those who have the *authority* to define something as natural. Those without authority or legitimacy may or may not agree with this definition of what constitutes the natural. Without such authority or legitimacy, Mexican Americans have hardly been asked to help define the "reality" of the American western and southwestern experience or help create what Benedict Anderson in another context has termed its "imagined communities" ([1983] 1987, 15). On the contrary, American literature has tended to define the Mexican American without pausing to consider whether the images it offers of their reality are images that the Mexican American can recognize as "truthful reflections of reality."[2]

It is also the case that all of the notions of unity, coherence, and causality associated with realistic plot lines tend to beg the questions that the devices of style are supposed to answer: can one tell the story of the fragmenting effects of contemporary postmodern life in an uncomplicated reflectionist way? Rivera's answer is to turn to narrative experimentation.

Despite narrative experimentation, and as is the case in the major Chicano texts after Paredes' short fiction and Villarreal's *Pocho*, Rivera faithfully situates his story in the day-to-day life of postwar social reality. The poverty, hardship, and exploitation that his characters endure is no more than that which Rivera himself experienced

2. See Cecil Robinson, *Mexico and the Hispanic Southwest in American Literature* (revised from *With the Ears of Strangers*) for the definitive study of the racial and sexual stereotyping of the Mexican American in American literature.

as a farmworker in and around Crystal City, Texas, during the 1940s and 1950s.[3]

In an interview with Bruce-Novoa, Rivera situated his work squarely within the bounds of the Mexican American's struggle for social and political justice:

> In . . . *tierra* . . . I wrote about [the life of] the migrant worker in [the] ten year period [between 1945 and 1955]. . . . I began to see that my role . . . would be to document that period of time, but giving it some kind of spiritual strength or spiritual history. . . . I felt that I had to document the migrant worker *para siempre* [forever], *para que no se olvidara ese espíritu tan fuerte de resistir y continuar under the worst of conditions* [so that their spirit of resistance and willingness to endure should not be forgotten], because they were worse than slaves. (Bruce-Novoa 1980, 148, 150–51)

Written during the period 1967–68, at the height of the politicization of the Chicano labor struggles and just prior to the takeover of political power by Mexican Americans of *La Raza Unida* political party in Crystal City, the novel is imbued with a sense of political urgency.[4] But apart from the reality of economic exploitation and social injustice, Rivera's novel also presents the anguish of a transcendentally spiritual exploitation. His anonymous narrator literalizes the "subjectlessness" of the corrido narrator, as he is born into a world of absence and loss, seeking to discover his identity, to inscribe his name in the text of history, and to recover what he calls "un año perdido [a lost year]."[5] *Tierra* functions aesthetically and ideologically as a memorial to and partial reconstitution of the forgotten history of a people's oppression and struggles. Simultaneously, it signifies a determining instance of the repressed "political unconscious" of American political and literary history.

Without a name, initially without a sense of his specific geographical space or real time, and unable to decide whether he wakes or dreams, the child calls out and turns, not realizing that he himself has spoken. The novel opens abruptly with this disembodied voice:

Aquel año se le perdió. A veces trataba de recordar y ya para cuando creía que se estaba aclarando todo un poco se le perdían las palabras. Casi siempre

---

3. See Rivera's comments in an interview with Bruce-Novoa, (1980, 140, 148–49).

4. See Acuña (1981, 360–62) for details concerning the political struggle in Crystal City, Texas; see also Sommers (1979, 100–101).

5. Tomás Rivera, . . . *Y no se lo tragó la tierra / And the Earth Did Not Part* (Berkeley: Quinto Sol Publications, 1971; reissued by Justa Publications, 1976): 1. Textual citations are from the Quinto Sol, bilingual, first edition and refer to the Spanish and English language texts.

empezaba con un sueño donde despertaba de pronto y luego se daba cuenta
de que realmente estaba dormido. Luego ya no supo si lo que pensaba había
pasado o no.

. . . [O]ía que alguien le llamaba por su nombre pero cuando volteaba la
cabeza a ver quién era el que le llamaba, daba una vuelta entera y así quedaba
donde mismo. Por eso nunca podía acertar ni quién le llamaba ni por qué, y
luego hasta se le olvidaba el nombre que le habían llamado. Pero sabía que
él era a quien llamaban.

(That year was lost to him. Sometimes he tried to remember, but then
when things appeared to clarify somewhat his thoughts would elude him.
It usually began with a dream in which suddenly he thought he was awake,
and then he would realize that he was actually asleep. That was why he
could not be sure whether or not what he had recalled was actually what had
happened.

. . . [H]e would hear someone call him by name. He would turn around to
see who was calling, always making a complete turn, always ending in the
same position and facing the same way. And that was why he could never
find out who it was that was calling him, nor the reason why he was being
called. He would even forget the name that he had heard. But he knew that
he was the one who was being called.) (*Tierra* 1, 3)

There is no clear beginning nor any motivated action in the first
scene of this story. Rather, like Abraham called by the insubstan-
tial voice of Yahweh to test his faith and confront his destiny, the
child is called to bear witness to and compose the testament of his
history. He is no patriarchal prophet, but he has apparently been
chosen, and the subtle echoes of the Book of Genesis will soon turn
out to be well-motivated foreshadowings of crucial later scenes. For
the present, however, situated between madness and chaos, the child
reacts to the chaos of his placeless, nameless isolation by beginning
to construct a context for order:

Una vez se detuvo antes de dar la vuelta entera y le entró el miedo. Se dio
cuenta de que él mismo se había llamado. Y así empezó el año perdido. . . .
Se dio cuenta de que siempre pensaba que pensaba y de allí no podía salir.
. . . Pero antes de dormirse veía y oía muchas cosas . . .

(Once he stopped himself before completing the turn, and he became afraid.
He found out that he had been calling himself. That was the way the lost
year began. . . . He discovered that he was always thinking that he was thinking, and that he was trapped in this cycle. . . . But before falling asleep he
would see and hear many things.) (1, 3)

What we have read on the first page of Rivera's novel is not a representation of insanity or of childhood confusion. Rather, he gives us

what we might liken to a phenomenological reduction to absolute consciousness, as the allegorical child undertakes a complex inner exploration in order that he might recover "a lost year," the absent history of his life. The "cycle" that the boy enters seems at this point a vicious circle of entrapment. In fact, the cycle turns out to be an entry into a hermeneutic circle of understanding that begins to parody and belie the certainty of the Cartesian cogito. In terms more grandly absolute than any imagined by Villarreal, Rivera thus sets the scene for his own portrayal of a radical revaluation of values. Through this stark reduction, Rivera's protagonist will experience the chaos of personal solitude in order to understand dialectically, "thinking that he was thinking," how his life fits into a pattern of labor commodification and class and racial oppression.

Through a series of wire-taut chapters of interior monologue repeating snatches of half-heard conversations that begin to articulate the protagonist-narrator's lost history, Rivera portrays a community's indomitable will to survive and flourish. We see glimpses of a stark world of class and racial oppression: the death of a child, shot when he pauses from working to get a drink of water; a mother anxiously praying for her son who is away fighting in Korea; another child's first shocking encounter with adult sexuality; an agoraphobic woman painfully venturing out into the marketplace; a truckful of migrant farmworkers speeding northward in the night toward the agricultural fields of the Midwest.

Rivera has confirmed that as he was preparing to write *Tierra*, he was "wandering through the library and I came across *With His Pistol in His Hand* by Américo Paredes, and I was fascinated . . . because . . . it was about a Chicano, Gregorio Cortez. . . . That book indicated to me that it was possible to talk about a Chicano as a complete figure. . . . More importantly, *With His Pistol in His Hand* indicated to me a whole imaginative possibility for us to explore" (Bruce-Novoa 1980, 150). Rivera's confirmation of Paredes' influence situates his novel within the province of socially symbolic acts of resistance initiated by the corrido form and extended by Paredes into narrative fiction. The proletarian world represented in Rivera's novel is hence that of the corrido, but without the moment in the corrido when the common working man is transformed into an epic-heroic projection of his community. But like the corrido, Rivera's novel is an ideological expression of cultural and political resistance. With the two core episodes of the novel, "La noche estaba plateada" / "It Was a Silvery Night" and the title piece, Rivera chronicles the rise of an intractable will to power and what José Saldívar has correctly termed the "dawning sense of solidarity with other members of [his] class and race."[6] But this dawning class consciousness must occur by degrees and first as a *personal* act of understanding the causes of his people's victimization and oppression by a common enemy. As José Saldívar has pointed out, this personalization of the political has occasioned decidedly existentialist readings of the novel, readings that go only part way in exploring the ideological implications of the characters' actions as they experience reification and the emergence of class consciousness (1985, 103).

One silvery night, the child awakens to walk through a nearby wood to summon the devil: "Lo del diablo le había fascinado desde cuando no se acordaba" ("The thought of the devil had fascinated him since he could remember") (*Tierra* 55, 61). Flashing back to another time, the child offers us a possible motive for this inexplicable desire to summon the devil and to violate one of the principal folk taboos of his culture when he recalls overhearing that

con el diablo ne se juega. Hay muchos que le han llamado y despúes les ha pesado. La mayoría casi se vuelve loca. . . . Hay unos que se mueren de susto, otros no, nomás empiezan a entristecer, y luego ni hablan. Como que se les va el alma del cuerpo.

(You can't fool around with the devil. There have been many who have summoned him and they've regretted it later. Most have been on the verge of going insane. . . . There are some who die of fright; there are others who are overcome with sadness and eventually stop talking altogether, as if the soul had left their bodies.) (55, 61)

But the child is of a mind to summon the devil: "Nomás quisiera saber si hay o no hay" ("All I want to know is whether or not the devil actually exists") (56, 62), he says in innocent simplicity. Alone in the middle of the dark woods, he calls repeatedly but nothing happens: "No se apareció nada ni nadie ni cambió nada" ("Absolutely nothing

6. José D. Saldívar, "The Ideological and the Utopian in Tomás Rivera's *Y no se lo tragó la tierra* and Ron Arias' *The Road to Tamazunchale*" (1985, 103). Rivera's work has had the good fortune of having been treated by exceptionally fine critics. In addition to the essay just cited, see Juan Rodríguez, "The Problematic in Tomás Rivera" (1967, 42–50), and "La búsqueda de identidad y sus motivos en la literatura chicana" (1979a, 170–78). In addition, readers may now refer to the useful collection, *International Studies in Honor of Tomás Rivera*, ed. by Julián Olivares (1985), for recent reinterpretations of this important author. See especially, Sylvia S. Lizárraga, "The Patriarchal Ideology in 'La noche que se apagaron las luces,'" Patricia de la Fuente, "Invisible Women in the Narrative of Tomás Rivera," Lauro Flores, "The Discourse of Silence in the Narrative of Tomás Rivera," and Erlinda González-Berry and Tey Diana Rebolledo, "Growing Up Chicano: Tomás Rivera and Sandra Cisneros."

appeared and absolutely nothing changed") (56, 62). Returning home, relieved and proud of his daring, it occurs to him that the devil has not appeared because "no había diablo" ("The devil did not exist") (56, 62). And since in the rhetoric of the child's Catholic doctrine evil is inseparable from good, the thought that the devil does not exist leads him to the partial conclusion that: "si no hay diablo tampoco hay . . . No, más vale no decirlo." ("and if there is no devil, there must be no . . . no, I'd better not say it") (56, 62). Such logic would not be foreign to Richard Rubio of *Pocho*.

The binary structure of what I have termed the "differential structure" of Chicano narrative necessarily brings into question the complement of evil and the supreme origin of value, God Himself. At this point, however, the child's inability to separate himself from the ultimate expression of imposed value systems, especially from an apparently beneficent one, is designated by the inconclusive ellipse and the conscious decision not to speak the words of denial. It is curious, moreover, that his intimation of the world as a place without devils or gods, *"No hay diablo, no hay nada"* ("There is no devil. There is nothing") (56, 63), does not lead him into existential despair. On the contrary, the boy unconsciously senses the possibility of freedom in the absence of devils and gods. He now understands that "los que le llamaban al diablo y se volvían locos, no se volvían locos porque se les aparecía sino al contrario, porque no se les aparecía" ("those who summoned the devil and later went insane did not do so because they had seen the devil. On the contrary, it was because the devil had not appeared") (56, 63). In an impressive rhetorical move, the narrator signals the sublimity of this partial recognition by transferring metaphorically the joyful serenity of the child's insight about the human constructions of ethical value to the moon hovering overhead, "contentissima de algo" ("extremely happy about something") (56, 63).

The protagonist's reticence before the annihilation of traditional value schemes in "La noche estaba plateada / It Was a Silvery Night," is overcome in the climax to the titular chapter. There, haunted by his inability to understand why a beneficent God would allow disaster to strike unremittingly a good and innocent people, the boy finally brings himself to do what he could not do earlier: deny and curse God. This rejection of the traditional ideology of acceptance and submission that his Catholic faith has taught him allows him now to elevate his own creative will to a higher sphere of existence and thus to produce his own history. Here too, as in *Pocho*, the act of rejection isolates a systematic distrust of any preexistent, transcendental rule of value because such systems contribute to the enslavement of the individual will. From the boy's precritical perspective, only in the context of present historical conditions and under the influence of its own productive intellect can the individual create a personal and cultural identity. The initial movement toward liberation is thus explicitly located immanently within the consciousness of the individual subject. In ". . . Y no se lo tragó la tierra" / "And the Earth Did Not Part," the existential dialectic that will eventuate in a full deconstruction of the sovereignty of individual subjectivity continues but is taken one step further away from individual being toward the context of social being.

Rivera's titular story places the reader in the full misery of a South Texas cotton field, parched by the noonday sun, as a small group of Chicanos weed a crop. The previous day, the child's father, working under these same conditions, has suffered a sunstroke. And earlier still, his aunt and uncle had also been struck. Trapped as much by his mother's passive faith that the meek shall inherit the earth as by the exploitative capitalist agricultural system that demands their cheap piece-rate wage labor, the child cries:

"¿Qué se gana, mamá, con andar [clamando la misercordia de Dios]? ¿Apoco cree que le ayudó mucho a mi tío y a mi tía? ¿Por qué es que nosotros estamos aquí como enterrados en la tierra? O los microbios nos comen o el sol nos asolea. Y todos los días trabaje y trabaje. ¿Para qué? . . . Tanto darle de comer a la tierra y al sol y luego, saz, un día cuando menos lo piensa cae asoleado. . . . Y luego ellos rogándole a Dios . . . si Dios no se acuerda de uno. . . . N'ombre a Dios le importa poco de uno de los pobres. . . . Dígame usted ¿por qué? ¿Por qué nosotros nomás enterrados en la tierra como animales sin ningunas esperanzas de nada?

[What do you gain by [praying to God], mother? Don't tell me that you believe that sort of thing helped my uncle and aunt? Why is it that we are here on earth as though buried alive? Either the germs eat us from the inside or the sun from the outside. And work, work, day in and day out. And for what? . . . After feeding the earth and the sun for such a long time, . . . one day unexpectedly he is felled by the sun. . . . And to top it off, praying to God. God doesn't remember us. . . . God doesn't give a damn about us poor people. . . . Why should we always be tied to the dirt, half buried in the earth like animals without any hope of any kind?] (67–68, 75–76)

His hapless mother is the innocent target of his anger since he cannot as yet see the source of his oppression. The despair and sense of helplessness that he felt earlier in the face of their victimization by those who would bind them to the earth are nothing compared to this day's rage, as his youngest brother now also falls from the sun's devouring rays: "¿Por qué a papá y luego a mi hermanito? . . . ¿Por qué?" ("Why my father, and now my little brother? . . . Why?") (70, 78).

Rushing home with his brother in his arms, the protagonist brings himself to do what he had done previously by indirection: "Maldijo a Dios" ("He cursed God") (70, 78). At this instant, he imagines that the earth is about to part and swallow him alive; but the earth did not part. Instead, he continues homeward carrying his brother, feeling the solidity of the material earth beneath his feet. With his accep- tance of his own universal isolation comes "un paz que nunca había sentido antes" ("a peace that he had never known before") (70, 78).

This almost Nietzschean serenity, a liberating joyful wisdom, is the direct result of his appropriation of the site of God's former exis- tence as the place for his own self-determined presence: "por primera vez se sentía capaz de hacer y deshacer cualquier cosa que él quisiera" ("for the first time he felt himself capable of doing and undoing what- ever he chose") (70, 78). The religion of Job reconciled or of Christ crucified here has not diminished but rather added to man's burden of suffering to the extent that it has been used as a justification for the historical crimes that people commit against other people. By rejecting that religion and its idealist metaphysics and moving as it were beyond good and evil, the protagonist implies that in this life *understanding*, the source of collective power, is the first step toward historical materialist salvation.

Jameson has suggested that "the vocation of the dialectic lies in the transcendence of this opposition toward some collective logic 'beyond good and evil'" (1981, 286). In this case, understanding, the product of the dialectic, survives and replaces the decay of faith in the divine and its transcendental strictures and works to create the preconditions of that collective logic. To be sure, this act of under- standing is still an individual one affecting an isolated subject and cannot readily be appropriated unproblematically as a model for the full reconstruction of a collective process of meaning. But it does foreshadow a mode of thinking that might prefigure an alternative social formation, one that does not tie men, women, and children in bondage to the earth through myths of transcendental peace. The proleptic quality of this dialectical resolution is not particularly sur- prising, especially "if we take dialectical thought to be the antici- pation of the logic of the collectivity which has not yet come into being."[7]

7. J. Saldívar (1985, 100), citing Jameson (1981, 286).

Freed now of those myths that have been used to underwrite and perpetuate the specific historical formation of postwar capitalist agribusiness, the child protagonist of ". . . y no se lo tragó la tierra" knows that the earth cannot "swallow" and the sun cannot "devour." He saves himself to act within the bounds of history by realizing that those anthropomorphic projections of human will onto unfeeling nature are, like the myth of God Himself, only the fraudulent means by which the force of individual will and collective action can be diminished and misdirected. His analysis is less a demand to abandon religion than a plea to give up a condition that requires illusions. Authentic life is now to be constituted by the will's interpretive act, the determination of its own fate. To paraphrase Paul Ricouer, Rivera's child protagonist begins to do away with idols when he begins to listen to the symbols by which his world is ordered.[8] His iconoclastic act, cursing God, speaking the unspeakable, is motivated by a double urgency: to liquidate oppressive idols and to articulate the power of self-determination. He may now truly do and undo whatever he chooses. Having attained this necessary protopolitical level of Feuerbachian dialectical insight through the reduction of his illusions, the child's full attainment of a political understanding of his place in a system of class oppression, of seeing the world as a product of socially interactive labor, of recognizing the need for collective action, and the subsequent recovery of his "lost year" cannot be far off.

With this reassertion of the active subject's—the proletariat's—creation of the historical world as part of the dialectic of subject and object, comes the possibility of the articulation of an authentic class consciousness. Rivera does not offer us so much a story of personal redemption as an allegory of historical crisis. The categories of individuality and personal subjectivity, under suspicion from the initial scenes of the novel where even the most basic markers of the traditional notion of the sovereign subject are absent, begin now to be attenuated even further as the boy's former intuitions concerning his "subjectlessness" undergo an even more drastic reconceptualization with his emergence from the isolation of his ego-centered alienation into the "collective utopian world of the human community" (J. Saldívar 1985, 105).

The two central episodes of the novel amount to critiques of religious idealism and ego psychology and show how tenacious and debilitating a precritical metaphysic can be. They dramatize that the

8. Paul Ricoeur, *Freud and Philosophy* (1970, 27).

making of a working-class consciousness is at least in part a reaction to a pacifying combination of imaginary, psychological, religious, and economic formations working to protect the status quo.
The tropological deconstruction of the ethics of "good and evil" reveals how effective ideological manipulation, the work of hegemony,
may be as it enforces the interests of the oppressors by having the
victims internalize and embrace the system of beliefs that justify
their oppression. At this moment, however, the child protagonist experiences the existential resolve not to believe and hence not to be
bought and sold like an animal or like the fields that he works. In
effect he begins to resist the literal commodification of his labor.
Taking the part of a human individual possessed of a will as well as of
working power, resisting the commodification of his labor, Rivera's
protagonist signals, if not the integration of his formerly fragmented
identity, at least the possibility of his future liberation. Representing crises that initially seemed expressions of a universal existential
homelessness, Rivera identifies the specific historical factors of the
workings of capitalist social and ideological life as the sources of
alienation.

The essentially negative demystifying work of ideological analysis
that characterizes crucial scenes of the novel and reveals the debilitating contradictions inherent in the developing capitalist agribusiness economic world of the 1940s and 1950s are counterpoised by
equally crucial scenes that seek to identify an affirmative ground for
a collective cultural unity beyond the realm of the individual subject.
The utopian possibility of transcending the logic of good and evil
toward some collective logic free of the limits imposed on language
and thinking now becomes the very substance of the concluding sections of Rivera's novel.

The closing sections of *Tierra* emphasize formally the thematic
concern with the dispersal of the subject that has been one of the
novel's basic themes and return us to the issue of narrative experimentation. While the temporal and compositional elements of the
narrative, short, episodic, nonsequential narrative frames that may or
may not develop into a string of causal sequences, have from the beginning of the novel made a traditional reading of character difficult,
the various sections of the text do tend to focus on the experiences
of single individuals. This narrative stratagem has a double purpose:
it allows the representation of personal alienation while simultaneously putting into question the very category of an unproblematic
individual identity. The final two sections of the novel, however,
alter the former configurations of subjectivity dramatically.

In the penultimate section, "Cuando lleguemos" / "When We Arrive," the single narrative voice and individual narrative focus give way to a complex choir of intermingling voices. The narrative form itself repeats the thematic move away from the singular subject as it calls for a responsive understanding on the part of the reader, encouraging that we listen to the voices that now become the subject of the story. And while we will return to the child protagonist's perspective in the final section of the novel, even there the point of view is no longer an inwardly directed one but is now explicitly focused on the place of the protagonist's life within the larger social world as he scans the scenes, people, and events that have formed the substance of his narrative and achieves an almost utopian lucidity of insight and transparency of identity.

The mood of "Cuando lleguemos" / "When We Arrive" is like the tense of the verb in Spanish, a conditional one: the completion of the action has been deferred. We hear the thoughts and voices of at least nine individuals packed into the van of a large truck with perhaps forty other migrant workers, men, women, and children, who are being transported from Texas to the farms of Minnesota. It is four o'clock in the morning, and after nearly twenty-four hours on the road the truck has broken down along a deserted stretch of Iowa highway "cerca de Dimoins" ("near Des Moines") (149, 157). People had stirred when the truck stopped but now silence reigns again as "unos estaban dormidos otros estaban pensando" ("some were asleep, others were thinking") (148, 156).

The separate voices speak their concerns: one is glad that the truck has broken down because he can hurry off into the bushes to relieve himself; a second commiserates with the children, who like the adults have had to stand for these past twenty-four hours; another hopes for a successful onion harvest so that next year he and his family might not have to travel "como vacas" ("like cattle") (150, 158). Yet a fourth hopes for a good beet harvest so that he might repay to "el señor tomson" (150) the two hundred dollars at 100% interest that he has borrowed to make the vegetable harvest trip, while another worries about his wife's kidney condition and hopes for her sake that "cuando lleguemos" they don't have to live in a chicken coop as they did the prior season.

Some of the voices are distinct enough that we can identify them when they speak again, as is the case for one angry voice: "Nomás que lleguemos al rancho y me voy a ir a la chingada. Me voy a ir a buscar un jale a mineapolis" ("Just as soon as we get to the ranch I'll get the hell out of here. I'm going to look for a job in Minneapolis") (149, 157). A few paragraphs later we hear again: "pinche vida, pinche vida, pinche vida, pinche vida, por pendejos, por pendejos. Esta es la última vez que vengo así como una pinche bestia parado todo el camino. Nomás que lleguemos me voy a mineapolis." ("This goddamn fuckin' life. This goddamn son-of-a-bitch's life. This is the last time I travel like a goddamn animal standing all the way. Just as soon as we arrive I'm going to Minneapolis") (150–51, 158–59). Similarly, the person in the bushes now speaks again, commenting on the beauty of the stars and wondering "¿Cuántos más estarán viendo la misma estrella? ¿Cuántos más estarán pensando que cuántos estarán viendo la misma estrella?" ("I wonder how many others are looking at the same star. I wonder how many others are wondering how many others are looking at the same star") (151, 159). The truck driver too is identifiable as he looks forward to their arrival when he might abandon his passengers and return to Texas: "Cada quien para su santo" ("Let each one look out for his own skin") (152, 160). And yet, the identity of the speakers is not the concern of the narrative at all. The separate voices meld beyond their individuality in their common refrain "cuando lleguemos":

—cuando lleguemos, cuando lleguemos, ya, la mera verdad estoy cansado de llegar. Es la misma cosa llegar que partir porque apenas llegamos y . . . Mejor debería decir, cuando no lleguemos porque es la mera verdad. Nunca llegamos.

(When we arrive, when we arrive. At this point, to tell the truth, I'm tired of always arriving someplace. Arriving is the same as leaving because as soon as we arrive . . . Maybe I should say when we don't arrive because that's the plain truth. We never really arrive anywhere.) (152, 160)

The economic life of the migrant farmworker bound to the seemingly endless cycle of arrival and departure here becomes itself the subject of the analysis. It offers us one more version of the differential structure that we have identified as basic to the ideological critique of contemporary life performed by Chicano narrative. The dynamics of this structure undermine fixed ethical conclusions and fixed categorical definitions, particularly of polar oppositions put forth as irreconcilable and insoluble in favor of what we might call a unity within difference. In this instance, arriving and departing are shown to be not absolute oppositions of one another but rather mutual differentials, differing from and deferring to the other sequentially, continuously. As there is no definitive origin to their journey, neither is there an absolute endpoint. The geographical space between Texas and Minnesota is thus collapsed into the temporal cycle lived in the

modes of human suffering and frustration that makes each place both
an origin and an end but neither one nor the other exclusively.

The political consequences of this deconstruction are significant
indeed. Read one way, the refrain "cuando lleguemos" serves a decidedly hegemonic end: it manipulates with the false hope that there
is a definitive end to the migratory cycle, that the new cars, the
comfortable rooms, and the good wages are there at journey's end
awaiting their arrival. Defusing and rechanneling the workers' dangerous angers and frustrations by promising them the rewards of
their labor at a constantly postponed journey's end, the cycle performs a powerful ideological function. Read dialectically, however,
with the recognition that, as the one voice puts it, "es la misma cosa
llegar que partir," the phrase carries quite another valence: when
we arrive we are no better off than we were when we departed. At
this point we are at a protopolitical level, one step away from the
recognition that the cycle of arriving and departing is itself part of
the corrosive system for guaranteeing the availability of cheap and
plentiful agricultural labor.

The possibility of this recognition is signalled both by the gram-
matical subject of the first-person plural ("cuando lleguemos") and
by the narrative form that has blurred the conventional boundaries
between the various speaking voices to form a harmonious ensemble
of thoughts, has dramatized the impossibility of plots with stable beginnings, middles, and ends, and has problematized linear narrative
itself as a dependable recorder of reality. In both the cases of char-
acterization and narrative form, individual experience is gradually
replaced by conditional solidarity with others who also suffer an in-
articulated victimization. The utopian hope for a better future that
does emerge from Rivera's narrative is based less on the characters'
expectations of attaining some personal dream than on the narrator's
confidence that the characters' metonymic ensemble of conscious-
nesses can express, even if only allegorically, the possible unity of
a collectivity. While working within the general paradigms of traditional narrative realism with its direct ties to the socioeconomic
framework of the real world, *Tierra* thus constructs a more complex
realism than do the texts that we have previously discussed.

In the last section of the novel, "Debajo de la casa" ("Under the
House"), the protagonist reappears but in significantly different form.
Underneath a house, looking for a quiet place to think, the child
focuses now not on "his lost year," but on the people, places, and
events that have constituted that year. One by one, communal voices
invade his story even more forcefully than before, affirming in their

presence the historical unity of the heterogeneous crowds that pass
through his mind. He now says: "Quisiera ver a toda ese gente junta.
Y luego si tuviera unos brazos bien grandes los podría abrazar a todos"
("I would like to see all those people together. And if I had long
enough arms, I could hug them all at the same time") (168, 176).
Having discovered himself as the creative documentor of South Texas
migrant life in the process of telling his nonsequential, disseminated
story, the child triumphantly reemerges from the flow of voices:

Se sintió contento de pronto porque . . . se dio cuenta de que en realidad
no había perdido nada. Había encontrado. Encontrar y reencontrar y juntar.
Relacionar esto con esto, eso con aquello, todo con todo. Eso era. Eso era
todo. Y le dio más gusto.

(Suddenly he felt very happy because . . . he realized that he hadn't lost
anything. He had discovered something. To discover and to rediscover and
synthesize. To relate this entity with that entity, and that entity with still
another, and finally relating everything with everything else. That was what
he had to do, that was all. And he became even happier.) (169, 177)

The narrator here describes the very process of dialectical analysis that has motivated his entire story: abstraction from specific real
conditions, followed by systematic analysis, and then by successive
reapproximations to the real, all made necessary because everyday
experience catches only the delusive appearance of things. If we continue to use the category of the subject in referring to the narrative
procedures of Rivera's text, we do so now "under erasure,"[9] with the
understanding that the term designates an as yet untheorized object—the collective folk self-identified as la raza (the people). Lauro
Flores is surely correct when he observes that "Rivera's characters
. . . predate the Chicano Movement . . . [and] inhabit a world in
which exploitation and denial are still the fundamental traits of their
existence" (1985, 106). But while granting the fact of an unachieved
class consciousness in the story that Rivera tells, we cannot ignore
the strength of the imperfect allusions to collectivity throughout
the narrative. Rivera accomplishes his portrait of the real working-
class experience of la raza not by attempting to transcend the historical terrain of repression but by working at the radical level of
historical and cultural specificity, attempting to show the working
class as what Lukács has called the self-emancipating subject of history (1968, 199). "Thinking that he was thinking," Rivera's narrator-
protagonist refers the question of knowledge to its concrete situation

9. See Derrida, Of Grammatology, for a full discussion.

in social reality and to the class affiliation of the subject. In their very alienation and their sense of themselves as commodities to be sold, Rivera's characters come to apprehend reality as a process and as a reification into separate and unrelated things. Unable to raise themselves above the role of object, their consciousness is what Lukács has termed "the self-consciousness of the commodity; . . . the self-revelation of the capitalist society founded upon the production and exchange of commodities" (1968, 168). Rivera's figures are thus not the pragmatic subjects who populate the myth of American individualism, nor are they romanticized symbols of the Worker engaged in a world-wide class struggle. Rather, his characters are fundamentally rooted in the stuff of South Texas social and economic history, lived out as the community of *la raza*. As a fluid and nonsubjectified character, *la raza* itself becomes an element in the larger ideological struggle between agricultural capital and social democracy. In Rivera's narrative, this fluidity is not a sign of its social and political elusiveness but the ground of its historicity and political force. It signifies, as Joseph Sommers claims, "the beginning of recuperation of historical experience" (1979, 105).

The Autobiography of a Brown Buffalo

If in Rivera's view life can be stabilized only after we have experienced its instability and dreamed its integration in a utopian vision, in Oscar Zeta Acosta's narratives life is constituted only as instability, as chaos. Around the chaos, order can be momentarily constructed, but precisely because this order is a human construct, it cannot be made permanent. In the tragicomic antics of his fictional persona, Buffalo Zeta Brown, lawyer, writer, and would-be revolutionary, Acosta attempts to transform the debilitating effects of psychic doubt into political action, to fashion out of the absence of absolute value a new hypothetical order. In the process, he creates two of the most outrageous and iconoclastic satirical narratives in Chicano literature.

The first of these books, *The Autobiography of a Brown Buffalo* (1972), tells of the transformation of Dr. Gonzo, "the 300-pound, pill-popping Samoan attorney immortalized in Hunter Thompson's *Fear and Loathing in Las Vegas*," into Oscar Zeta Acosta, a new-left, psychedelic, radical Chicano lawyer.[10] The first view we are offered of

---

10. Oscar Zeta Acosta, *The Autobiography of a Brown Buffalo* (New York: Popular Library, 1972), publisher's information, p. 1. Héctor Calderón argues persuasively that

the Brown Buffalo is a revealing one, as he stands tableaulike before the mirror of introspection:

I stand naked before the mirror. Every morning of my life I have seen that brown belly from every angle. It has not changed that I can remember. I was always a fat kid. I suck it in and expand an enormous chest of two large hunks of brown tit. . . . I enter into the toilet. With my large, peasant hands carefully on the rim of white, I descend to my knocked knees. I stare into the repository of all that is unacceptable and wait for the green bile, my sunbaked face where my big, brown ass will soon sit. (11–12)

as partly Ulysses?

It is July 1, 1967, and as he will now explain, Acosta, in the guise of his fictional persona Buffalo Zeta Brown, has been brought to this expiatory position (his "sunbaked face" and "big brown ass" sharing a joint excremental function) in the thirty-third year of a life of wasted potential by the accident of being born poor and Mexican American. Racked by pain from an ulcerated stomach brought on by alcohol, tranquilizers, poor nutrition, and the frustrations of his job as a Legal Aid attorney, Acosta is desperate, burned out, and in the phrase of the day about "to turn on, tune in and drop out," seeking for himself that elusive oneness with the cosmos that the burgeoning love generation seems to have found. He leaves behind a very different world. The unending stream of poor blacks and Chicanos seeking temporary restraining orders against eviction notices, repossession claims, or querulous spouses, seeking declarations of bankruptcy, the restitution of wages, or child support payments, seeking in other words whatever meager justice is afforded to impoverished minority men and women attempting to allay the domestic tragedies of mid-century American life, has driven Acosta to the very edge of sanity:

For twelve months now all I have done is stuffed myself, puked wretched collages in the toilet bowl, swallowed 1000 tranquilizers without water, stared at the idiot-box, coddled myself, and watched the snakes grow larger inside my head while waiting for the clockhand to turn. For twelve months now, since I first became an attorney, a man who speaks for others . . . *time* has been nothing but a never-ending experience that meets me in the morning just like it left me off the night before. . . . I used to have the answers. . . . (28–29)

On this day, the "angst" (28) will not stop. He can speak for no one as he feels that no answers are available, and only the road beckons as a possible way out. The rest of Acosta's *Autobiography* tells of his

---

Brown Buffalo and *Revolt* should be read as satires (1982, 6–7). On satire, see also Guillermo E. Hernández, *Chicano Satire*, forthcoming.

search for answers in the altered states of consciousness brought on by excesses of sex, booze, LSD, mescaline, peyote, hashish, cocaine, amphetamines, and anything else that he can encounter on the road, as if in an attempt to make his very physical being the experimental canvas of an excremental artform, the fashioning of a self. In the course of this restless, near suicidal trip through the counterculture scene of the late 1960s, we learn by way of a series of flashbacks that Acosta's crisis has been developing since childhood in the 1940s and early 1950s, through a stint as a Baptist missionary in Panama in the early 1960s, and through two nervous breakdowns and ten years of psychoanalysis. Yet, whatever answers might exist for him are not to be found solely in personal terms. On the contrary, Acosta's satire reasserts what Jameson has termed "the specificity of the political content of everyday life and of individual fantasy-experience" (1981, 22). His descent into the nightmarish underworld of the American dream will reclaim the force of individual experience, restore it to the status of psychological projection, and will lead him by a roundabout path back to the active struggles of the beginnings of the Chicano Movement in East Los Angeles and the beginnings of a wholesale critique of the assimilationist, consensual American ideological hegemony. In the process, he will produce an identity for himself. But first he must confront himself.

Interspersed with the series of drug- and alcohol-induced binges that form the core of the satire are a series of flashbacks to Acosta's childhood as a "peach-picker's boy" (66) in Riverbank, California. Acosta's sense of himself as an "outlaw," an "outsider," and an "outcast" (94, 95) comes from the first days of his family's arrival in Riverbank from El Paso, Texas, his birthplace:

California, then, was a land of *Pochos*. . . . when we left *El Segundo Barrio* across the street from the international border [in El Paso], we didn't expect the Mexicans in California to act like gringos. But they did. We were outsiders because of geography and outcasts because we didn't speak English. . . . And so we had to fight every single day. (95)

Apart from fighting the other Mexicans who didn't consider him and his brother "*real* Mexicans" (95), Oscar also finds that "we had to fight the Oakies because we were Mexicans!" (96). In a town where "there were only three kinds of people: Mexicans, Oakies and Americans. Catholics, Holy Rollers and Protestants. Peach pickers, cannery workers and clerks" (96), Acosta must accept his contradictory niche as "a fat, dark Mexican—a Brown Buffalo" (107), even while the California *pochos* never quite acknowledge him "as part of their

tribe" (96). His fantasy of being accepted by his "American" school-
mates and especially by a "pig-tailed American girl" (109) who has
been friendly to him, is exploded one day when she tells the teacher
that Oscar "stinks" (117). He is forced to recognize that "I *am* the
nigger after all. . . . I am nothing but an Indian with sweating body
and faltering tits that sag at the sight of a young girl's blue eyes"
(118). As will continue to be the case throughout the remainder of
the story, Acosta's sense of his own being as man of color in a white
supremacist society is focused sharply on his sensual being and on
how he imagines it to be perceived by blue-eyed, pony-tailed American women.

Back in the present through Idaho, Montana, and Colorado, with
an assorted company of hippies, bikers, hitchhikers, druggies, and an
outlaw journalist modeled after Hunter Thompson, Acosta pushes
his alcohol- and drug-consuming capacities to the limits, often unconsciously flirting with death, while coming no closer to a resolution of the doubts with which he began. The romantic collectivism
of the Timothy Leary, flower child, love-in generation has turned
him into "a recorder of the past with a sour stomach" (18): "I was
thirty-three years old . . . and I had no idea where I was" (180). From
the chaotic ruins of his life, he now makes one last effort to salvage
some sense: "I decided to go to El Paso, the place of my birth, to see
if I could find the object of my quest. I still wanted to find out just
who in the hell I really was" (234).

He finds El Paso to be nothing like the town that he remembers
having left as a child twenty-five years earlier. But he is struck by
the people and their language: "All the faces are brown, tinged with
brown, lightly brown, the feeling of brown. . . . And they are all
speaking in that language of my youth . . . a language perfect in every
detail for people who are serious about life and preoccupied with
death only as it refers to that last day of one's sojourn on this particular spot" (236–37). The unusual feeling of being an insider rather
than an outcast intensifies as he crosses the bridge into Juarez, but
so too does his fear that he is only "impersonating a *mexicano*":

All my life someone or another had made such accusations. The kids from
the West Side fought Bob and me because we were from the East. . . . The
Oakies spit on my prick because I was a nigger faking it as a Mexican. And
the Americans wanted me to forget I was ever a savage with secret codes.
(238)

When a Mexican prostitute approaches him in a bar and he is unable
to flirt with her in Spanish or respond to her question of whether he

is Mexican or not, Acosta realizes that his old joking response that he
is "Samoan" (242) is no longer very funny. The consequences of his
search for his "fucked-up identity" (242) get even more serious when
he is arrested and thrown into the Juarez jail, where he is humili-
ated by the Mexican police and terrorized by the Mexican prisoners.
The ultimate humiliation occurs, however, when even though he is
a lawyer he is unable to plead his case before the Mexican magistrate
because his Spanish is too weak. He must meekly speak his apologies
in English. As he is being led out from the courtroom after having
been found guilty of a misdemeanor offense, the Mexican magistrate,
a dark-skinned woman, calls out to him in perfect English: "Why
don't you go home and learn to speak your father's language?" (247).
His homelessness is made all the more vivid when, as he crosses
the bridge back to El Paso, the U.S. Immigration officer admits him
into the country but with the comment that he should carry identification papers since "You don't *look* like an American, you know"
(249). It is January 1968 and Acosta has descended as far into hell as
he will go.

Acosta's story ends as it began: he stands naked before a mirror,
wallowing in self-pity, and completely lost to himself: "I am a brown
buffalo lonely and afraid in a world I never made" (249). He is forced
to admit that he has "failed to find the answer to my search. One son-
ofabitch tells me I'm not a Mexican and the other one says I'm not
an American" (250). In the midst of his inability to resolve his schiz-
oid identity, neither Mexican nor American, and as he is planning to
leave the country for Guatemala to write about the Sandinista revolution, Acosta learns from his brother about "some group called the
Brown Berets [who] are going to have a school strike [in East L.A.]"
(250–51). His brother suggests that Acosta go to East L.A. and write
about that revolution. The narrative ends none too optimistically as
we find our hero factitiously dreaming about the rousing speeches
by which he will stir the coming Chicano revolution:

No one ever asked me or my brother if we wanted to be American citizens.
We are all citizens by default. They stole our land and made us half-slaves.
. . . Now what we need is to give ourselves a new name. We need a new identity. A name and a language all our own. . . . I propose that we call ourselves
the Brown Buffalo people. (253)

His search for personal identity has led him uneasily to the possibility of a transpersonal solution to his questions. But, in fact, as
he readily admits, what he really wants is "to speak for his people"
as "Moses, Mao, and Martin" did for theirs (253). The patent inau-

thenticity of his resolve to join in a collective enterprise is revealed ✓
in his grandiosely overblown self-denial in the name of *la raza,* a
community he does not yet really understand.

The Revolt of the Cockroach People

The next chapter of Acosta's life finds him back in East Los Angeles
in 1968, working again as an attorney for the Public Defender's office,
caught up in the newly politicized Chicano movement, and sporting
a new name, "Buffalo Zeta Brown."[11] *The Revolt of the Cockroach
People* is, as the stinging irony of its double-edged title suggests, a
profane, ambiguous attempt to reconstruct the mood of the heady
days of the Los Angeles Chicano high school blow-outs (walkouts)
in 1968, the founding of the militant Brown Berets, the protests of
the Católicos Por La Raza (CPLR) in 1969, and the general politicization of the Chicano community by the farmworkers' labor struggles
and the alliance of the Chicano Movement with the anti–Vietnam
War movement in the Chicano National Moratoriums of 1970.[12] The
consolidation of the feminist movement, protests against academic
regimentation, racial discrimination, workers' exploitation, religious
alienation, dehumanization, sexual repression, environmental destruction—the entire panoply of seemingly unrelated "disorders"
that formed the core of the social crisis of the 1960s and early 1970s
are exposed in confusing array as the substance of Acosta's novel.

The Revolt of the Cockroach People places us in the midst of the
turbulent scenes of the demonstrations by the CPLR on Christmas
Eve of 1969 at St. Basil's Cathedral, protesting the Church's refusal to
involve itself in the cause of social justice for Mexican Americans. It
follows with trial scenes where Brown serves as the defense attorney
first for the Chicanos accused of conspiracy in the school blow-out
case, and then for those arrested at the St. Basil's Cathedral demonstration. The climactic scene of the novel dramatizes Brown's role as
defense lawyer in the trial of the Chicanos tried for conspiracy and
inciting to riot at the National Chicano Moratorium antiwar demonstration at Laguna Park in East Los Angeles on August 29, 1970.
In each of these cases, *The Revolt of the Cockroach People* uses the

11. Acosta, *The Revolt of the Cockroach People* (San Francisco: Straight Arrow
Books, 1973; New York: Bantam Books, 1974), 30.
12. See Acuña, "New Nationalism—Youth Movement" and "Major Demonstrations" (1981, 355–60, 366–71) for discussion of the early days of the Chicano movement in Los Angeles.

historical events of the day as the context for the construction of
a Chicano identity and the realization of a revolutionary class consciousness. In the role of Buffalo Zeta Brown, Acosta remains out-
rageously, even arrogantly, self-oriented in the course of his story,
but finds that despite himself the answers to his personal questions
continue to lead him in an extrapersonal direction.

"While the novel may hold up a mirror to life," notes Héctor
Calderón, "the satirist uses the mirror to distort" (1982, 7). Despite Brown's overt sexism, his blatant anticlericism, and his heavy-
handed egoism, no single feature of his satire is likely to offend the
common reader more than his assessment of the American legal
system as an arbitrary weave of semantic threads created to hide
the empty forms of notions such as "justice" and "natural rights."
Whereas we would expect Law, at least in its ideal form, to permit us
an approximation to the state of transcendental right, Buffalo Zeta
Brown shows us, in a series of increasingly allegorical trial scenes,
that the truth of justice is intimately tied to its differential opposite,
the lie of justice: "All of them," he tells us in the climactic scene of
the novel's closing trial:

every single witness, both prosecution and defense . . . is lying. Or not telling the whole truth. The bastards know exactly what we have done and what
we have not done. . . . But they have all told their own version of things as
they would like them to be. (272)

Brown's version of the law as he has come to understand it in the
course of the various trials in which he participates offers us two
correlative qualities: Law is *arbitrary* because it is constituted by
a systematic difference between truth and lies and not by its own
individual, *de jure*, fullness. It is *differential* because law does not
function from the compact force of meaning at the core of "truth"
and "lies" but by the *de facto* network of oppositions that distinguish
them and relate them to one another. The major consequence to be
drawn from this double recognition, as Brown realizes, is that an objective truth, sufficient unto itself and available for all to see, can
never be made present, either in the courtroom or elsewhere. Brown
does not mean that there are not statements that we can judge "true"
or "false." He does suggest, however, that every attempt to specify
"truth" forces us to define it in terms of an abstract entity that is
only a cultural convention: All speak "their own version of things as
they would like them to be." From Brown's point of view, truth and
falsehood are not by-products of the direct adhesion between a word
and some actual state of the world but are instead functions of co-

incidences or discrepancies between multiple versions of the same event. This recognition is at once frightening and exhilirating for Brown, for it allows him to fashion, if only crudely and temporarily, the answers to his earlier schizophrenic questions, and to meld his double desires both to counsel at law and to write "THE BOOK" of his life (14). He now sees the former antithesis between his private desires and his public responsibilities to be as factitious and as reductive as his former sense of *law* as simply an instrument of class domination. Law may well serve as a tool of repression but it may also be used to project a radically new form of legality that cannot be achieved within present institutions. The result of this realization is that Brown's overly facile resolutions of his personal identity crisis by subsuming it to ethical politics of "right" and "wrong" is totally negated. He now finds that ideological commitment to a cause or to an identity is not a matter of moral choices tied to absolute standards of "truth" and "falsehood." The matter resolves to the more fundamental issue of taking sides in a struggle between embattled groups (Jameson 1981, 290).

The reconciliation between his contradictory impulses is possible because Brown comes to see living, like lawyering and authoring, as a play of stylistics. The play allows the fashioning of a formal context into a thematic content. And all three activities finally entail a play with "lies" so that "truth" might be revealed. But all also entail the possibility that in the play with form, the form itself can become an end and seduce one away from the hard-won recognition of its foundation upon arbitrary *difference*. The flow of judicial, as well as fictional, language points to no meaning other than its own pleasurable self-reproduction. Legal and artistic truth depend not on a direct relation between a linguistic expression and a real object or state of affairs, but rather on the process of continuously displaced sign functions that attempt to name the truth.[13] His understanding of the arbitrariness of truth statements, however, does not lead Brown either to his former "angst" nor to a sense of powerlessness. On the contrary, his understanding of the arbitrary difference of truth statements permits him to establish meanings as cultural units *materially* accessible to the individual will itself.

The hallucinatory dream of romantic collectivism he pursues in his satiric *Autobiography* bursts into full political consciousness in *The Revolt of the Cockroach People*. Brown there comes to realize

13. On the relationship between legal and literary discourses, see the excellent essay by Susan Heinzelman (1988).

that forms of law, and of political, philosophical, religious, or artistic ideology are products of the concrete social relations into which people enter at a particular time and place. As products, they can also be reproduced. His aesthetic creation of "the Book" of his life is just one such cultural production. Stéphane Mallarmé had dreamed of a universal "*Livre*" to serve as the "spiritual instrument" in which all earthly existence might ultimately be contained. In a manner quite unanticipated by Mallarmé, Buffalo Zeta Brown's "Book" functions as a material instrument, attempting not to contain existence but rather to forge a symbolic or imaginary solution to the unresolvable social contradictions of our times (Jameson 1981, 79). For Acosta, too, reality remains a shocking montage of dissimilar qualities, but one that the revolutionary artist can nonetheless help transform. Through the fictional mask of Buffalo Zeta Brown, Acosta accepts this possibility and uses it to convert chaos into a utopian anarchy of both forensic and poetic form.

5. Migrant farmworkers and hiring agents gathering at an informal employment agency advertising work in Michigan for "beet pickers" in Corpus Christi, Texas, April 1949. (Russell Lee Collection, courtesy of the Eugene C. Barker Texas History Center, University of Texas at Austin)

6. Farm laborer and his grandchild pausing near San Angelo, Texas, on the migrant path from the border town of Laredo, Texas, to the sugarbeet fields of Wyoming, May 1949. (Russell Lee Collection, courtesy of the Eugene C. Barker Texas History Center, University of Texas at Austin)

7. Migrant farm-laboring families of the era depicted in Rivera's *Tierra*, San Angelo, Texas, May 1949. (Russell Lee Collection, courtesy of the Eugene C. Barker Texas History Center, University of Texas at Austin)

8. Sign of the times: enforcing the Jim Crow laws and the segregation of "Mexicans" and "Spanish" in San Antonio, Texas, June 1949. (Russell Lee Collection, courtesy of the Eugene C. Barker Texas History Center, University of Texas at Austin)

5
Romance, the Fantastic, and the Representation of History in Rudolfo A. Anaya and Ron Arias

While Rivera's novel retains vestiges of the corrido tradition, Acosta's satirical narratives irreverently explode the myth of the reticent, humble hero and deflate what by the 1960s has become an empty stereotype. Rudolfo Anaya and Ron Arias offer further variations on heroic identity and the formation of the Chicano subject in its position of resistance to the dominant American culture. Anaya's *Bless Me, Ultima*, for example, rejects the symbolic social force of the corrido and its celebration of direct, confrontational resistance in favor of a romantic, mystical celebration of a racial collective unconscious unity with the world spirit. He presents this choice of romantic coalescence as an alternative sanctioned by the indigenous myths of his beloved New Mexico. Nowhere are the regional differences among Chicanos and their cultural productions highlighted more clearly than in Anaya's and Arias' different narrative choices and representations of history.

In Anaya's text, the radical tendency of Chicano narrative to explore the material conditions of psychological and cultural production appears surreptitiously, working against the unpolitical "conscious" levels of the narrative. Arias' fantastic narrative, similarly, seems to depart from the high realism of the corrido tradition represented in Paredes, Villarreal, and even in the formally experimental Rivera. Unlike Anaya's romance, however, Arias' fantasy invests the world of the imagination with the stuff of history and the imagined reality of urban *barrio* life. In its concern with the pathos of the imaginative life and the ideological formations within which the subject recognizes itself, *The Road to Tamazunchale* extends the critique of American cultural hegemony expressed in the corrido to the realm of the symbolic. Here I follow Jameson's suggestions about the ideological implications of the conventions of romance and the fantastic as narrative genres, and of how these conventions serve as strategies of containment against history and the political.

Bless Me, Ultima

The critical reception of Rudolfo A. Anaya's *Bless Me, Ultima* (1972) has been almost as uniformly positive as the popular reception of the work. Winner of the second annual Quinto Sol literary award, Anaya's novel is surely the best-selling Chicano literary work, having gone through eighteen printings totaling sales of over 220,000 copies as of 1989. Reasons for this phenomenal success (relative to the usual market for Chicano works) are various and complex. Certainly, the fact that *Bless Me, Ultima* follows a Joycean high literary pattern, offering a New Mexican portrait of the artist as a young boy, makes the story more accessible to the traditional literary establishment and to audiences beyond the Mexican American community. Also, as critics have rightfully pointed out, Anaya's novel, while deliberately set within the social and geographical parameters of rural New Mexico, self-consciously strives to attain "universal" significance. Its symbolic patterns, myth structures, and ideological system are drawn from the venerable traditions of Western European high culture. Blending these traditions with indigenous belief, folk legend, myth, and poetically crafted scenes of local color, Anaya's book creates a uniquely palatable amalgamation of old and new world symbolic structures. Describing the coming to maturity of the young protagonist in the years during and immediately following World War II, Anaya offers a highly romantic representation of the growth to artistic and ethical consciousness. In detailing this growth, Anaya leads his readers through an enchanting, mystical landscape, animated by spiritual forces that seem to affect the course of personal destiny.[1]

The rural New Mexican world Anaya describes is alive with the most fundamental of originary forces: old gods and new still compete for the allegiance of mankind, Edenic gardens still flower, milk and honey still flow from the fields, and the radical separation between man and nature has not yet occurred. But this cluster of images tells

---

1. Anaya discusses his sense of "landscape" and its significance for his works in an interview with Bruce-Novoa (1980, 184–202) and in an essay on "The Writer's Landscape: Epiphany in Landscape" (1977, 98–102). See the excellent discussion of this topic by Héctor Calderón, "Rudolfo Anaya's *Bless Me, Ultima*: A Chicano Romance of the Southwest" (1986).

only one half of Anaya's story. For in opposition to the Edenic myths
that animate the protagonist's world, devils and witches also walk
the earth, evil itself awaits to devour the innocent, and the powers
of nature are capable of turning against humanity as in some postromantic vision of apocalypse. The legendary past and the mythic
present can recoil against humanity with terrifying force. In the
midst of these wild, untamed elements, Antonio Juan Márez y Luna,
at the beginning of the story a child already wise beyond his years
and soon to be even wiser, is called upon to make the crucial choices
that will determine the course of his life and of his community. Like
his literary forebears from Paredes' boy heroes to Villarreal's and
Rivera's artists in the making, Antonio must live an apprenticeship
year in life before he may turn to his momentous destiny in art. But
unlike his literary predecessors, Antonio looks not to history but to
myth, magic, ritual, and symbol as the sources of the stuff of life and
as the contexts of his growth to artistic maturity. Such anyway, is
apparently what the novel *Bless Me, Ultima* seems to offer.

Antonio is seven years old when his *Lehrjahr* begins. It ends after
an intense period of experiencing the world and of spiritual growth
under the tutelage of an old *curandera* (folk-healer) named Ultima,
who has come to live with the Márez family. In the year of narrative time, Antonio experiences in rapid succession the brutality
perpetrated by man against man and man against woman, the loss of
childhood innocence, the horror of evil, doubts about his traditional
Catholic faith, and eventually, through the mediation of Ultima's
persona, a powerful reconciliation with the forces of good. Ultima,
with her magical ties to the unconscious powers of unadulterated
nature, has been described as a "pantheistic priestess, good witch
of the South, earth mother, life force and universal spirit, all com-
pactly molded into one small, ageless woman with glossy braids and
a magical owl."[2] She senses something of her own spiritual tie to
the mystical life in Antonio and since she is the last ("última") of
her kind she uses her time with the boy as a surrogate mother to
teach him about the awesome powers of the metaphysical, supernatural life. Ultima's good works are obstructed by the power of pure
evil in the person of Tenorio Trementina, father of three witchlike
daughters, who together with the satanic old man set out to destroy
Ultima.

Antonio's father, Gabriel Márez, a fiercely independent *llanero*

---

2. Dyan Donnelly, "Finding a Home in the World" (1974, 115); cited in Tatum (1975, 118).

(plainsman) who proudly claims an ancestry of sixteenth-century Spanish conquistadores who tamed the New Mexican wilderness, laments the waning of his people's independent spirit and hopes to imbue the boy with his racial wanderlust and his dream of migrating to the promised land of California. The Márez clan, a people associated with the sun and the oceanlike plains (*mares* translates as "seas"), live near the community of Las Pasturas ("the pastures"). Antonio's mother, María Luna, traces her lineage to the hardy farmers who settled the New Mexican territory, transforming the wilderness into a fertile garden. The Lunas ("moons"), associated with the moon and its cycles of fertility, live in a river valley near the garden community of El Puerto de los Luna. Her clan is earth-rooted, domesticating, and allied with the civilizing arts. Her husband's is a free-spirited, exuberant, adventurous people. The conflicts set up by the polarities crossing in Antonio's soul and complicated even further by Ultima's mystical interventions form the basis of Anaya's novel.

Critics have rightly dealt with *Bless Me, Ultima* as a novel that departs radically from the traditional realism of other Chicano literary texts. Roberto Cantú has claimed that *Bless Me, Ultima* chronicles the construction of "a new life," offering as its "message" an ideology of "regeneration" activated through an "adaptation to circumstances, an invention of a style of life, and an ethnic revindication" (1979, 387). Elsewhere, he argues that "Anaya has marked out his work within a temporo-spatial dimension of mythic character" (1973). He points out that the novel is set in locales that ring with allegorical significance: Guadalupe, Las Pasturas, El Puerto de los Luna, names with clearly symbolic associations with El Tepeyac (scene of the miraculous appearance of the Virgin of Guadalupe, the national saint of Mexico), idyllic pastorals, and the Garden of Eden. And despite the fact that the novel is set in the historical time of World War II, he claims, "the war serves only to underline the evil that is preying upon mankind; its function is simply symbolical and subsidiary to the manichean theme of the work, given that, the town of Guadalupe is at the margin of history" (1973).

Other critics offer different insights. Elaine Johnson views *Bless Me, Ultima* as a story of cultural experience: "Antonio Márez y Luna's odyssey is a search for his own identity, a spiritual journey which in the course of the narrative is developed into an allegory for the whole Chicano experience" (1978, 92). Anaya's point of departure as well as his endpoint are thus apparently mythic in quality. Jane Rogers emphasizes the significance of archetypes from world mythology in Antonio's year of growth: he is "symbolically both Christ and Odysseus" as he "moves from the security and from the sweet-smelling warmth of his mother's bosom and kitchen out into life and experience" (1986, 200). Linked to the Christ and Odysseus myths, and the associated images of Scylla and Charybdis, the Wandering Rocks, the Siren, and Narcissus, myth critics find the folk legends of Native American and Mexican oral culture, especially the myth of *la llorona*, the wailing woman of the rivers, who mourns the deaths of the children she herself has murdered, as crucial to an understanding of the novel.[3] According to Rogers, as Antonio comes to "face the reality of his manhood," he must first learn to elude the call of death (1986, 205). The shamanic power of the old faithhealer Ultima and of her tremendous influence on the outcome of Antonio's life have led David Carrasco to see *Bless Me, Ultima* as a text of revisionary religious power (1982). Vernon E. Lattin takes Antonio's relationship to Ultima as a paradigmatic instance in American literature of the transcendental desire to recuperate the separation between man and nature (1979). In each of these readings, Antonio is seen as the organizing center around whom the New Mexican bicultural, bilingual situation is synthesized: "Antonio moves toward being able to write the novel; the reader moves toward being able to read it" (Dasenbrock 1987, 16). The heightened poetic style of Anaya's novel, the sharp delineations between the forces of good and evil, and the precritical acceptance of legend, myth, and popular belief all tend to make the story seem a fantasy or a romance rather than a realistic depiction of contemporary life.

In the best single reading of the novel to date, Héctor Calderón argues that *Bless Me, Ultima* is not a novel at all but a self-consciously crafted romance that uses all of the generic possibilities available to it as romance: "It is the romance whose formal possibilities and stylistic features can accommodate mythic and religious materials, as well as folk beliefs, and then project them in almost any age as ideals and wish-fulfillment fantasy, that will give us greater insights into *Bless Me, Ultima*" (1986, 22). Calderón's reading is an important one for it does not simply answer the question of the narrative's genre but, more important, it explains "under what conditions

3. The legend of *La Llorona*, "the wailing woman," takes many forms and is widespread throughout Greater Mexico. Américo Paredes writes: "La Llorona, the wailing woman in white [seeks] her children who died in childbirth. Originally an Aztec goddess who sacrificed babies and disappeared shrieking into lakes or rivers, La Llorona usually appears near a well, stream, or washing place. The Hispanicized form has La Llorona murdering her own children born out of wedlock when her lover married a woman of his own station" (1970, xvi).

[it is] possible to conceive of this literary form." Using Jameson's notions of "metacommentary" and the "political unconscious," Calderón goes on to show that romance is possible during periods of cultural transformation when myth is displaced toward the aesthetic realm:

As a written form, romance follows in the wake of the dissolution of a world conceived through mythic or . . . magical consciousness and whose dominant form of discourse is oral and formulaic. Displacement means that beliefs in foundation myths are depragmatized, removed from their original collective context, deprived of their truth effect and transformed into the metaphors and archetypes of imaginative literature. (1986, 23)

Bless Me, Ultima thus can be said to capture in the form of romance a critical and complex transition period in the literary-cultural history of the Southwest: the simultaneous existence within Chicano communities of pre-Columbian myths, beliefs, legends, and superstitions, and mid-twentieth-century technological, literate, mass-media culture. It may seem paradoxical that certain precapitalist social formations should exist into the mid-twentieth century. But the apparent incongruity of these separate symbolic structures for the organization of life only suggests the compatibility of distinct types and rates of development and the coexistence of various modes of production within contemporary mass-market economies and capitalist societies.

In *Bless Me, Ultima,* Anaya depicts those incongruities while offering a displaced and marginalized reprise of the social realism and the ideological critique in the form of the dialectics of difference that we find in texts such as the nineteenth-century corrido, Paredes' short fiction, and Rivera's and Acosta's novels. In the following discussion we will consider *Bless Me, Ultima* as one very interesting dramatization of this complex interaction between "mythic or magical consciousness" and mid-twentieth-century technological social formations and as an allegory of the repressed space of the worlds of work, of history, and of protopolitical conflict. Jameson's notion of the "political unconscious" is especially suited for reading such a narrative.

We have noted that *Bless Me, Ultima* narrates the crucial events in the life of the seven-year-old Antonio. The narrative voice itself, however, is that of an adult speaker, presumably Antonio himself, as he recollects his childhood and transcribes its effects. And, in fact, time is the issue with which the narrator chooses to begin his tale:

Ultima came to stay with us the summer I was almost seven. When she came the beauty of the llano unfolded before my eyes, and the gurgling waters of the river sang to the hum of the turning earth. The magical time of child-hood stood still, and the pulse of the living earth pressed its mystery into my living blood. She took my hand, and the silent, magic powers she possessed made beauty from the raw, sun-baked llano, the green river valley, and the blue bowl which was the sun's home. My bare feet felt the throbbing earth and my body trembled with excitement. Time stood still, and it shared with me all that had been, and all that was to come. . . .[4]

The opening passage of the narrative illustrates at least four levels of temporality, levels that will continue to play a significant role in the development of Antonio's story. First, we see the narrated past of the boy's childhood, "the summer I was almost seven." This nar-rated past implies a second temporality, the duration of the story that we are about to hear. Both of these moments are counterpoised momentarily by a third temporality, the static time associated with Ultima's timeless presence and ageless demeanor, when "time stood still." This nondurational temporality is certainly the temporality of myth itself, capable of being emplotted and narrated but imply-ing no necessary procession. It is also shortly to be linked to what Antonio calls "the time of dreams" (4), as he begins to narrate the first of ten prominent dream sequences. Against these represented and implied temporalities figures yet another temporal dimension, the temporality of history itself, marked out over the following pages by references both to the history of nineteenth- and twentieth-century New Mexico, and especially to World War II, as when Antonio men-tions the socially dislocating impact of "the big rancheros and the tejanos [who] came and fenced the beautiful llano" (2), thus breaking up the open range and destroying the tradition of commonly held range lands, or as when Antonio's father laments the changes to their serene village brought about by "the winds of war" (3). Freeing itself from the most restrictive aspects of linear time, Antonio's narrative immediately sets out to explore the hierarchical levels that form the depth of temporal experience.[5] His narrative detects temporalities that are more or less extended, and that offer in each instance differ-ent figures of recollection, of eternity, and of the relation between myth and history, all against the backdrop of death.

4. Rudolfo A. Anaya, *Bless Me, Ultima* (Berkeley: Quinto Sol Publications, 1972), 1. I cite the third printing (1974) of the novel.

5. Ricoeur, *Time and Narrative* (1985, 2:101).

The initial instance of this complex interaction between narrative time, mythic time, and historical time occurs in the context of the first of ten narrated dreams.[6] I have already mentioned the conflict between Antonio's parents over their son's fate, one desiring for him the free-spirited *vaquero* life of the Márez, the other hoping that he will choose the quiet agricultural life of the Luna. Antonio's first dream takes him to the original scene of that conflict, the moment of his birth, as both the Márez and Luna families bring to the child gifts symbolic of their different work. The farmers solemnly offer the fruit of their fields, anointing his forehead with "*the dark earth of the river valley,*" hoping that the newborn child will "*keep our customs and traditions*" (5) and become a farmer and perhaps also a priest, thus reenacting the life of the legendary founder of their clan, a heroic farmer-priest who lead them through the wilderness to a land of milk and honey. The wild Márez enter smashing the fruits of the fields to offer instead the implements of their work, "*a saddle, horse blankets, bottles of whiskey, a new rope, bridles, chapas, and an old guitar*" (5). They too have a history for Antonio to replay: "*His forefathers were conquistadores, men as restless as the seas they sailed and as free as the land they conquered*" (6) and they desire that life for the child, too. With pistols drawn on both sides to settle their conflict over the ritual disposition of the child's afterbirth, whether it will be buried in the fields to renew their fertility or burned and its ashes scattered by the wind on the "*ocean of the plain,*" to celebrate the spirit of freedom, the old woman who has delivered the baby claims the child, saying, "*Only I will know his destiny*" (6). The nature of that destiny is not very mysterious, as we will soon find out when Ultima offers the child the implements of several trades, and he chooses pen and paper (51). Ultima's own ambiguous status is questioned by Antonio's two sisters, "Is it true she is a witch?" (7), but is resolved to Antonio's satisfaction by the logic of his dreams, which link Ultima, her companion owl, and the Virgin of Guadalupe into one ensemble figure (12).

Antonio's dreams effectively set up the conflicting qualities of his young life. In schematic form they break down into some such symmetrical pattern:

6. Antonio's ten dreams form a coherent narrative sequence in their own right, following Anaya's admitted influence by Jungian psychology. See the discussion by Roberto Cantú, "Estructura y sentido de lo onírico en *Bless Me, Ultima*" (1974, 27–41).

LUNA		MÁREZ
farmer	Ultima	vaquero
river	Virgin	plain
moon	mother	seas
El Puerto		Las Pasturas

These oppositions, basically functions of the historically real New Mexican forces of production and the resultant division of labor, ✓ serve initially as the fundamental discrepancies in Antonio's life. Given the pastoral and idyllic character of the rhetoric of romance and the prominence of the binary oppositions it creates, it is easy to see why critics have taken the figural resonances of these oppositions liberally as the machinery for the production of an interpretive myth based loosely on Jungian psychology and the notion of a racial collective unconscious.[7] As Calderón has shown, romance, as a literary institution, authorizes readers to attempt to reconstruct the totalizing imaginary entity behind the polarities that would reconcile their differences. Those factitious oppositions, mediated by the presence of the old *curandera* in her several guises and through her link to mythic time, are the objects of the deconstruction that the narrative proceeds to perform.

Following immediately on the arrival of Ultima, Antonio's lessons in life begin in earnest:

She taught me the names of plants and flowers, of trees and bushes, of birds + *genesis* and animals; but most important, I learned from her that there was beauty in the time of day and in the time of night, and that there was peace in the river and in the hills. She taught me to listen to the mystery of the groaning earth and to feel complete in the fulfillment of its time. My soul grew under her careful guidance.

I had been afraid of the awful *presence* of the river, which was the soul of the river, but through her I learned that my spirit shared in the spirit of all things. (14)

The serenity of this idyllic time is completely shattered by the intrusion of events from the real world. Soon after Ultima's arrival, one of the townspeople, Lupito (diminutive form of the name Guadalupe), a returned veteran made "crazy" by the war in the Pacific, flashes back to the horror of combat and in a fit of frenzy kills the sheriff.

7. Anaya's sense of a collective unconscious appears in an interview with Bruce-Novoa, when he comments that "what we must not forget is that beneath the surface [of particular cultural symbols] we will find the archetypes and the values and the primal symbols which we share in common with all mankind" (1980, 196).

Now he is to be himself hunted down. Having sneaked out to follow his father and the other men, Antonio is present when Lupito is cornered and killed. The dying man crawls to Antonio, who is hiding in the reeds by the river, and pleads for his blessing. In his fright at the sight of death and "the horror of darkness" (20), Antonio runs from the scene, having heard "the soft wail of a siren" (21), ambiguously the sound of the police cars or of the spirits who summon him to share Lupito's death.

Safe in bed, thinking about the dead man and "the war [that] made him crazy" (22), Antonio now dreams about his three older brothers who are themselves away at war. León, Andrew, and Eugene are truly Márez men, as Antonio is not. In the dream Andrew recalls that their forefathers *"were men of the sea . . . they were conquistadores, men whose freedom was unbounded"* (23). He points out how their father, forced to give up the life of his people and live in the city of Guadalupe to make a living for his family as a highway construction worker, still yearns for that freedom: *"He builds highways that stretch into the sun, and we must travel that road with him"* (23). Having given up the sweet life of the vaquero, Gabriel hopes to recapture it, his former freedom, and the tie to unspoiled nature by migrating to "the land of the setting sun, to the vineyards of California" (13). But "the war had ruined his dream" (14) by having taken his three sons. In the dream the older brothers suggest that they possess their father's independent ways to his detriment, for when they return from the war they will follow their own highways "with their carpenter tools" (24), apart from his, suffering their own very real "war-sickness" (61). They taunt Antonio with the fact that he is *"a Luna . . . you are to be a farmer-priest for mother!"* (23). As Calderón has noted, both "families belong to a romantic pastoral, a village life when men lived unalienated from nature and in harmony among themselves" (1986, 27). Despite their apparent differences as ranchers and farmers, the two families share a fundamental base: both lead a communal, patriarchal life in an Arcadian setting untouched by the outside Anglo world, and together they offer allied versions of the myth of the Golden Age and the Earthly Garden. Antonio's narrative would have us believe that in Las Pasturas and El Puerto de los Luna men once worked freely together toward one common goal and in control of the means of production. Joined into direct relationships for the production and exchange of goods that satisfied qualitatively defined needs, Márezes and Lunas once lived as whole human beings. The products of their work acquired lifelike qualities and were so animated that they became enmeshed with the

people who created them, implying a direct connection between the
ego and the phenomenal world. This symbolic relationship is evident
in Antonio's dream of his birth, when the Lunas and Márezes bring
the child the emblems of their respective work. Spiritual unity with
all things is precisely the universal connection that Ultima's mysticism promises to Antonio. Now, however, both clans desperately
need the rejuvenating presence of a leader who will return them to
the full vigor and symbolic plenitude of that former age and fullness
of being. Antonio thus stands as the messianic figure, possessing the
best qualities of each who will eliminate their superficial differences
and underwrite the continuation and expansion of their pastoral existence by standing above their differences: "I love them both, and yet
I am of neither" (38).

To be sure, the nostalgic myth of an organic social structure that
Antonio's narrative wishes to recreate through the resolution of differences within his own mediating presence is a preciously fragile
one. Even as Antonio attempts to shore it up and live its authenticity,
the myth of pastoral stability, either in its Márez or Luna manifestations or in some synthesis beyond them, is throughout his narrative
continually assaulted by the incomprehensibility of history: World
War II and its effects on those who fought it, and on the communities to which they returned. Lupito, León, Andrew, and Eugene have
been touched by history and have become for Antonio "lost men"
(60). Antonio's response to the corrosion of the Golden Age is to look
for a symbolic reconciliation of the contradictions occasioned by the
loss of pastoral stability, by contact with the outside world, and by
the loss of harmony among men. When in the dream his brothers
cower before the wail of "la llorona . . . the old witch who cries along
the river banks and seeks the blood of boys and men to drink" (23),
Antonio protects them with his understanding that his spirit shares
in the spirit of all things, even the mystical "presence *of the river*"
(24). This universal "presence," in various manifestations, will be a
motif throughout the novel, an emblem of the sublime timelessness
of nature and a barrier against the force of history.

The most startling version of this motif appears in the myth of the
Golden Carp. One of Antonio's precocious friends, Samuel, prophet-
like, shares with him a legend about the origins of the world. According to Samuel's story, an originary people wandering through the
wilderness are given a fertile valley by the gods. Only one restriction
is imposed upon them: they are not to fish the carp of the river, for
this fish is sacred to the gods. The people obey at first; but after a
drought of forty years' duration they are forced to eat the sacred fish.

In their anger the gods are ready to destroy the people. "But one kind god who truly loved the people argued against it, and the other gods were so moved by his love that they relented from killing the people. Instead, they turned the people into carp. . . ." (74). To protect them in their new home, the one kind god becomes a carp himself and goes to live among his carp people. Later, when Antonio actually sees the Golden Carp, he realizes that he has "witnessed a miraculous thing, the appearance of a pagan god" (105).

He also finds that the Golden Carp has its own dialectical opposite, in the form of an evil black bass. Before he hears this myth Antonio recognizes only one God—the God of the Roman Catholic faith. Slowly, he begins to accept, however, that the Carp too is a figure of regeneration—a symbol of salvation. In fact, both myths, the Christian and the pagan, are versions of the same story. As Antonio realizes, to admit of more than one God is sacrilege. Compounded with the unmistakably real healing powers of the *curandera* Ultima, who has saved people from possession by the devil where parish priests have failed, Antonio seems willing to risk breaking the commandments, believing in the existence of more than one God, in order to create a synthetic, transcendental unity of godly powers, to which he above all might have access.

Everywhere in the text the events of history attempt to break through the transcendental barriers that Antonio and Ultima erect against it. While he ponders the nature of the Golden Carp and the black bass, "Lupito's soul, or la Llorona, or the *presence* of the river," and wonders about "the terrible burden of dark mortal sin" on men's souls (26), or the peculiar evil of Rosie, madame of the brothel in the town of Guadalupe (31), black-dressed women mourn the local victims of "the far-off war of the Japanese and the Germans" (30). Even the Arcadian village of El Puerto de los Luna is touched by its effects, as Antonio's grandfather, Prudencio Luna, acknowledges: "This war of the Germans and the Japanese is reaching into all of us. . . . There is much evil running loose in the world" (46–47). The war is not, however, the unique agency of the evil changes occurring around them. Antonio's father identifies the passing of the pastoral Golden Age as the moment during his own childhood when "the tejano [Anglo-Texan] came and built his fences, the railroad came, the roads—it was like a bad wave of the ocean covering all that was good" (51). Antonio's desire is to hold off the corrosive effects of history, to protect Arcadia himself through Ultima's agency in the refuge of the timelessness of myth and art and the "mystery" and "magic" of letters (59). In the process of effecting his desire, Antonio must live out a fantasy in art that subordinates his family's wishes to his own, marginalizes the real world of labor and class conflict, and in short, denies the history of his beloved New Mexico. As in the case of his literary model, Stephen Dedalus, for Antonio history is the nightmare from which he is trying to escape.

The nightmare caused by the encroachment of twentieth-century industrial society and global conflict, incomprehensible in scope and power, is made manageable when it is personified in the figures of Tenorio Trementina and his three evil daughters. While neither Ultima, nor the Virgin of Guadalupe, nor the Golden Carp can alter the fragmentation of Antonio's mythic world, a world whose organic existence is already very much in doubt, in myth the romantic powers of good can triumph over the prince of evil. This is the compensatory manipulation that Antonio and Ultima must effect in order for their utopian vision to endure. Our first glimpse of this symbolic transposition occurs, significantly enough, at El Puerto de los Luna. Antonio is to spend a summer with the Lunas to learn their ways, "before he is lost, like the others" (47), as his uncle Juan Luna says. At this precise instant, Antonio looks across the river and sees "witches" dancing in a grove of trees: "In the form of balls of fire they danced with the Devil" (47).

The Trementinas have compacted with the Devil so that they may lay their curses upon men and "tamper with fate" (88). "Tampering with fate" is a meaningless concept within the confines of the utopian temporality of an Arcadian farm or ranch, where, as in El Puerto de los Luna, people are "happy, working, helping each other" (47) or where, as in Las Pasturas, the people "were like the wind, and the fragrances they carried on their clothing shifted as the wind shifted" (118). The cycles of time in such places are governed by imperturbable, immutable natural laws, not unlike the temporality Antonio identifies with Ultima's presence and with the magical duration of his childhood and his dreams. But if such a temporality ever existed outside of myth and dreams, it certainly no longer exists. Since in post-Edenic time man's fate can and does change with bewildering force, Tenorio and his daughters are "dancing with the devil" (47, 77, 81) so that they may acquire agency and control over the changes in men's fates. In the absence of the dependability of natural agency, with the loss of control over the means and forces of production, and in the face of the awesome incomprehensibility of the forces of change unleashed by twentieth-century technological society, Tenorio's dance with the devil becomes a substitute evil, a symbolic simulacrum, that can be controlled.

When Arcadian farmers and herdsmen become landless wage-laborers, they sometimes invoke the devil as part of maintaining control of their own destiny.[8] Where before the advent of "the railroad" and "barbed wire" (119) and the break-up of communal lands the fertility spirits of nature and the imagery of benign Gods dominated the ethos of production in the peasant mode of production, the devil and evil are now associated with the capitalist mode of production (Taussig 1980, 13). The organic fetishism that allowed the products of precapitalist labor to seem to embody the very people who produced them stands in stark contrast to the commodity fetishism of twentieth-century capitalist society, where the products of wage-labor are not only completely dissociated from the life and social milieu of the people who produce them but even seem to be independent and self-empowered. The "railroad" and the "barbed wire" (119), symbols of capitalist market economy, are the implements of a first phase of the disruption of the organic life, just as Antonio's brothers' "really nice Chevy" (173), and the "highways" and towns and cities of contemporary New Mexico are the ways and means of the post–World War II dislocation of their pastoral life in an even more drastically disruptive second phase of change.

Historian Rodolfo Acuña insists that "New Mexicans have historically found security in believing that they assimilated into Anglo-American culture and that they effectively participate in the democratic process":

> This myth has been articulated so often that they believe it. The reality that a small oligarchy of Anglo-Americans, aided by a small group of *ricos* [rich people], established their privilege at the expense of the Mexican masses has been conveniently ignored. (1981, 48).

The peculiarly New Mexican myth claims that the original settlers of the territory were purebred Spanish conquistadores. According to the popularly held belief, New Mexico was isolated from the rest of the Southwest and Mexico during colonial times. As a result, the present-day descendants of the original settlers remain racially pure Europeans, in contrast to the *mestizo* Mexicans who arrived after the original colonists. Calling themselves *Hispanos* or *Spanish*, the descendants of the original New Mexicans managed to carve out a safe racial and economic niche for themselves by denying their mestizo identity and escaping Anglo racial discrimination at the expense of later Mexican immigrants after the Anglo takeover in 1848 (Acuña

---

8. I am indebted here to the argument about the relationship between devil belief and the introduction of capitalism made by Taussig (1980, 3–38).

1981, 48). George Sánchez, Carey McWilliams, Américo Paredes, and others have exploded this "fantasy heritage," showing that the majority of the original settlers from Mexico in 1598 were mestizos (Acuña 1981, 48). Nonetheless, New Mexicans continued to deny their Mexican identity, especially after the early years of the twentieth century and the great influx of Mexican laborers. Integral to this myth of racial purity, is the belief that "Spanish" New Mexicans willingly and peacefully joined the Anglo-American nation and worked with Anglos as racial brothers and friends to create a garden in the wilderness.

This rewriting of history ignores the fact that considerable anti-American feeling existed among native New Mexicans before, during, and after the invasion by the American "Army of the West" in the mid-nineteenth century. Anglo-Texas had claimed portions of the New Mexico territory before the War of 1846 and had sent an expedition to make good that claim. A "nasty guerilla war with racial overtones" (Acuña 1981, 50) followed the failure of that expedition. Even after the American victory, New Mexicans, including the controversial Padre Antonio José Martínez, conspired to drive their oppressors out of the province, with rebels assassinating the American governor in 1847. American retaliation resulted in the massacre of the rebel army outside Taos and the execution of the rebel leaders (Acuña 1981, 51–52). Armed resistance by small bands of rebels continued, however, inflamed by the organized American seizure of land after the conquest when the Anglo newcomers "established their privilege, controlling the territorial government and administering its laws to further their political, economic, and social dominance" (Acuña 1981, 53).

Padre Antonio Martínez, the beloved and legendary "priest of Taos," ordained in 1822 after the death of his wife, was an important leader of the opposition to this dominance. In the course of his life, he established a seminary, published a newspaper, opposed Anglo encroachments on communal lands, and after the Anglo occupation, continued to take part in liberation movements within the Church and in state politics, defying the Anglo power structures until his death in 1868 (Acuña 1981, 55–56).

Whereas the Anglo-American pioneering experience had been based on "the movement of individuals into new areas with the accouterments of civilization following" (Acuña 1981, 53), Mexicans had moved to the frontiers collectively and had worked the land communally. Far from an idyllic reenactment of the Golden Age, life in the pueblos was patriarchically rigid and organized along definite class lines. A few rich families owned large tracts of land and exploited their fellow villagers and the native American Indians. These elites were able to retain power and influence after the war "through alliances with Anglos in ranching, railroading, and banking" (McLemore and Romo 1985, 9). Despite the pressures before the war from the New Mexican *ricos* and after the war from the Anglo oligarchy, many other families did share in communal grants, acquired water rights, farming rights, and rights to use the communal pasturelands and forests. "Necessity bound them together" and even allowed for intermarriage with native American Indian population (Acuña 1981, 53). But by the end of the nineteenth century the transfer of land and power from the native New Mexican communities to Anglo individuals was in full force. Organized armed resistance on the part of societies like *Las Gorras Blancas* (the White Caps) failed to stop the appropriation of communal lands or stop the transfer of power to Anglo capital interests. By 1900, with few exceptions, Mexicans no longer shared in the control of production (Acuña 1981, 69). The full impact of the loss of communal lands and the increase of wage labor was not to become apparent until the depression of the 1930s (Acuña 1981, 69).

Against this far from peaceful or idyllic real history of New Mexican life, Anaya attempts to create a substitute history around the figure of the young boy, Antonio Márez y Luna. His story, set in the wake of the socioeconomic events of the nineteenth and early twentieth centuries, and at the crest of the total expansion of technological, military-industrial American mass-culture after World War II, must be read as a nostalgic projection of utopian wish-fulfillment. As José Monleón has correctly insisted:

In the second half of our century, New Mexico is to see its socio-economic structure radically altered, owing principally to the influence of the military-industrial sector which, after the selection of Los Alamos as the center of nuclear research, will expand notoriously throughout the state. . . . [Anaya's choice of] the period of the Second World War as the setting for his novel, far from being a casual choice, is rather a reflection of a moment of historical transition, the expression of the origin of a series of conflicts. From the 40s on, the small self-sufficient agricultural pueblos will depend on new forces of production and their former patterns of social relations will have been weakened considerably.[9]

9. Monleón, "Ilusión y realidad en la obra de Rudolfo Anaya" (1986, 176). My translation. With Calderón's essay, Monleón's discussion clears up much of the mysticism that criticism has layered on Anaya's work.

In *Bless Me, Ultima*, the sense of organic unity between persons and their products, between persons and their social milieu in the pueblos, stands in stark opposition to the alienating effects of mid-twentieth-century capitalist society. Only Antonio and Ultima seem to stand as barriers against the complete decline of the Golden Age. At stake in the course of Antonio's narrative is thus not simply the outcome of one sensitive boy's life, but the fate of an entire community and its way of life. Upon the success or failure of Antonio's apprenticeship in Ultima's shamanistic wizardry depends the very life or death of the world represented by Las Pasturas and El Puerto de los Luna.

This is one explanation for the apocalyptic imagery that punctuates Antonio's narrative. At an early point in his story Antonio tells us, for example, that "the days grew heavy and ominous. Nobody seemed to know except the kids that the world was coming to an end. We talked about the signs we had seen. . . . We looked at the clouds and waited" (70). That the catastrophic and perhaps revelatory end of the world is continually put off does not dull the edge of Antonio's anxiety. Later, the signs of destruction enter his subconscious as he dreams of *"a howling wind"* whose *"powers pulled at the still waters of the lake. Thunder split the air and the lightning bursts illuminated the churning, frothy tempest. . . . I thought the end had come to everything"* (112). Shortly before the climactic confrontation between Ultima and Tenorio Trementina with which the narrative ends, yet another nightmare gathers together in one powerful apocalyptic scene many of the themes that we have been discussing:

A loud peal of laughter boomed and rang out in the valley of flames. It rolled in clouds of dark smoke like the thunder of the summer thunderstorms. . . . My father and mother and my sisters perished in the flames. [The Trementina sisters] killed the owl and made Ultima powerless, then they beheaded her and drank her blood. When they were bathed in blood they tied her to a post, drove a stake through her heart, and burned her. They went to the river and caught the carp that swam there, and brought the fish back and cooked it in the fires of Ultima's ashes. And they ate the flesh of the carp.

Then there was a thundering of the earth, and a great rift opened. The church building crumbled, and the school collapsed into dust, then the whole town disappeared into the chasm. . . .

The wind blew dusty now, and the sun turned blood red. The people looked upon each other and they saw their skin rot and fall off. Shrieks of pain and agony filled the air, and the whole countryside cried in mourning

as the walking-dead buried their sleeping-dead. A putrid, rotting smell was
everywhere. There was disease and filth throughout. (165, 167–68)

The depth of Antonio's fear of the Trementinas is apparent in this
dream of mayhem and anarchy loosed upon the world. And yet,
echoes to the destruction of Sodom and Gomorrah in the dream are
also appropriate, for Antonio has already decided that his brothers'
visits to Rosie's brothel in Guadalupe are one aspect of their fall from
grace. Indeed, the nightmare occurs the day that Antonio sees his
brother Andrew refuse to leave the company of one of Rosie's girls
to aid Narciso, a friend of the family, who seeks to warn Ultima that
Tenorio is going to kill her. Beyond this identification between sexuality, sin, and death is the very real fear that supernatural forces have
been unleashed upon the earth and threaten its very existence. The
source of this scene of mass destruction turns out to be, however,
not supernatural but all too human.

The apocalyptic force of Antonio's nightmare spills over from the
world of omen and dream into full reality very late in the narrative
when Ultima and Antonio go to the aid of a man named Téllez from
the nearby village of Agua Negra. Téllez seeks the powers of the
curandera in fighting an evil power that is destroying his home: pots
and pans and dishes are being lifted into the air and crashed against
the walls (214), and now "stones rain from the skies" (215). Ultima
explains that a curse was long ago laid on Agua Negra and Téllez is
witnessing the outcrop of its traces. Agua Negra "was the land of the
Comanche Indian . . . then came the Mexican with his flocks" (216).
When the Comanches raided the Mexican flocks, Téllez's grandfather helped hunt down and hang the offending Comanches. But,
"they left the bodies strung on a tree; they did not bury them according to their custom" (216). According to Ultima, the three tortured
spirits still wander the earth, manipulated by witches to do evil.
This story tells in brief a very different version of the history of New
Mexico than the one that Antonio's narrative proposes: the settling
of the llano was initiated and accomplished by force and the effects of
that violent history continue to the present, even if felt now only as
guilt expressed in the dream symbols of their collective unconscious.

Arriving at Téllez's ranch, Antonio, his father, and Ultima witness
first-hand the evil that Téllez has reported: "A cloud passed overhead and darkened the house. . . . A few moments ago the sky had
been clear, and now in the gloom we saw each other as dark bultos.
. . . Then the pounding began. . . . [Ultima] stood quietly, listening
to the devil's bombardment that held us with such terror that we

could not move. . . . Téllez groaned, 'it is the devil dancing on my roof—' " (221). When Ultima announces that what they have experienced is not the devil but the "work of man" (221), she means that the Trementinas are behind the cloud and its rain of stones. Since the Trementinas are agents of the devil, however, her explanation continues to be tied to the mysteriously spiritual realm and is therefore only partly demystifying. As in earlier scenes, the devil belief of this scene makes the Trementinas in their alliance with the devil substitute symbols of the pain and havoc caused by the very real effects of the dissolution of the principles of reciprocity and organicity represented by the decline of the former life of the pueblos and the growth of wage labor under capitalist conditions. This symbolic substitution allows Antonio through Ultima to personify and overcome what might otherwise remain awesomely unconquerable.

Ultima's explanation is correct; what they have witnessed is "the work of man" and not of the devil, as we have stepped into the entirely new epoch of New Mexican and contemporary American history with the development of the instruments of thermonuclear warfare at Los Alamos in 1945. As Calderón (1986) has pointed out, the people of Guadalupe are aware of the resemblance between the events of Téllez's ranch and the explosion of the first atomic bomb: "many grown-ups blame[d] the harsh winter and the sandstorms of spring on the new bomb that had been made to end the war. 'The atomic bomb,' they whispered, 'a ball of white heat beyond the imagination, beyond hell—' And they pointed south, beyond the green valley of El Puerto" (183). With brilliant insight, Calderón notes that south, beyond El Puerto, lie Agua Negra and point Trinity, where on July 16, 1945, the inhabitants of the remote village of Carrizozo "were awakened by a roar to witness a pillar of fire six miles high just thirty miles away" (1986, 41). The apocalyptic visions of Antonio's nightmares and the cloud and falling rocks that pummel Téllez's home are indeed in the logic of Antonio's narrative devilish, but not supernatural, for they represent, as Calderón insists, "the ultimate tampering with the destiny of the world" (1986, 41). It is human action and not supernatural agency that is the cause of this devilishness and the source of its symbolism is not the collective but the political unconscious. Ultima's death at story's end and Antonio's loss of innocence are inevitable to the extent that the two have represented the last bastions of a mythic response to the real forces of history, one by appealing to the mysteries of the spiritual world, the other by turning to the consoling confines of romance beneath which the text of history may be subsumed. Only in the context of Antonio's self-consciously nurtured narrative recreation of the Golden Age myth can their victory over history and the dawning of a truly apocalyptic thermonuclear age be guaranteed.

The schema given earlier revealed that despite the significant differences among the various readings of the text, it is possible to abstract from them a common structural model of resolved binary oppositions within which the ideological and semantic content of Antonio's narrative makes sense: Luna versus Márez; farmer versus vaquero; El Puerto versus Las Pasturas; moon versus sun; river versus plain. The typology generated by the narrative can then be extended beyond the problematics of Antonio's inner struggles to explain, again in binary terms, the recurring clashes between good and evil that Antonio is continually called upon to witness: Ultima versus the Trementinas; the Golden Carp versus the black bass; the Virgin of Guadalupe versus Rosie's prostitutes; *la llorona* versus Antonio's mother.

This structural model also emphasizes with no ambiguity the patriarchal nature of Antonio's traditional world view, as it assigns the women in his story to either one of only two possible roles: women are either saintly or evil. There can be no doubt as to the phallocentric quality of Antonio's emphatically gendered and romantic repression of history, despite the fact that Ultima herself authorizes it. Plainly, Ultima is made into an agent of the patriarchy.

In the end, with Ultima's death, we are to see Antonio's turn to art in the form of the writing of the story we have been discussing, as the full incorporation into his own being of the mystical (feminine) powers of the old *curandera*. As in the polarity he sets up between myth and history, Antonio expresses a wish for a clean, undistorted, hierarchical relationship between the dichotomies that order his world (so that we end with myth over history, romance over realism, male over female). His narrative serves to justify his view by providing a pleasing reconciliation of these polar oppositions within his own soul and in the book that will chronicle the closure of opposition, incongruity, and doubt.

But we can reinvest the language of Antonio's narrative with an alternative ideological and semantic content. Rather than depending on the binary structure of Antonio's logical oppositions, oppositions that are awesomely static and far from dialectical, we might notice that the oppositions set up by the narrative rarely hold up as binary oppositions under the light of close analysis, as in the case of the purported duality between the Márez and Luna clans, who turn out to share a far more important common pastoral base and mode of production. Such is also the case for Antonio's opposition between myth and history, between good and bad gods, or between saintly and evil women—the oppositions obtain only within the confines of the logic of romance, with its generically constrained requirements of symmetrical closure, and could never be found acceptable either as realistic fictions or as historical interpretations of contemporary New Mexican society.

Rather than taking the structural polarities Antonio offers as the fundamental categories of reality, we might notice that his narrative posits these polarities as functions of two elementary, foundational principles: (1) that the pastoral world is organically, wholly unitary, and (2) that various overarching, transcendental myths govern the original pastoral world. These two concepts work together to provide the romantic machinery by which Antonio will elude history. The two value systems at work within the narrative, also generate their negative oppositions, that is, a world that is decidedly *not* organically pastoral, and one that is *not* transcendentally mythic. These opposites are indeed subsumed to the first-level terms, but not as categories of static thought. In contrast to the structural schema with which we began, we can project this alternative graphic pattern for Antonio's narrative:

organic pastoral world (+ value)   transcendental myths

not-myths   not organic pastoral world (− value)

Figure 5.1

When viewed in this fashion, the ideological closure of Antonio's narrative becomes understandable. A. J. Greimas's "semiotic rectangle,"[10] as Jameson has shown, "furnishes the graphic embodiment of ideological closure as such, and allows us to map out the inner limits of a given ideological formation" (1981, 48). This alternative schema does not simply posit the logical permutations of the text, but affords a way into the text that employs the terms implicit but unrealized in the surface of the story, terms that have failed to become manifest in the logic of the narrative. It brings to the fore precisely what the text has wishfully projected and what it has re-

---

10. Greimas elaborates the four-part schema by which a narrative's logic may be elucidated in *Du sens* (1970, 135–55).

pressed. It is in the underside of the narrative's chart that we will find those terms that Antonio's story has sought desperately not to think or express.[11]

The opposition between the organic pastoral world (as a positive value projected by Antonio's narrative into the Golden Age of a pre-capitalist world) and the transcendental myths that still have agency in the contemporary world is not, strictly speaking, a logical contradiction. It is rather a symptom of the dilemma, the aporia, expressed in the form of Antonio's desperate wish for resolution and reconciliation in the form of his own mediating spirit, that marks the concrete social contradictions that his narrative cannot openly confront. The two superior terms thus necessarily posit subsidiary negations that accompany the primary terms throughout the text. None of the terms by itself can serve as a "slot" for characters, character systems, themes, motifs, imagery, or any other narrative category. The place of characters and narrative categories is opened up rather by the combination of these four principal terms through the various possible combinations marked out among them in figure 5.1.

To follow our chart around clockwise beginning on the lefthand side, we can see how the Márez and Luna clans, far from being binary oppositions, share a common ground as emblems of Antonio's desire to see the two halves of his soul as the unity between the positively valued organic pastoral world and a realm that is *not* mythic. Moving to the upper horizontal combination, between the organic pastoral world and transcendental myths, we see another part of Antonio's fantasy—the desire to retain a world of purity and permanence, figured most prominently by Ultima herself, who unites the Christian and the pagan, the Virgin of Guadalupe and the Golden Carp, in one symbol of overarching good.

The next possible combination, on the righthand side of our diagram, shows how we are to understand the mysteriously threatening qualities of the spiritual world, represented by *la llorona*, the presence of the river, the sirens of the lakes, and the black bass. These elements function as symbolic syntheses of transcendental myths that are emphatically not part of the organic pastoral world but serve as its manichean background, the necessary evil to be vanquished by the hero's power of good.

Moving to the lower horizontal opposition, the interaction be-

---

11. Here, as in many places throughout my discussion of Chicano narrative, my debt to Jameson, even when I differ from him, is obvious. I refer especially to *The Political Unconscious* (46–49, 167–69, and 253–57).

tween the negative values of the narrative's superior, positive terms, we find precisely those elements that serve as the sources of conflict, discord, fragmentation, and indeed contradiction, throughout Antonio's narrative. This subtext, constituted by the union of elements that are *not* myth and *not* the organic pastoral world, tells the story of contemporary New Mexico with all of its most problematic features. In contrast to the romance of Antonio's achieved artistry and growth to ethical maturity, this lower story serves as the degraded version of the reality principle denied by the force of Antonio's wish-fulfillment projection of resolved contradictions. It is here that we will find history, World War II, the atomic bomb, the Trementinas, in short, all of the elements of the plot of *Bless Me, Ultima* that work against the romantic stability that Antonio so desperately desires.

+ hist

We may now chart the basic pattern of the novel:

Ultima
Golden Carp
Virgin of Guadalupe

organic pastoral world (+)   *transcendental myths*

Márez/Las Pasturas   llorona
Luna/El Puerto de los Luna   presence
                                                sirens
                                                bass

                        Antonio

not-myths   *not-organic pastoral world* (−)

history
World War II and the bomb
Trementinas (father & daughters)
town of Guadalupe
Lupito (Guadalupe)
three brothers
Rosie and her brothel

Figure 5.2.

The schema represented in figure 5.2 stages the fundamental problems of the text and articulates the generation of the characters, the representation of themes, and the synthesis of the problematic in the central figure of Antonio. The ego-centering quality of this project also explains why Antonio himself does not fit into any of the combinational categories of his narrative. He stands outside of, or above, the schematic representation of the story that he tells because he is its creator, himself the cause without a cause of narrative action and narrative time.

Our chart also suggests the ideological service that his narrative of romance performs by repressing the worlds of history and work (by ignoring the effects of the forces and forms of production on New Mexican history) and of protopolitical conflict (by assigning the conflicts between Spanish colonialism and Native Americans, between Mexicans and Anglos, and between New Mexican workers and capitalist interests to the margins of the text and to the subconscious realm of Antonio's mind). History is vanquished in Antonio's superior narrative by being subsumed to only one of the four levels of temporality with which we began our discussion, the level of nondurational myth and dream.

Unlike other Chicano narratives with which we have dealt, *Bless Me, Ultima* cancels out "realism," attempting to cross it out and lift it up to a higher realm of truth, as in some Hegelian dialectic. The facticity of this precritical idealist venture is nowhere more evident nor more dissatisfying than in Anaya's writings, which impose upon us the burden of restoring the whole socially concrete subtext of nineteenth- and twentieth-century Southwestern history, mythified and reified on so many levels of utopian compensation. The popular and critical success of his narrative, making it the most widely read of Chicano works by both Mexican American and Anglo audiences, emphasizes the difficulty of maintaining history and the extent to which we all desire to turn away from it.

The Road to Tamazunchale

Oscar Zeta Acosta's novels are probably the most concerted attempts by a Chicano writer to create a truly "radical" art that is "historical," albeit filtered through the screen of fiction. But as we have seen in the works of Paredes, Villarreal, and Rivera, the general impulse of Chicano narrative is toward root concepts and toward understanding the fundamental links between historical and aesthetic categories. Thus the radical tendency of Chicano narrative can emerge in various ways, even when they must do so subversively and surreptitiously by working against the "conscious" surface elements of the text as in Anaya's *Bless Me, Ultima*.

With Ron Arias' *The Road to Tamazunchale* (1975), the Chicano novel begins to exploit its privileged position at the juncture of the North and South American novel, and to perform the deconstruction of value in yet another way.[12] The hero of Arias' novel wanders

12. On the possibilities of a comparative study of the Chicano and Latin American novel, see Tatum, "Contemporary Chicano Prose Fiction: Its Ties to Mexican Lit-

imaginatively from the barrios of East Los Angeles to the rain forests and mountain clearings of Peru, as he attempts to track down
the scene of his own death. In this novel the realism of American
literature is mixed with the "magical realism" of Latin American literature to create a supernatural Chicano realism.[13] As Pablo Neruda
has shown, the supernatural musings of the solitary poet at Macchu
Picchu can have significant effect on the course of events in the communal world. Arias seeks to create just such a synthesis of poetry and
life through the figure of his protagonist, the dying eighty-year-old
man, Fausto Quiroga.

While the texts that we have examined begin with a moment of
spiritual doubt or decay, Arias' novel begins with a dream of material
decay:

> Fausto lifted his arm and examined the purple blotches. . . . He tugged at
> the largest one, near the wrist. . . . Slowly it began to rip, peeling from the
> muscle. No blood. The operation would be clean, like slipping off nylon
> hose.[14]

A life of smog, poverty, and emptiness behind him, Fausto amuses
himself in his last days "waiting for the end" (14), by metaphorically
stripping the shreds of his life from his skeletal frame. Readers have
pointed out that Fausto here literalizes the metaphoric title of Carlos
Fuentes' 1972 novel *Cambio de piel* (*A Change of Skin*) and refers
to "Xipetotec, the Nahautl deity who suffers flagellation in order to
change skin and thus undergoes a transformation into a new life"
(Nieto 1986, 242). A retired encyclopedia salesman who has walked
the streets of the Chicano barrio Quixote-like peddling the dreams
of a better life, Fausto at the end of his days is beaten, tired, and no
closer to his elusive dreams than at any other point in his life; he
is ready to transform to a new life. Thus, of late, he has begun to
hear again what he calls "the song of life . . . somewhere beyond the
house" (14). Seized with a sudden "monstrous dread of dying," Fausto
begins his unlikely quest. Pursued by the death of life, Fausto decides
to find, in present real terms, a life within the bounds of death. But
what he seeks is not that of traditional Christian theology; Fausto's
life-in-death is to be one of his own making.

---

erature" (1975, 432–38), and Monsiváis, "Literatura comparada: Literatura chicana"
(1973, 42–48).

13. See E. Martínez, "Ron Arias' *The Road to Tamazunchale*: A Chicano Novel of
the New Reality" (1986) for a survey of the relation between Arias' novel and Latin
American "magical realism" and the French "nouveau roman."

14. Ron Arias, *The Road to Tamazunchale* (Reno, Nev.: West Coast Poetry Review,
1975), 13. All subsequent citations are to this edition of the novel.

Once the old man sets out on his wanderings through the sur-realized landscape of East L.A., accompanied only by Mario, a weird "goateed teenager . . . dressed all in black" (25), we cannot be certain when "real" events end and hallucinatory Faustian or Quixotic ones begin. In fact, in scenes such as that of Fausto's self-excoriation at the beginning of the novel, of his escape from the police by hiding and later reemerging from an occupied coffin (chapter 3), of the ap-pearance of a singular snow-cloud over Los Angeles (chapter 5), of the figurative rebirth of David, an undocumented worker who has drowned but spends a night of love with Mrs. Rentería (chapter 7), or of Fausto's attempted wholesale smuggling of hundreds of "moja-dos" ("wetbacks") across the U.S. border and his subsequent obses-sion to protect them (chapter 8), the normal lines between the real and the imaginary have totally disappeared. Fausto's masque, the play-within-the-novel entitled "The Road to Tamazunchale" that is enacted on the stage of his imagination in chapter 11, sums up the fact that what persists is a metaphor of reality.

In Fausto's play-within-the-novel we are, as in Rivera's and Acosta's novels, on the road in search of a lost or never fully present plenitude of being. "Tamazunchale" is a real Mexican village, but, more sig-nificantly, it becomes for Fausto a figure for the inaccessibility of that plenitude. In fact, the road to Tamazunchale may be, as one character tells us, the road to no place at all: "You see," says the stage director of Fausto's play, "whenever things go bad, whenever we don't like someone, whoever it is . . . we simply send them to Tamazunchale. We've never really seen this place, but it sounds better than saying the other, if you know what I mean" (84). The director thus sees the name of Tamazunchale as signifying, without actually denoting, "the other" unnameable resting place. In contrast, Fausto's personi-fied self-presence, the "Tío" of the play, makes Tamazunchale sig-nificant in its own right. Responding to a child's question, "What's [Tamazunchale] like?" Fausto's alter ego claims:

Like any other place. Oh a few things are different . . . if you want them to be. . . . [If] you see a bird, you can talk to it, and it'll talk back. . . . If you want to be an apple, think about it and you might be hanging from a tree. . . . You can be the sun. . . . You can be the stars. . . . No one dies in Tamazun-chale. . . . Tamazunchale *is* our home. Once we're there, we're free we can be everything and everyone. If you want, you can even be *nothing*. (89–90)

Before he too vanishes "between the horizon and the stars," Fausto thus succeeds in doing something that he has never before accom-plished—he isolates a place of free and absolute self-presence. He does not need someone to die for him to bring him everlasting life because he is perfectly willing to die, and to live, his own death. Through the various transformations Fausto experiences in the moments before his death, he realizes that death is the ultimate mirror against which life is reflected and in the face of which life's only values exist. By sheer force of will, he manages to carve from the give and take between life and death, from the difference between being and nothing, a fleeting point of eternal space, unaffected by the decaying effects of time.

Thus, even in this most fantastic and abstract representation of Chicano life, we find the dialectics of difference at work, reevaluating, restructuring, and reinterpreting the nature of human existence.[15] The novel's abstractions and ambiguous time relations are precisely intended to be read in situation, as neither fantasy nor reality, against the reader's urge to reduce their complexity. In fact, the complexity of the interaction between life and death as Fausto envisions it not only provides the novel's aesthetic base, but it also serves as a clue to its ideological direction. The novel's complexity demands a descent on the reader's part into what Jameson has called "the materiality of language and the consent to time itself in the form of the sentence" (1971, xiii). The reader's descent into the materiality and temporality of the text is the concomitant of Fausto's production of life from out of the tightly woven fabric of life's interaction with death. By making us work through the concrete details of this interaction in the form and content of the text, Arias removes his work from the simple bounds of either reality or abstraction in isolation. Through the very act of reading, Arias forces the dialectical method upon us. Far from bearing no relation to the real world, Arias' text registers in its very structural and thematic forms the phenomenological fact of the density of contemporary life. In this very different sense, then, Arias employs the tactics of fantasy that animate Anaya's narrative. While fantasy works to disguise history in *Bless Me, Ultima*, in *The Road to Tamazunchale* fantasy works to subvert the closure of history. Arias' text continually foregrounds the sedimentary levels of consciousness that create a sense of history. As Nieto has pointed out, this emphasis on the constructive activity involved in history begins with the epigraph to the novel, from Fran-

---

15. The "fantastic" quality of Arias' novel has led some readers to ignore its substantial critique of both Mexican and American ideologies of death. A more subtle reading is offered by J. Saldívar, "The Ideological and Utopian in Tomás Rivera's *Y no se lo tragó la tierra* and Ron Arias' *The Road to Tamazunchale*" (1985, 109–12).

cisco López de Gómara's *Istoria de la Conquista de México*: "not only are we involved with the word 'historia' in terms of a personal history or account, but the question of fictional narrative versus history is also being raised. By alluding to the chronicle genre, . . . the invention of history, the fictionalization of 'truth,' becomes a part of the problematic structure within the work" (Nieto 1986, 241).

In contrast to the density of historical life, the simplicity of Fausto's death becomes an act of revolutionary art: it allows the ground of life, which is death, to become visible and manageable. And it makes the gap between subjective experience and the empirical world collapse in a moment of pure insight. Fausto's creation of "Tamazunchale" as the symbolic place of life-in-death forces upon us the view that reality is a changing, discontinuous process, produced by men and women and so transformable by them. It demonstrates how character and action can be different and need not be conceived of as historically fixed.

Writing about how the storyteller "borrows his authority from death," Walter Benjamin notes that "the novel is significant . . . not because it presents someone else's fate to us, perhaps didactically, but because this stranger's fate by virtue of the flame which consumes it yields us the warmth which we never draw from our own fate. What draws the reader to the novel is the hope of warming his shivering life with a death he reads about" (1973, 94, 101). Seen as the storyteller who can let the wick of his life be consumed by the flame of his story, Fausto thus joins the ranks of poets and revolutionaries who produce their own valid reality. In effect, Fausto transforms his death into the triumphant life of art, which is the difference between life and death. In doing so, he manages to invest the world of the imagination with the pathos of history and the materiality of life.

While in the great majority of Chicano narratives the political is precisely what is most conscious and, indeed, what determines consciousness, Anaya's *Bless Me, Ultima* is unique to the extent that it manages to repress the force of the political into the unconscious. Jameson's hermeneutics are amply appropriate for reading canonic texts and, as evidenced in this discussion, appropriate too for reading some from the opposition. But to the extent that Chicano narrative may be said to represent, like other Third World literatures, a resistance to the experiences of colonialism and cultural imperialism, it severely challenges any attempt to account for the possibility of a uniform cultural paradigm or "national allegory" that might be theorized under one universal formulation of a "cognitive aesthetics of third world literature" (Jameson 1986, 65, 83). Aijaz Ahmad has argued that "this 'cognitive aesthetics' rests . . . upon a suppression of the multiplicity of significant differences" (1987, 3) evidenced by various Third World literatures. As Arias' novel and other narratives that we have discussed show, Chicano narrative, correspondingly, does not reduce to a single ideological formation. Nor may its narratives all be read as local expressions of one master narrative, even when they function under the comparable forms of romance and fantasy.

The political and ideological struggles represented by the narratives of Chicano women and men exhibit no necessary homogeneity, allegorical or otherwise. This means that the narrativization of the real, in turn, cannot exhibit a singular ideological instance, but offers instead a nonunitary, differential complex of social practices and systems of representation that do have political significance and consequence even when they operate, as *The Road to Tamazunchale* does, within the realm of the fantastic. Jameson, to his great credit, has shown us how to theorize this differential and to see how monological readings and interpretive codes, even his own, might become "strategies of containment" (1981, 10) that seek to project an illusion of self-sufficiency to the detriment of the richness of history and the complexity of texts such as those we consider in this study.

6

Rolando Hinojosa's
Korean Love Songs
and the *Klail City Death Trip*

A Border Ballad and Its Heroes

The seven published novels of Rolando Hinojosa form an ongoing, multivolume novel in the tradition of Trollope, Galsworthy, Proust, and Anthony Powell. As a whole, Hinojosa's *Klail City Death Trip* series is a dynamic, living chronicle of twentieth-century Chicano life and minutely reflects the various stages of the history of the Lower Rio Grande Valley of South Texas. As individual works, the novels appear "fragmented, static, and monocentric" (R. Sánchez 1985, 76). The first two, *Estampas del Valle (The Valley)* (1973) and *Klail City y sus alredededores (Klail City)* (1976), reflect the heterogeneity of the Mexican origin community of the valley in the fictional "Belken" County. *Mi Querido Rafa (Dear Rafe)* (1981) and *Rites and Witnesses* (1982) focus on the private and public affairs of the ruling Anglo families of Klail City. Later volumes, *Partners in Crime* (1985) and *Claros Varones de Belken / Fair Gentlemen of Belken* (1986), depict the social, class, and race contradictions embedded in the social life of Hinojosa's imaginary South Texas terrain. Much attention has been devoted to these six narratives.[1]

The third text in the series, an extended narrative in verse entitled *Korean Love Songs* (1978), strangely, has not been read as carefully as

---

1. See, for instance, the fine collection of essays in *The Rolando Hinojosa Reader*, ed. José David Saldívar (1985). In addition to having "recast" several of his own earlier Spanish language novels into English, Hinojosa has also "rendered" Tomás Rivera's *... Y no se lo tragó la tierra* into English as *This Migrant Earth* (1987). These "recastings" and "renditions" are not translations of the Spanish originals, but different versions of the original narrative. In recreating the texts in English, Hinojosa foregrounds the question of bilingualism. For an excellent reading of Hinojosa's *Claros Varones de Belken* (1986) from the perspective of "cultural studies," see José D. Saldívar, "The Limits of Cultural Studies" (1989).

have Hinojosa's other works. Set during the years of the Korean War, *Korean Love Songs* is the crucial text of the series, serving to help turn what seem monocentric and fragmented texts "developing on one plane only" (R. Sánchez 1985, 76), into a richly layered, multiply developed work that expands across the several planes of class and race ideologies and world-historical geopolitics. Reading Hinojosa's *Korean Love Songs* in the context of those other songs of class and race conflict, the corridos of Border conflict that we have already discussed, will allow us to see how Hinojosa's theme of war becomes an allegory for the Gramscian "war of position" (1971, 108), the strategy of indirect cultural resistance that Chicanos assume after the end of the period of direct armed resistance chronicled in the heroic corridos.

I examine here the transformation of the complex of issues raised by corridos such as "Gregorio Cortez" in Rolando Hinojosa's novels and narrative poem. Hinojosa's poem roughly parallels the formal and thematic features of early-twentieth-century corridos. But in the intervening years between the production of songs such as "Gregorio Cortez" and *Korean Love Songs*, historical circumstances have changed dramatically. As a consequence, while racial conflict and class struggle continue to be the concerns of the sensitive artist, the formulation, confrontation, and attempted reconciliation of that struggle by the poetic hero have also changed.

Not the least of the factors involved in our understanding of the difference between Mexican American narrative verse of the early twentieth century and that of late century are the changing notions of literary modernism with its attendant sense of so-called high culture, and of folk art, with its different sense of cultural valuation. I think that a brief consideration of these issues will help us to understand why in his contemporary manifestation in Hinojosa's long narrative poem the mid-century Mexican American ballad hero remains the analogue of the hero of the earlier corrido in vastly redressed form. Like *El Corrido de Gregorio Cortez*, Hinojosa's *Korean Love Songs* has as its underlying impulse—albeit in symbolic and unconscious form—some of our deepest fantasies about the nature of social life, both as we live it and as we would like to have it be. The difference is that in the earlier song this impulse can be expressed directly and literally, whereas in the later song the impulse can be expressed only indirectly and figuratively.

I begin my discussion at a theoretical remove by turning first, and briefly, to the theory of culture worked out by the Frankfurt

School in the work of Adorno and Horkheimer. Additionally, Stuart
Hall has shown how the work of Antonio Gramsci can have relevance for the study of race and ethnicity (Hall 1983). Together, the
work of these various theoreticians provides an important working
methodology for the close analysis of the literary products of culture in the contemporary American scene. As Jameson points out in
an essay on "Reification and Utopia in Mass Culture," the work of
the Frankfurt School can be characterized "as the extension and ap-
plication of Marxist theories of commodity reification to the works
of mass culture" (1979, 130). Similarly, Gramsci argues that "there
are already proletarian forces of production of cultural values" (1985,
41) that should be put to use as the crucible where the spirits of a
new age might be forged. When addressed from these perspectives,
the function of art, its unique and distinct "ends" or values, must be
understood in terms of its *use function*, its "instrumentality."

Under capitalism, older forms of human activity, including aesthetic ones, are instrumentally reorganized and analytically fragmented in order to be reconstructed according to models of effi-
ciency and profitability. In traditional activity, artistic or otherwise,
as Jameson suggests, "the value of the activity is immanent to it,
and qualitatively distinct from other ends or values articulated in
other forms of human work or play" (1979, 130–31). It is only with
the commodification of labor power that all forms of human work
can be "separated out from their unique qualitative differentiation
as distinct types of activity" (1979, 131). Once this separating out of
the differentiating aspects of human work has occurred, all work can
be reclassified and hence reunderstood in terms not of its immanent
value but of its instrumentality.

In a world where everything, including labor power, has become
a commodity or an instrument, the purpose of cultural productions
becomes to create the conditions for their own consumption. The
commodity produced by human labor "no longer has any qualitative value in itself, but only insofar as it can be 'used'" (1979, 131).
The objects of the commodity world of capitalism, as Jameson goes
on to suggest, "shed their independent 'being' and intrinsic qualities and come to be so many instruments of commodity satisfaction"
(1979, 131). A similar fate is accorded the subjects of capitalism.
Horkheimer and Adorno note, for instance, that "Kant's formalism
still expected a contribution from the individual, who was thought
to relate the varied experiences of the senses to fundamental concepts; but [the culture] industry robs the individual of his function.
Its prime service to the customer is to do his schematizing for him"

(1972, 124). Everything in consumer society thus takes on an aesthetic dimension, to the extent that its consumption becomes literally or figuratively a sensual experience.

Simultaneously, this new sensual experience of consumption becomes curiously devalued, as "the whole world is made to pass through the filter of the culture industry," thereby causing "the stunting of the mass-media consumer's powers of imagination and spontaneity" (126). "To this extent," Horkheimer and Adorno add, "the claim of art is always ideology too" (130). In mass-media culture, then, art works in the crudest ideological way to produce but one end: "obedience to the social hierarchy" (131). With a polemical flourish bred of their vehement reaction to the fascist regimentation of culture in the 1930s and 1940s, Horkheimer and Adorno thus conclude that

to speak of culture was always contrary to culture. Culture as a common denominator already contains in embryo that schematization and process of cataloging and classification which brings culture within the sphere of administration. And it is precisely the industrialized, the consequent, subsumption which entirely accords with this notion of culture. By subordinating in the same way and to the same end all areas of intellectual creation, by occupying men's senses from the time they leave the factory in the evening to the next morning with matter that bears the impress of the labor process they themselves have to sustain throughout the day, this subsumption mockingly satisfies the concept of a unified culture which the philosophers of personality contrasted with mass culture. (131)

Although a fuller discussion of the applicability of the theories of the Frankfurt School to contemporary conditions would have to qualify and reformulate some of that group's conclusions, taking into account, for instance, Adorno's elitist and Eurocentric biases, for the present discussion this survey of their notion of cultural theory provides a convenient beginning point. It helps us to specify, at the very least, some of the basic differences between popular folk art, and in particular the folk art of the past, and the products of contemporary high art or mass culture. For example, as Américo Paredes has so definitively established, the border ballads of the early twentieth century reflected and depended on for their production a social reality different from that which produces mainstream "high" or "popular" art in the late twentieth century. And while it may still be the case that contemporary Chicano literature is the "organic" expression of a distinct community, a unified social group with its own cultural specificity not yet totally compromised by the effects of mass market economy, the historical effect of late capitalism to dissolve and

fragment organic communities into isolated and atomized agglom-
erations of private individuals is too well known to be ignored. The
individualized voice of the unique artistic sensibility represented
among Chicanos by Richard Rodriguez is one example of this disruption of the organic Mexican American community. It thus behooves
us to understand the conditions under which the ideological force
of the border ballad of the peaceful man struggling for social justice
"with his pistol in his hand" has been preserved, even if in altered
form, in late-twentieth-century Mexican American narrative verse.

As we have seen in chapter 2, the typical corrido situation depicts
a common working man put into an uncommon situation by the
power of cultural and historical forces beyond his control. In style
and form, the corrido is the product of the collective imagination of
a community whose environment was border conflict. The corrido
hero's individual life sequences have not yet become totally distinct
from those of his community; the private sphere of interior consciousness has not yet become the concern of the balladeer; the private quality of life has not yet coalesced into a central, independent
identity that is distinct from the identity of the community.

Hinojosa's *Korean Love Songs* tells the corrido story of border conflict and social justice in the symbolically displaced form of the long
narrative poem and the ideologically different context of the Korean
War. The hero in this case, however, is not an idyllic figure of communal solidarity like Gregorio Cortez, but rather the orphaned and
eccentric Rafa Buenrostro, one of the two Janus-like protagonists of
the *Klail City Death Trip*. The issue is not the conflict inherent in a
cultural and political border but a real war precipitated from an abstract conflict between world powers and their surrogates. And yet,
what remains constant, and links Hinojosa's poem with the grand
tradition of the corrido, is the poem's thematization of cultural integrity, communal identity, and social justice. As paradoxical as this
claim may seem, given that the entire action of *Korean Love Songs*
is set in Japan and Korea, it can be shown that Hinojosa's poem, like
the corridos that form its generic model, is about South Texas and
Mexican American life in a moment of crucial self-formation.

Unlike the situation of contemporary "high" art, in which capitalism has so dissolved the fabric of all cohesive social groups that
an authentic aesthetic production having its source in group life is
practically impossible, *Korean Love Songs* is an example of Chicano
narrative struggling to maintain its existence as an expression of an
organic social life. In Hinojosa's poem we are offered a moment in
this struggle to understand and retain a genuine cultural and his-

torical class consciousness within the ever-encroaching insistence
of late capitalist social life. But unlike its own folkloric base, Hinojosa's poem must enact its representation of this struggle not from
the outside, as one between Anglo-American cultural and political
institutions and Mexican American ones, but from within, as the
central Chicano characters become representatives of American cultural and political power as embodied in its armed forces. Hinojosa's
Korean Love Songs represents the tradition of folk art even while it
differs greatly from it, just as it draws from the tradition of literary
modernism even while it sets its own separate course. To see this set
of issues at work we should situate Hinojosa's poem in the context
of the earlier novels.

In Hinojosa's first stories, narrative time and space are fluid so that
characters in the present seem to coexist temporally and spatially
with others from the past and in different places. The narrative of
Estampas del Valle (The Valley) cuts from one character to another,
without apparent logic or motivation, and instantiates the places and
times alluded to in two prefatory maps depicting the political terrain of the struggle for ideological position depicted in his text (see
figure 9). The first of these maps is open to the world at large, as it
places Tokyo and Kobe, Japan; Panmunjon, Korea; Fort Ord, California; and Fort Sill, Oklahoma—all settings for *Korean Love Songs*—
schematically before the reader. Below this schematic drawing and
superimposed upon a map of the fictional Belken County appear the
names of Texas, Arkansas, Illinois, Missouri, Indiana, and Michigan, the route that the great stream of migrant farmworkers take to
the agricultural fields of the Midwest. Finally, we get the imaginary
geography of Belken County itself, with its fictional cities and towns
of "Jonesville-on-the-River" (a reference to the setting of Paredes'
stories), Klail City, Flora, Bascom, and the rest.
    The narrative thus begins pictorially, presenting in a single visual
moment the multileveled geopolitical topography with which it will
be concerned. But instead of establishing a privileged beginning that
could be displaced along a temporal axis following out the linear geographical axes promised in the maps, the narrative unhinges time as
it stretches out according to the rhythms of associative similarities.
Tied as it is to the realistic details of everyday South Texas life, Hinojosa's narrative proceeds to name that reality in decidedly unrealistic
ways.
    The first and third parts of *Estampas del Valle* refer to well over a
hundred characters by name in separate vignettes of varying length.

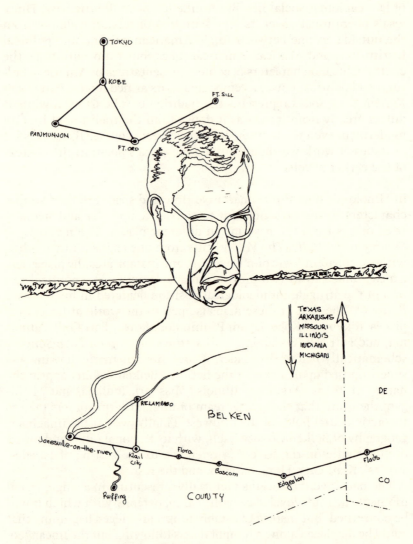

9. Schematic map of the fictional Belken County and the Lower Rio Grande Valley area from the first edition of *Estampas del valle*. (Courtesy of Rolando Hinojosa)

The links among these characters are established gradually, by re-
iteration, allusion, and simple juxtaposition, for the narrative rarely
names these links directly. The two axes along which the text develops, a metonymical linear one of time and geography, and a metaphorical one of associative substitutions, form the narrative loom
upon which Hinojosa's at first unnamed narrator weaves his tale.
And as the narrative proper begins, it turns again to pictorial script
to instantiate past and present time, absent and present characters
within the narrative "now."

The first section, entitled "Braulio Tapia," is not a privileged point
in history or a necessary origin for the many tales that are to unfold
before us in the coming volumes of text. It is simply an arbitrary moment in the lives of these characters, as if one moment could serve
as well as any other as the "introduction" to their story. Here is the
beginning of the narrative:

> Chaparro, fornido y pisando fuerte a pesar de venir con el sombrero en la
> mano, Roque Malacara me pone cara de vaqueta y dice que no es por falta
> de respeto pero ¡qué le vamos a hacer! no tiene padrino y por eso viene a
> pedirme a Tere él solo.
>
> Me recuerdo que ya hace año y medio que tiene entrada en la casa y que
> ahora viene a pedir mi consentimiento para casarse. Le digo que sí, choca-
> mos la mano, y le hago pasar. En el umbral de la puerta deviso a mi difunto
> suegro, don Braulio Tapia, con su bigote lacio y patilla larga, saludándome
> a mí como cuando yo vine a esta casa a pedirle a Matilde. Para ese tiempo
> ya estaba viudo de doña Sóstenes como yo ahora lo estoy de Matilde. Don
> Braulio me dice que sí, me choca la mano y me hace pasar a su casa.
>
> ¿A quién vería don Braulio en el umbral cuando él pidió a su esposa?
> (EV 16)

> (Squat, what the Germans call *diecke* and thus heavy of chest and shoul-
> ders, Roque Malacara carries his hat in his hand. . . . I'm standing on the
> doorway on the east porch of a hot Thursday afternoon, and he says: My
> coming here alone isn't a matter of disrespect, sir, it's just that I've no money
> for sponsors. He then asks me for my daughter Tere's hand; I nod and point
> to the living room. Hat held in a firm hand, he follows with the same and
> sure unwavering step. . . .
>
> Turning my head slightly to the right, I catch a glimpse, or think I do, of
> my late father-in-law, don Braulio Tapia: long sideburns and matching black
> moustache à la Kaiser; don Braulio raises his hand to shake mine as he did
> years ago when I first came to his house to ask for Matilde's hand.
>
> By that time, with doña Sóstenes's death, he'd been a widower as I now am
> and have been since Matti's death three years ago. Don Braulio nods, takes
> my hand, and bids me enter.
>
> Who did don Braulio see when he walked up these steps to ask for his
> wife's hand?) (V 12)

As we enter the historical and ideological space of Hinojosa's characters, we watch with the anonymous narrator as his future son-
in-law, Roque Malacara, approaches to ask for the hand in marriage
of the narrator's daughter, Teresa. All of this is in the "present" of
narration. Simultaneously, the narrator remembers the day that he
approached his future father-in-law, don Braulio Tapia, to ask for his
daughter's hand in marriage. One page into the narrative, we have
entered a cultural-historical space where the past is starkly visible,
as in broad panorama. And that past too serves as a window to still
other past moments, even as it implies the future. Don Braulio Tapia,
the title character of the scene, is not even present. Yet, in another
sense he is. In this one single moment of multiple presents, the wide
context of history that the narrative is to dramatize is flashed before our eyes: we see at the same time four generations of history.
The map of this history can be traced out as a genealogical chart,
proceeding backward in time from the unnamed speaker (soon to
be identified as Jehú Vilches), and forward toward his still-unborn
grandson, Jehú Malacara, one of the two central figures of the *Klail
City Death Trip*. In diagram, their genealogy reads:

Braulio Tapia   m.   Sóstenes Calvillo
                |

       Matilde Tapia   m.   Jehú Vilches
                        |

         María Teresa Vilches   m.   Roque Malacara
                                   |

              Jehú Malacara

The genealogical diagram, like the prefatory maps and charts of *Estampas del Valle*, extended along syntactic lines in the narrative
proper, establishes narrative unity through the analogy of biologi-
cal identity. It also seems to offer the unambiguous identity of Jehú
Malacara, the other of the two linked protagonists of the *Klail City
Death Trip*. At one point Roque Malacara even says: "my son and my
late father-in-law are one and the same person" (*V* 14). But it is just
such identities and certainties that the narrative proceeds to put in
question.

The simplest of all narrative patterns, the genealogical, takes the
principle of succession literally: we can know who we are because
we know our past. Hinojosa's first narratives undo this certainty as
they investigate the transformations that occur within and acquire

predominance over succession in the search to know who we are. *Estampas del Valle* collapses the metaphorical and metonymical axes of narration, leaving the figurative possibility of identity indistinguishable from the literal one of difference within the narrative line.

Because of their narrative temporal and spatial instability, Hinojosa's novels create less a history of individual subjects and unique personalities than a history of the collective social life of the Mexican American community of the Lower Rio Grande Valley of Texas. That collective social life becomes a "character" in its own right, a kind of disembodied consciousness that attains almost heroic proportions. In *Korean Love Songs* this pattern continues and serves as perhaps the single most important difference between this work and the traditional corrido. Whereas in a song like "Gregorio Cortez" the actions of the hero serve at least initially as the organizing focus of the story, in Hinojosa's poem there is no "hero" in the traditional sense. The action represented must be read not as the story of "individuals," nor as the chronicle of a generation and its destiny, but as the dispersed history of impersonal forces. The central narrative of the work is not simply Rafa Buenrostro's but is immediately deflected on the opening pages of the text to "the four of us" (*KLS* 5), that is, David "Sonny" Ruiz, José Vielma, Rosalío "Charlie" Villalón, and Rafa Buenrostro. Jacob Mosqueda and Cayo Díaz Balderas later join this initial group. As the narrative proceeds, the personal identity of this cluster of characters is superseded first by the impersonal anonymity of the 219th Field Artillery Battalion in which they serve, then by the institutional identity provided by the U.S. Eighth Army, and finally by the masking quality of the Korean and Japanese cultures within which these displaced Chicanos find themselves.[2]

Although Rafa Buenrostro commands our attention as a singular voice, he is not the central actor precipitating the outcome of historical action. He is, rather, a peripheral mediator, serving as a link between his own Mexican American culture, the Anglo-American institutions represented starkly by the demands of army life, and the ritualized Japanese way of life. In one significant scene Rafa must swear before an army board of inquiry that Sonny Ruiz, whom he knows to be alive and well and living in Japan, is dead. Rafa, the literal and symbolic orphan of the story ("two orphans, she and I," Rafa later says in reference to his friend Hanako Kokada and himself [*KLS*

---

2. Goulden, *Korea: The Untold Story of the War* (1982), recounts the history of the events that Hinojosa's poem dramatizes.

48]), serves the odd function of giving Sonny Ruiz a new Japanese life
by taking away his former Mexican American one.

Having been wounded by a rocket blast that has killed his friend
Joey Vielma, Rafa is given an "R & R Medical leave" in Japan after his
release from an army hospital. He has arranged to meet Sonny, who
has gone AWOL and disappeared into Japanese life, at the Tanaka
Tea Gardens in Nagoya, Japan. Because the passage is so important,
I quote it at length:

> Many uniforms around us, but again no familiar patch or face.
> It's eight forty, and the Tanaka Tea Gardens, a mile off,
> Is where I'm to meet Sonny Ruiz,
> Who these many months
> Has been AWOL (and reported missing sometimes, and dead
>   at others).
> They'll never find him; to begin with,
> To Americans he looks Japanese; For another,
> No one really give a damn, one way or another. The Army,
> For all its pretense,
> Is not led by divine guidance.
>
> Sonny of the *old*, old 219th and twice wounded, made corporal
>   and stopped;
> One day he filled out and signed his own Missing-In-Action cards,
> Just like so much equipment;
> He personally turned them over to battery HQ,
> Then simply walked away to the docks.
>
> Army efficiency being what it is immediately produced a replacement
> Who promptly went mad during practice fire,
> And that was the end of that.
> Not long after, cards started to arrive from Nagoya and signed
> By Mr. Kazuo Fusaro who, in another life,
> Had lived as David Ruiz in Klail City,
> And who, in his new life,
> Was now a hundred and ten per cent Japanese.
>
> There he is, punctual as death: Business suit, hat, arms at his side,
> And as I approach, he fills the air with konnichi wahs,
> As he bends lower and lower, arms still at his side, smiling the while.
>
> He and I are the only ones left:
>   Charlie Villalón, Joey Vielma, Cayo Díaz
>   And a kid named Balderas
> Have all been erased from the Oriental scene. . . .
>
> Business is fine, and he is marrying later in the fall;
> A schoolteacher, no less.

And home?

"This is home, Rafe. Why should I go back?"

(43-44)

This passage may be easily misread. On one hand, we have Sonny's apparently complete assimilation into Japanese society. Rafa's words that "to Americans he looks Japanese" are bolstered a few lines later when an American M.P. looks straight at Sonny and his flower bouquet and "grunts" to his friend: "Pipe the gook and them flowers, there. / Damndest place I've ever seen" (45). From the Anglo-American perspective, all non-Anglos look and are alike. Given this uniformity, we might be lulled into believing that the assimilation of a cultural identity is indeed simple. Interestingly enough, this view that filters out the real historical differences between Mexican American and Japanese life and their cultural expressions is also Sonny's, who is "now a hundred and ten per cent Japanese." From Sonny's perspective, the cultural affinity between Japanese and Mexican American life allows for this assimilation and its resulting turn away from an oppressed, self-negating home in South Texas.

And yet, Rafa, who will return "to Klail, And home. Home to Texas, our Texas, / That slice of hell, heaven, / Purgatory and land of our Fathers" (53), uses his narrative material to sharpen our senses of the historical differences between Anglo-Americans and Japanese, Chicanos and Japanese, as well as between Anglos and Chicanos, and to stimulate an apprehension of what happens and what we would have happen when cultures meet. Sonny Ruiz has found the utopian opposite to "That slice of hell, heaven, / Purgatory and land of our Fathers" to which Rafa will return.

A few pages later, before the army Board of Inquiry into Sonny Ruiz's "death," Rafa says:

> The Board of Inquiry wishes to ascertain
> Facts relative to
> The matter of Cpl. David Ruiz's death
> In battle action in the summer of 1951.
> On a Government Issued bible, I swear
> That, to the very best of my knowledge,
> Cpl. Ruiz is dead.
>
> At parade rest,
> Before the Board,
> I think of old, mad Tina Ruiz, the widow of Ortega,
> Who lost another son, Chano,
> On a sixth of June, a few years back.

> She's Sonny Ruiz's sole beneficiary, and she's worth a howitzer
> or two;
>
> And so I lie. . . .
>
> It comes down to this: we're pieces of equipment
> To be counted and signed for.
> On occasion some of us break down,
> And those parts which can't be salvaged
> Are replaced with other GI parts, that's all.
>
> (49–50)

In the face of a depersonalization which is also dehumanizing, Rafa's lie before the board of inquiry paradoxically gives Sonny back an identity of his own, albeit not the one in which he lived his former life in Klail City. Rafa's lie before the board of inquiry on behalf of Sonny Ruiz overcomes both one aspect of Sonny's isolated, autonomous subjectivity and the anonymous absorption of that subjectivity by the American army. As Rafa realizes: "I work for the State" (51), and he may acquiesce to its transformation of his own identity into forms it approves of, or he may subvert its deindividualizing intentions by reinventing a character for his friend. In having become "just like so much equipment" (43) "to be counted and signed for" (50), Rafa in Korea and Japan begins to feel a sense of the way in which capitalist institutions use human lives in terms of their "instrumentality." He even acquires the words to begin to understand his predicament: As a chaplain reads from the Introductory Rubric to the *Burial of the Dead* ("violent hands upon themselves," Rafa mulls:

> . . . [H]e's reading it from a book,
> And I suppose anyone of *us*,
> Could have done *that*,
> Except
> For the fact
> That we don't belong to the same union;
> Our guild furnishes the bodies;
> And his, the prayers. Division of labor it's called.
>
> (51)

Classical Marxist analysis shows that the division of labor inside a nation leads to the separation of industrial and commercial from agricultural labor, and then to the separation of town and country and to the conflict of their interests. Its further development leads to the separation of commercial from industrial labor. At the same time, through this division of labor, there develops within the various separated branches of labor, divisions among the individual laborers which now preclude the cooperation of individuals in definite kinds of labor.[3] Out of the unity of laboring men and women, the separation and division of singular and competing individuals is thus created. These same conditions of separation operate at the level of the production of ideas, as expressed in the language of politics, laws, morality, religion, or aesthetics of a people. Separated into "guilds," Rafa recognizes, individual action is parceled out and reconstituted into efficiently controllable instrumentalities. Some kill while others pray; these distinctive activities define them consequently as one or the other exclusively, a soldier or a priest: "Our guild furnishes the bodies; / And his, the prayers." Stating the situation in this manner allows Rafa to understand that to assert himself as an individual he must regain that preseparatist collective expression which has been the legacy of his people. The police action in Korea thus becomes an analogue of the commodification of labor power and its resultant separation of the differentiating aspects of human communities which Rafa's homeland must resist—prey to a system in which everyone and everything are replaceable parts.

These scenes in *Korean Love Songs* are crucial because they seem to project a utopian fantasy about cultural synthesis. Sonny Ruiz is able to find in Japan what he cannot possess at home: "Why should I go back?" he asks. "Why, indeed?" answers Rafa, as he too seems drawn to the fantasy of annihilating the past and starting absolutely anew. This alien world seems rich to them in contrast to the one to which they must return, especially as men like Rafa's company commander Captain "Tex" Bracken and General Walton H. ("a lot of Mexicans live in Texas") Walker "reminded [us] who we were / Thousands of miles from home" (11). Objects of prejudice and exploitation at home, dying in Korea, "creating history by protecting the world from Communism" (11), it is no wonder that they are charmed by the allure of Japanese self-sufficiency, integrity, and family solidarity in the face of an occupying American army.

Rafa begins to understand that as little as he knows about the Chinese troops he kills by the "hundreds," so too the army knows or

---

3. Of the several places where this issue is developed, the early formulation of the concept of the "division of labor" in Marx and Engels' *The German Ideology* (1845–46) is one of the most succinct. See *The German Ideology*, Part 1, in *The Marx-Engels Reader* (1978, 150). See also Marcuse's introductory essay, "The Foundation of Historical Materialism" ([1932] 1972).

cares little about him. But he chooses not to turn against his American home. As we already know from the previous novel in the series, *Klail City y sus alrededores*, the Texas home to which the Korean War veterans will return is no different from the one to which the World War II veterans returned. It is a place where veterans like Ambrosio Mora, who saw Chano Ortega, the half-brother of Sonny Ruiz, die at Normandy, can be murdered by the local sheriff's deputy in broad daylight "en frente de la J. C. Penney en el centro de Flora un domingo de palmas" ("in front of the J. C. Penney in downtown Flora on a Palm Sunday afternoon") (145). We know too from that novel that while the veterans will protest that "ellos también habían ido a la guerra y que bastaba con 'ese pedo de la *descreminación*' [*sic*]" ("they too had served and gone to war and that they had had enough of 'this damned discrimination'") (147), the deputy will go free, leaving old Mora only the futile protest gesture of destroying with a crowbar the monument in honor of the local war dead erected by "las damas auxiliares de la American Legion" ("the Ladies Auxiliary of the American Legion") (147). The marker is an empty sign and, like the mass grave with its innumerable neat crosses that Rafa and Joey Vielma once visited to pay their last respects to Charlie Villalón, no one should believe "that the marker is reserved for you" (24).

And yet, at the moment he is wounded, Rafa's thoughts turn not to rage over the deaths of his friends or to his own possible death, or to the lack of social justice in South Texas. Instead:

> For me, there was the thought of home and friends, and,
> Strangely enough,
>   Of an Easter picnic near the river
> Where I met a girl named Nellie
> Now long dead and, I thought,
> Quite forgotten.
>
> (39)

The solution to the confusion of serving one's own oppressor is evidently not the assimilation to another world, but rather the determination to return to the contradictory but familiar one.

It is in the crucible of death that were the Korean battlefields that Rafa Buenrostro at mid-century, like Gregorio Cortez "with his pistol in his hand" in the early part of the twentieth century, resolves to take on the duty to live justly in Texas. Gregorio Cortez identifies himself in opposition to the Anglos who victimize him and his family. Rafa and others like him renew their solidarity by serving first as voluntary agents of American military power. The index of their song's ideology is thus not to be found in its apparently inno- cent story, but in its ideological commitment to collective solidarity. No less surely than in *El Corrido de Gregorio Cortez*, the under- lying symbolic impulse of *Korean Love Songs* turns out to be the resolution to reawaken in the midst of a privatizing and alienating dominant culture, even while half a world away, a continuing sense of the drive toward community and collectivity which has been the historical heritage of the border communities of South Texas. Like their corrido folk art base, Rolando Hinojosa's "songs" thus align themselves with the most ideologically vital artforms of Mexican American culture. The songs serve to highlight and hold off the dis- solving and fragmenting effects of contemporary American life while attempting to represent the conditions necessary for the retention of organic community life. It is a task that Hinojosa continues to chart in symbolic form in his other exemplary works.

10. Chicana worker at "La Malinche" tortilla factory, Corpus Christi, Texas, May 1949. (Russell Lee Collection, courtesy of the Eugene C. Barker Texas History Center, University of Texas at Austin)

11. Commissioned to photograph the people and living conditions of the "Spanish-speaking people of Texas," Russell Lee captured typical scenes such as this of low-cost housing units, home for approximately twenty Mexican American working-class families of the post–World War II era, Corpus Christi, Texas, May 1949. (Russell Lee Collection, courtesy of the Eugene C. Barker Texas History Center, University of Texas at Austin)

12. Mexican American child in the courtyard of an urban working-class housing unit, Corpus Christi, Texas, May 1949. (Russell Lee Collection, courtesy of the Eugene C. Barker Texas History Center, University of Texas at Austin)

13. Chicana schoolgirl, San Angelo, Texas, May 1949. (Russell Lee Collection, courtesy of the Eugene C. Barker Texas History Center, University of Texas at Austin)

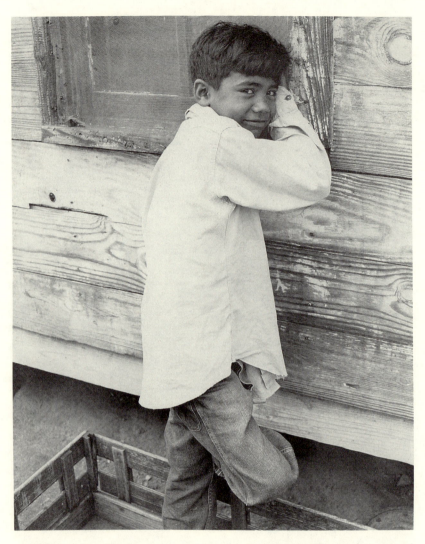

14. School-age boy, San Angelo, Texas, May 1949. (Russell Lee Collection, courtesy of the Eugene C. Barker Texas History Center, University of Texas at Austin)

15. Chicano laborer and his daughter, San Angelo, Texas, May 1949. (Russell Lee Collection, courtesy of the Eugene C. Barker Texas History Center, University of Texas at Austin)

7

Ideologies of the Self

Chicano Autobiography

Autobiography has a long, distinguished history as a narrative form. Because of its historical viability from the classical era through Augustine, the Middle Ages, and Romanticism, and on to the modern era, one might well use autobiography and its discourses to chart the historical, cultural, and psychological factors surrounding the development of an ideology of the self. But aside from its historical roots, autobiography is of immense interest to students of literature and culture in general because of the special way it assimilates real historical time and space (what Bakhtin has called the "chronotope" [1981, 84]). With their capacity to articulate historical time and space in critical discourse—especially discourse of the kind that has come to be known since the writings of Benjamin, Adorno, and the rest of the Frankfurt School as cultural criticism—works of contemporary autobiography can have special relevance to literary theorists. From this theoretical perspective, autobiography can be used to advance a critical attitude toward social institutions, turning what seems an inherently private form of discourse onto the public social world. This turn on the part of autobiography to the social world makes it a discourse rich with the kinds of questions pertinent to students of literature, criticism, and cultural studies.

Because of its fundamental tie to themes of self and history, self and place, it is not surprising that autobiography is the form that stories of emergent racial, ethnic, and gender consciousness have often taken in the United States and elsewhere. One thinks, for instance, of the powerful influence on self-definition that books such as those of Frederick Douglass, Malcolm X, Claude Brown, and Maxine Hong Kingston have had. Gramsci has thus pointed out that

154

autobiography can be conceived "politically." One knows that one's life is ✓
similar to that of a thousand others, but through "chance" it has had opportunities that the thousand others in reality could not or did not have. By
narrating it, one creates this possibility, suggests the process, indicates the
opening. Autobiography therefore replaces the "political" or "philosophical
essay": it describes in action what otherwise is deduced logically. Autobiography certainly has a great historical value in that it shows life in action
and not just as written laws or dominant moral principles say it should be.
(1985, 132)

Speaking of a particular kind of politicized autobiography, Michael
M. J. Fischer furthers Gramsci's point by noting that "ethnic autobiographical writing parallels, mirrors, and exemplifies contemporary
theories of textuality, of knowledge, and of culture. They are postmodern in their deployment of a series of techniques: bifocality
or reciprocity of perspectives, juxtapositioning of multiple realities, intertextuality and inter-referentiality, and comparison through
families of resemblance" (1986, 230).

In its canon Chicano literature includes books that are either semiautobiographical, such as Villarreal's *Pocho*, Acosta's *The Autobiography of a Brown Buffalo* and *The Revolt of the Cockroach People*,
and Isabella Ríos' *Victuum*, or specifically autobiographical, such
as the two works to be discussed in this chapter: Ernesto Galarza's
Barrio Boy: The Story of a Boy's Acculturation (1971) and Richard
Rodriguez's *Hunger of Memory: The Education of Richard Rodriguez*
(1982). A comparison of these two works will be instructive, providing significant insight into the rhetoric of autobiographical discourse
as such—and "ethnic autobiography" in particular—as well as into
its importance for understanding the features of the ideologies that
surround it.

I have taken Caliban's advice. I have stolen their books. I will have some
run of this isle. . . . (In Beverly Hills will this monster make a man.)

I begin with this passage from Richard Rodriguez's autobiography
rather than with Ernesto Galarza's work, in part because readers are
much more likely to be familiar with Rodriguez's work than with
Galarza's. Rodriguez's autobiography has been reviewed favorably
everywhere from the *Village Voice* (Marzán 1982) to the *Los Angeles
Times* (Miles 1982), and selections from it are now anthologized in
practically all new college freshman composition course readers in
this country. Rodriguez has become in the span of a few years' time
the voice of "Hispanic America," as is indicated by his many short ✓

articles on a variety of topics and in various publications, such as a recent one in the *Wall Street Journal* on language policy, and another in *Mother Jones* on immigration policy.

The allusion in Rodriguez's introductory sentence is of course to *The Tempest*, one of Shakespeare's final plays and often held to be the most autobiographical of his works. In *The Tempest*, Prospero, unjustly deposed as Duke of Milan by his treacherous brother, finds himself exiled to a distant and strange island. Prospero there creates a new kingdom, peopled only by himself; his daughter, Miranda; Ariel, a spirit who commands a submissive crew of other spirits; and, at the bottom of this weird social heap, a half-man half-monster named Caliban. Prospero desires to revenge himself against his brother and to regain his crown. Caliban desires only to usurp Prospero and regain his homeland.

In traditional studies, Caliban is taken as Shakespeare's version of the "natural" man, a version of Montaigne's "cannibal," the not-so-noble savage, whom society and culture must discipline and tame. From this perspective, Caliban is not entirely a negative figure (Shakespeare hardly ever creates one-dimensional characters). As a child of nature, Caliban is used to show us civilized men and women what is unnatural in our own domesticated lives. Caliban performs a positive function; he is a good example, in other words, of our own savage natures, which we must control. This is fine from the point of view of Prospero and Miranda and of all the good noble people who make their way through the enchanted isle.

But it is not so fine from Caliban's point of view. Poor Caliban is not so fortunate—he may be a man, too, but he is also a slave, and Prospero has given him the tools to understand the fact that he is a slave:

> "You taught me language; and my profit on't
> Is, I know how to curse you. The red plague rid you
> For learning me your language!"
>
> (I, ii)

Unable to organize his own rebellion, Caliban goes out and finds wandering the island the greedy, drunken, shipwrecked Stephano to do it for him: "Be my god," Caliban tells him. Still, Caliban shrewdly senses that Prospero's power comes from the force of his language, his words, and his books, and he also realizes that to share in some of Prospero's power he needs "first to possess his books" (III, ii).

Precisely because of moments such as this in the play, it is not surprising to find that Caliban has been the focus of some of the

best critical discussions of *The Tempest* by Third World scholars. A
notable case is an essay entitled "Calibán" by the emminent Cuban
theoretician Roberto Fernández Retamar. Retamar sees the plight of
Shakespeare's half-man half-monster as an allegory for the status of
the Third World: Prospero invaded our lands, killed our ancestors,
enslaved us, and taught us his language to make himself understood.
He has possessed us with his books. "What is our history, what is
our culture, if not the history and culture of Caliban?" asks Retamar
(24). Similarly, Houston Baker, Jr., calls Caliban's curse on Prospero
a "metacurse." His utterance is " 'meta' because its semantics are
marked by economies (implied or explicit) of *ob-scenity*—they speak
against the scene of an intruder's tongue. Not 'self' discovery, but
the impossibility of feeling anything other than cursed by language
is the sense of Caliban's utterance" (1985, 39).

There are many links, then, between Shakespeare's monster Caliban and Rodriguez's autobiography: ideas concerning the "natural"
man, human monsters, education, language, political power, and so
forth. But in the light of my concern here with a culturally specific
form of autobiography represented not only by *Hunger of Memory*
but also by Galarza's *Barrio Boy*, I shall restrict my comparative
focus to what these works can teach us, either through positive or
negative example, about (a) autobiography, in general, (b) the "private" and "public" roles of individuals in society, and (c) the power of
language, rhetoric, and education as elements of political ideology.

Hunger of Memory is an autobiography in the standard sense of the
word: it tells the story of Richard Rodriguez's journey from social
disadvantage to social acceptance, from public alienation to public
integration, from working-class Mexican America to middle-class
white America. Richard is the son of *mexicanos* who settled in Anglo
neighborhoods in Sacramento, California, in the 1950s. They meet
only limited hostility from their new neighbors and are for the most
part simply ignored by them. The real problems begin for Rodriguez
only when he begins his formal education at the parochial Catholic school. He feels himself an outcast, alienated in the classroom.
Midway through the first school year, the nuns from the school visit
the Rodriguezes, wanting to know if they speak only Spanish at
home. The nuns explain to Mr. and Mrs. Rodriguez that the "difficult progress" Richard and his brothers and sisters are making at
school could be explained by the fact that the Rodriguezes are not
practicing their English enough. Richard sees this moment as crucial
in his life—from the moment that English enters the "private" world

inside the home, he is well on his way to becoming the assimilated "middle-class American man" (7) who thirty years later will write the story of his life.

Once Rodriguez learns a public language, he acquires a public identity. But he realizes that in his transformation from the private person of the home-centered Mexican culture to the public assimilated man of the Anglo society he has lost something. Each world's language brought out different emotions. Spanish radiated family intimacy but also provoked shame and embarrassment. English opened doors to society's networks, rewards, and recognitions, but also subverted the family's sense of intimacy. His life then becomes a tenuous attempt to hold off these contradictions, to accept the benefits of his Mexican-ness while rejecting its demands, until he must irrevocably choose between them.

And choose he does. He chooses with great anxiety and precious sadness to reject the duality of his working-class origins and his middle-class manners; he chooses to market his existential anguish to the most receptive audience imaginable: the right-wing establishment and the liberal academic intelligentsia. His writings against bilingual education (because it is a hindrance to the access to a "public" language) and against affirmative action (because it denigrates the achievements of those who have made it on their own merits) involves him, whether he admits it or not, in a political service to the Right. Rodriguez chooses to assimilate without ever considering whether he acted by will or merely submitted to an unquestioned grander scheme of political ideology. In instance after instance, he emphasizes the absolute separation between the private and the public life of men and women, the priority of the individual private inner self over the social public outer self. As a consequence, he feels himself capable of functioning only as an isolated and private individual, deprived of any organic connection with his ethnic group, his social class, and finally even his own family. He is a solitary man, and he does not feel himself part of the social whole. Privacy and isolation are his essential features, even when he functions in the public arena, in the role of what Rodriguez terms the "public individual" (26).

Yet at the same time, Rodriguez does behave like the public man, as throughout the autobiography he fashions set pieces which are, as he admits, rhetorically structured acts of contrition and confession, written in the form of public accountings. These moments of exculpation are not moments of intimacy between the reader and the autobiographer but, rather, are like public apologia attempting to establish legal and moral justification of the public self he has chosen to be. As a result, the Richard Rodriguez we come to know in the autobiography is less the inner secret man he declares he wishes to present than the rhetorically highlighted, publicly apologetic voice of interplay between the allegedly distinct private and public selves that the book actually presents. In this inconsistent interplay, however, no dialectic develops. Thus even though he sets his life story among the political and historical events of the 1960s and 1970s, private life is not interpreted in the light of cultural-historical events, but the other way around. Social and political events gain meaning in Rodriguez's life *only* because of their connection with his private life.

Now, this privileging of the private viewpoint is significant, but not, I would stress, because autobiography has to be either public or private in purview. Autobiography is demonstrably capable of embracing both perspectives and putting them into dialogue, as we will see when we turn to Galarza's book. In Rodriguez's story, this privileging of the private is significant because of what happens to the assumed binary relationship between the "private" and the "public" self. His vision reduces the interplay between these two constitutive human realms to the overpowering order of the *private* world. The social, political, historical world of bilingual education and affirmative action is illuminated only insofar as it relates to his private fate. The essence of that world in itself remains, therefore, peripheral to the central concern of his story.

But curiously enough, while he would deny social or political significance to his life as a private phenomenon and see it so only as he became a public man, it is the very private quality of his confessional mode that has made his book of political consequence to the Right. Who would read another editorial on affirmative action? But who can turn away from an anguished denunciation of it by one who has benefitted from affirmative action? What Bakhtin has said of the subject of classical Greek romance—that "the public and rhetorical unity of the self he presents is to be found in the contradiction between it and its purely private content" (1981, 109)—we might just as well say of *Hunger of Memory*. It is this contradiction upon which we must seize.

In relying upon the pastoral form to structure his autobiography (the prologue is subtitled "A Middle-Class Pastoral"), Rodriguez cannot generate "form and unities that [are] adequate to the [complexity of] the private individual and his life" (Bakhtin 1981, 110). The homogeneity of this public and rhetorical side and the purely private side of the individual is huge, abstract, schematized, and tends to pro-

duce archetypal images. It is thus not surprising that when we last
see Rodriguez he is leaving the last supper of familial discontent
—a depressing Christmas feast—alone and aware of his isolation,
ready to suffer for our collective, bilingually educated and affirma-
tively enacted sins, and equally ready to be reborn as the published
autobiographer of assimilated middle-class Mexican America. With
Rodriguez we are now far removed from the paradigm of the folk
corrido hero. His narrative paradigms lie elsewhere.

As in Christian hagiography, where we are given two basic images
of the individual, that of the sinner *before* rebirth and that of the saint
after crisis and rebirth, joined by a middle period of *askesis*, or puri-
fication through suffering (Bakhtin 1981, 115–16), so Rodriguez's life
story is structured on the archetypal pattern of redemption, albeit
in Rodriguez's case, a secular redemption. His life story is thus not
set in a biographical time that chronicles personal history in social
history. As Bakhtin says of the saint's life, "it depicts rather only the
exceptional, unusual moments that are short compared to the whole
of a human life. But these moments *shape the definitive image of
the man, his essence, as well as the nature of his entire subsequent
life"* (1981, 116). Beyond these moments that have shaped his destiny, Rodriguez enters upon his biographical life as an essayist and
autobiographer. In Beverly Hills indeed has this Caliban made a man.

Contemporary scholarship on autobiography such as that of Elizabeth W. Bruss (1976), Jeffrey Mehlman (1974), James Olney (1972,
1980), and Paul Jay (1984) shows that from its original form in St.
Augustine's *Confessions*, through Dante's *Vita Nuova*, Rousseau's
Confessions, and into its nineteenth- and twentieth-century styles,
autobiography has tended to make similar demands on those who
would write their own life story. William G. Spengemann (1980) has
argued that authors of autobiography posit generally at least three
methods of self-presentation: (1) a historical self-explanation, (2) a
philosophical self-analysis, and (3) a poetic self-expression. Rodriguez's autobiography is remarkably problematic in all three categories. He seems persistently uncritical when he deals with the historical factors affecting Mexican American life in general and his
own life in particular. He mentions in several places, for instance, the
connection between race and social status (115–25, especially), but
overlooks the subtleties of the relation between a dark complexion
and a life of poverty. Autobiographers like Augustine and Rousseau
knew that such historical questions were inseparable from authentic
self-understanding, since the autobiographical act is at least in part
a publicly rhetorical one. Even in its most private and self-indulgent

confessional style, a published autobiography is after all addressed to a public, historically real readership. Rodriguez's autobiography, however, speaks to us from a position beyond history, as if the dynamic forces of historical change could no longer touch him.

In other words, the story Rodriguez tells us lacks the verisimilitude of autobiography's second demand: philosophical self-analysis. He fails to consider, as autobiography might induce him to, that the author lives, moves, and has his being in historical projections that constitute him as a subject. And an author cannot simply tell us the "truth" about himself, a truth that will "resonate with significance for other lives" (7), without undertaking some kind of philosophical reflection on the place of his private life in public history. I wish to emphasize this point in particular because Rodriguez seems so certain about the innocence of the split he makes between the "private" and "public" self. The desire to extract ourselves from the world, either to conceive it or to command it, only anchors us more deeply in it. In fact, one might argue as Michael Ryan has that the "private" philosophical and "private" historical are always public through and through. The "private" is always already a familial institution and a linguistic network that form a person. Rousseau and Augustine knew this.

I would also suggest that Rodriguez's autobiography suffers as a poetic self-expression. He offers his autobiography as a "pastoral," a kind of literature that draws a contrast between the innocence and serenity of the simple life and the corruption and chaos of urban life. But even in its most naive forms, the pastoral always recognizes that the desire for the innocent and serene past is unfortunately always nostalgic. Poetic self-expression requires the autobiographer to confront nostalgic desire with present circumstances. Out of this confrontation a new recognition can emerge: that future conditions are collectively created, by individuals and groups of individuals. Augustine and Rousseau knew this, too.

Paul de Man has argued that one way by which we might circumscribe the nature of autobiographical discourse is by contrasting it to fiction: "Autobiography seems to depend on actual and potentially verifiable events in a less ambivalent way than fiction does. It seems to belong to a simpler mode of referentiality, of representation and of diegesis" (1979, 920). Autobiography may very well contain fantasy, dream, and illusion but these turns away from reality at least "remain rooted in a single subject whose identity is defined by the uncontestable readability of his proper name" (920). But can we be so certain of this referentiality and of this centrality of single subjectivity? As de Man goes on to argue, "We assume that life *produces* the autobiography as an act produces its consequences, but can we not suggest, with equal justice, that the autobiographical project may itself produce and determine the life and that whatever the writer *does* is in fact governed by the technical demands of self-portraiture and thus determined, in all its aspects, by the resources of his medium?" (920).

Now, as is typical of de Man's inquiries in all of his essays, there is a lot at stake in this last question: our ways of accounting for the production of a life, for intention and causality, and for the mimetic mode of figuration by which we attempt to explain and justify our troubled lives. Let me put it this way, still paraphrasing de Man: in the case of the autobiography of Richard Rodriguez, can we be certain that the referent, his life, his anguished search for self-definition, determines the figure, the pastoral/hagiographical rendering of it in the text of *Hunger of Memory*, or is it the other way around? Is it because he writes his life story as a nostalgic desire for lost innocence and a sublime search for personal redemption that through his artful prose we come to believe in the lost innocence and personal redemption of his life? If so, then the referent of his autobiography is not simply a referent at all but something more akin, as de Man suggests, to a fiction.

I am not criticizing *Hunger of Memory* because it is at least in part a fiction. I think that de Man is also convincing when he argues that fiction is always involved in autobiography, just as the obverse is also true, "that any book with readable title page is, to some extent, autobiographical" (922). What I am suggesting is that the *genetic* relationship Rodriguez establishes between the self he offers in his book and the self outside the book, as between those "private" and "public" roles he ascribes to us all, is fundamentally open to question. If this alignment of textual and historical selves is problematic, are there perhaps other modes of figuration through which an alignment between the textual and the historical subject may be rendered? The autobiographical moment happens as an alignment between the historical and textual subjects involved in the process of understanding themselves as one subject that is determined by their "mutual reflexive substitution" (921). De Man argues that this doubling structure "implies differentiation as well as similarity, since both depend on a substitutive exchange that constitutes the subject" (921). It is not, then, the doubling of the subject that is at issue because the autobiographical moment is precisely, in all cases, a reflexive one when, as de Man suggests, the author "declares himself

[margin handwritten note: But isn't this true / to a minor / to an extent, / in any / autobiog?]

the subject of his own understanding" (921). What I am concerned with is not the fact of the reflexive subject but with the elaboration and the outcome of the figuration of selves in autobiography "as a discourse of self-restoration" (925). Both the reflexive and the elaborative moments entail representation and figuration, as the subject simultaneously imagines and projects the "real" and an image of the "real" that carries over into life as a particular kind of self-figuration.

Ernesto Galarza's *Barrio Boy: The Story of a Boy's Acculturation* (1971) is everything that Rodriguez's autobiography is not precisely insofar as it offers us another mode of self-figuration. The differences between the two works suggest unmistakably why Rodriguez's has been such a greater commercial and literary success than Galarza's. While Galarza's story is also one of a boy's education, the manner and substance of his education are wholly different from Rodriguez's. Born in a small Mexican village along the Pacific coast at the turn of the century, Galarza tells us his life story in its historical context. Uprooted by the events of the Mexican Revolution (1910–17), the boy, his mother, and his uncles make their way by stages from the village of Jalcocotán, to Mazatlán, to Nogales, and Tucson, and, finally, to Sacramento, California (coincidentally, the same town later to be Richard Rodriguez's hometown). Whereas the narrative strategy of Rodriguez's text is not that of biographical time, Galarza's is rooted in the temporality of traditional autobiography, but with a difference. The five parts of his books are in fact stages of a peregrination and form the organizing centers for the fundamental narrative events of his life story. From "In a Mountain Village," through "Peregrinations," "North from Mexico," "Life in the Lower Part of Town," and "On the Edge of the Barrio," the controlling discursive mode is that of journey literature. The author's life takes him on the road from his birthplace to his adopted American home.

On the road Galarza encounters representatives of virtually all social classes, religions, ages, and many nationalities as the turmoil of the Mexican Revolution has broken down the traditional rigid boundaries of prerevolutionary society. This collapse of social distance allows human fates to intersect in complex and distinctive ways, revealing the sociohistorical heterogeneity of both Mexican and American life. The difficulty of rendering these complex intersections and this heterogeneity makes the choice and orchestration of narrative strategies vitally significant. As de Man notes, the "doors" through which an autobiographer enters his work may be appropriately regarded as "revolving" ones because the metaphor "aptly connotes the turning motion of tropes and confirms that the specular moment is not primarily a situation or an event that can be located in a history, but that it is the manifestation, on the level of the referent, of a linguistic structure" (1979, 922).

As in journalistic accounts of travel or in the picaresque novel, the chronotope of the road functions in Galarza's autobiography precisely as the trope by which the multiply dispersed circumstances of a life may be appropriated to create the possibility of the condition of subjective identity. The interest of Galarza's autobiography over Rodriguez's is not that it has necessarily succeeded in unproblematically translating "events" into discourse, or that it reveals a more reliable self-knowledge than Rodriguez's, but that it dramatizes in a striking way the "motion of tropes" involved in the invention and projection of an identity within the heterogeneity of sociohistoric and psychological life. That Galarza is aware of the extent to which the specular moment that is part of all understanding, including knowledge of the self, is a tropological structure is evident from his choice of an epigraph to his autobiography. He quotes Henry Adams' words: "This was the journey he remembered. The actual journey may have been quite different. . . . The memory was all that mattered." The context of that "memory" is undeniably historical and discursive.

In contrast to the pattern of exceptional time functioning in an autobiography such as Rodriguez's, *Barrio Boy* offers a different temporal structure—that of everyday time. We follow the young Ernesto through the events of his everyday world, witnessing his gradual acculturation to, first, a Mexican world, and later, to an American one. This change from one culture to another corresponds to the actual course of travel, to his wanderings "north from Mexico." Thus, the basic plot of Galarza's autobiography is not the epiphanic revelation of an idiosyncratic destiny, as it is for Rodriguez. Rather, the life story is presented in the simple form of a travelogue and character reminiscence. Within this simple form, however, are subsumed the themes of transformation (especially human transformation through symbolic acculturation) and identity (particularly group identity). The motifs of transformation and identity, which might have been offered in terms of the individual, are transferred instead to the entire community within which individuals exist, by which they are created, and which they in turn dialectically transform.

In this way, Galarza realizes the metaphor of the "journey" of life. His writings *are* the course of his early life, as he travels with his mother and uncles through familiar territory to alien places. The road from Jalcocotán to Mazatlán and Nogales (mimetically mapped out for us on the cover of the book of his life) is not merely a road, but suggests the itinerary of his life. The intersections and cross-roads he experiences are literally signifiers of some turning point in the life of the autobiographer. Road markers are thus indicators of his fate. Bakhtin argues that "in the literary artistic chronotope, spatial and temporal indicators are fused into one carefully thought-out, concrete whole. Time, as it were, thickens, takes on flesh, becomes artistically visible; likewise, space becomes charged and responsive to the movements of time, plot, and history. This intersection of axes and fusion of indicators characterizes the artistic chronotope" (1981, 84). In this sense, Galarza's use of the chronotope of the road is specific, organic, and deeply infused with the ideological implications of his story, spread out along the edge of the road itself, and along the sideroads of revolutionary Mexico. As the guiding chronotope of the first half of the autobiography, the figure of the road allows Galarza to describe the sociohistorical heterogeneity of the culture that has nurtured him as a child (see figure 16).

Once he arrives in California the chronotope shifts. Instead of the road, now the parameters of the barrio form the locus of narrative, the place where the knots of narrative are tied and untied. From the enclosure of the dark musty rooms of their first residence in the lower part of Sacramento, "a prison even more confining than the alley [off of which they had lived] in Tucson" (133), the Galarzas slowly begin to explore their new world. Ernesto and his mother begin "to take short walks to get [their] bearings" (197). This innocent action is the sign of the new chronotope, as they map out the border of the barrio which they now inhabit:

It was a block in one direction to the lumber yard and the grocery store; half a block in the other to the saloon and the Japanese motion picture theater. In between were the tent and awning shop, a Chinese restaurant, a second-hand store, and several houses like our own. We noted by the numbers on the posts at the corners that we lived between 4th and 5th streets on L. Once we could fix a course from these signs up and down and across town we explored further. On Sixth near K there was the Lyric Theater with a sign we easily translated into Lírico. . . . Navigating by these key points and following the rows of towering elms along L Street, one by one we found the post office on 7th and K; the cathedral, four blocks farther east; and the state capitol with its golden dome. (197)

What is described in this passage is not incidental scenery, divorced from the substance of their lives. The placing of their lives in these surroundings and in this temporality provides the ground for

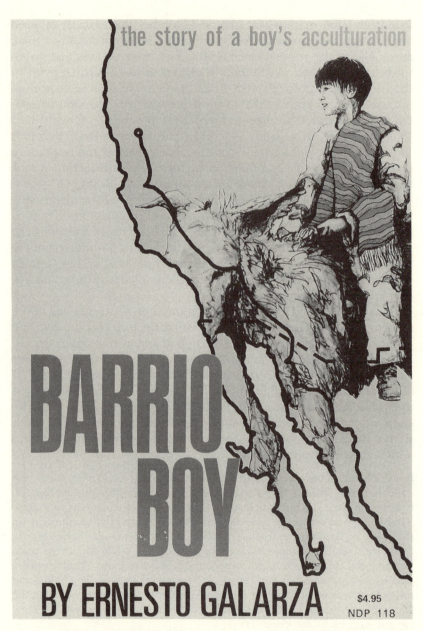

the story of a boy's acculturation

BARRIO
BOY

BY ERNESTO GALARZA

$4.95
NDP 118

16. Cover illustration of Ernesto Galarza's *Barrio Boy*. (Courtesy of Notre Dame University Press)

the very representability of the people they will have to become in these alien surroundings. As the passage points out, the process of acculturation is at first a conscious act of "translation," a reflexive representation that serves to help them "find their bearings" in this brave new world. Later, the acculturative translation becomes an unconscious and immensely significant imaging and projecting of a reality that now serves as the compass of their new identities as Mexican Americans. In this manner, as Galarza points out, "with remarkable fairness and never-ending wonder we kept adding to our list the pleasant and the repulsive in the ways of the Americans. It was my second acculturation" (205). The temporal and spatial dimensions of the barrio become the source of personal identity, as is borne out by the title of the autobiography. More than mere exposition, these sections of the autobiography describing the family's new surroundings carry great weight. They serve as the primary means for materializing time in space and serve as the center for concretizing representation and ideological awareness.

These were the boundaries of the lower part of town, for that was what everyone called the section of the city between Fifth Street and the river and from the railway yards to the Y-street levee. Nobody ever mentioned an upper part of town; at least, no one could see the difference because the whole city was built on level land. We were not lower topographically, but in other ways that distinguished between Them, the uppers, and Us, the lowers. (198)

The topographical metaphor puts into stark relief the ideological distinction between "Them, the uppers" and "Us, the lowers." Galarza's conception of the dialectic between the immediate perception of geographical terrain and the imaginative or imaginary sense of the city as an *invented* reality provides a striking instance of what Jameson has termed "cognitive mapping" (1988, 353). Galarza's capacity to map the literal city now allows him also to map it socially and experience it politically. His cognitive map is thus a powerful spatial analogue of Althusser's formulation of ideology itself as "the imaginary relationship of individuals to their real conditions of existence" (1969, 162). In a later essay, Galarza is thus able to note that "the urban barrios like the colonias of the countryside, started as cultural enclaves in the Anglo world. . . . In the barrios ethnic identity was strongly provided" (1972, 276).

In *Barrio Boy* we are not offered a tale of assimilation; instead, we see the complex historical-psychological process of acculturation unfold, as a discursive formation in which the historically constituted possibilities for identity are complexly dispersed. The difference between Galarza's and Rodriguez's versions of the discursive possibilities of autobiography is crucial. Galarza finds that he must hold off the contradictory impulses of his Mexican origins and his American growth to maturity. But differently from Rodriguez, he handles this turmoil not by rejecting his Mexican world as he develops a public self, but by "navigating" precariously between both worlds, inhabiting both in good faith, and finally by forging a span between his original Mexican and his acquired American enculturations.

This forging of identity does not take place as a simple binary opposition between a "private" and a "public" self. It does not require the rejection of the "intimate" sounds of Spanish in favor of the distanced forms of English. It does not assume the form of hagiography. Still less does it present itself as a pastoral, as a confession, or as an act of contrition. Rather, as Renato Rosaldo has noted, Galarza's autobiography "is marked by heteroglossia, a play of English and Spanish, and by an understated, often self-deprecating deadpan humor through which his political vision becomes apparent" (1987, 76). Replacing the political or philosophical essay, his autobiography is a personal document where historical self-explanation, philosophical self-analysis, and poetic self-expression merge to tell with irony and humor a social story: an individual's participation in one of the grandest migrations of modern times—the influx of Mexicans into the American Southwest. Here, the private self is as appropriated by its public role as the public self is fashioned by its private experiences. The opposition between the two versions of selfhood has become fluid, dynamic, and open to the shaping forces of cultural and political history. In this way, Galarza establishes a continuing correspondence between personal identity and a radical ethnic identity. The momentous undertaking that such a radical identification is entrusted with is, as R. Radhakrishnan puts it, nothing less than "the creation of a future where oppression will be not just immoral or unconscionable, but virtually 'unthinkable'" (1987, 220).

Our postromantic organizational framework for thinking about the self presupposes the duality of existence (into subjects and objects) and also presupposes the integrity of subjects and objects as independent entities. In this view, the self is certainly not untouched by the collective object-world around it. At the same time, that object-world is also seen as being organized into its institutional contexts by the intentional conceptualizing acts of the subject. The self is the result of the harmonious interaction between its "inner private" subjectivity and its "outer public" objective roles. Identity is the unity of these divergent spheres around the central cogito.

Against this view, Adorno has argued that if the "personal" is seen as already being public, then the will to keep the separation of the political from the personal loses its convincing force. This is precisely what Ernesto Galarza's autobiography teaches us and what Richard Rodriguez's would have us forget.

These days it has almost become a cliché to say that the personal, "private" self is political. But perhaps it is more accurate (and less clichéd) to put it the other way around: that the "public" philosophical and the "public" political are personal through and through. When we phrase the relationship in this way, we emphasize that, as Jean Baudrillard has suggested, the "private" is also the name for the cultural, the material-historical, the social, the familial institutions, the enculturating symbolic and rhetorical structures, in short, the very linguistic-conceptual systems that constitute a person.

Hence the importance of an autobiography like Ernesto Galarza's. What we read in *Barrio Boy* is an implicit critique of precritical ideologies that support the myth of innocently separable "private" and "public" roles of the self. The interior self that Galarza describes does not exist in empty space but in an organic human collective, in what he calls *la raza*. For this reason, the self Galarza lays bare is not something alienated, exiled from itself. It is his own native folk. "To be exterior meant to be for others, for the collective, for one's own people," says Bakhtin in reference to a certain kind of classical autobiography (1981, 135). We might say that from Galarza's perspective, to be for the collective meant also to be for oneself.

I would add only one further point to the comparison I have offered of the two autobiographies. This has to do with the ideologies implicit in the two texts. Both tell their stories as "educations" about "society." But one, Rodriguez's, implies that "education" and "society" stand against each other undialectically, with education standing as the valuative term, directing its critique and its lessons for transforming society from somewhere "outside" the social space and therefore free from the contaminating things it would change. In this view, Frank Lentricchia has argued, society is a function of the educated individual's intentional actions (1983, 4–5). The educated individual is thus seen as an unsituated, self-created function of nothing at all. Rodriguez's uncritical celebration of the autonomous individual is perhaps the most obvious expression of his investment in the American middle-class myth of individuality.

Locating subjectivity outside sociohistorical reality, Rodriguez cannot conceive of a form of subjectivity that would draw upon existing social practice, the life of the collective folk (of *la raza*), for an alternative critical society. When read against Galarza's life story, however, Rodriguez's undialectical opposition between self and society demands dialectical integration. That Rodriguez has been embraced by the liberal American media and by the humanistic academy while Galarza has not tells us much about the socializing function of education and about the political ideologies that operate within American higher education, from its freshman composition courses to its graduate seminars on autobiography. *Hunger of Memory* is a perfect example of our tendency to disguise the force of ideology behind the mask of aesthetics.

Against the ideology of individualized self-interest, we can read other stories, real American stories like Ernesto Galarza's that tell us something else: that the act of knowing and writing the self is an act of critical consciousness, an act of knowing oneself as a product of historical processes that can be interrogated, interpreted, and perhaps even changed. It is impossible not to see in stories such as this a repudiation of the imposition of Prospero upon Caliban, or of the false insularity of the "private" and the "public" selves, or even of an Ariel-like acquiescence to the master magicians who control us with their books.

8

The Dialectics of Subjectivity

Gender and Difference in Isabella Ríos, Sandra Cisneros, and Cherríe Moraga

Our discussion of contemporary Chicano narrative has not been intended as an exhaustive one. The contributions of Miguel Méndez, Alejandro Morales, John Rechy, Arturo Islas, Alberto Ríos, Max Martínez, Dagoberto Gilb, and Genaro González, for instance, will need to be included when the full literary history of Chicano narrative comes to be written. These authors constitute an alternative to the writers with whom we have dealt.

But no study of Chicano narrative, not even one attempting as this one does only to outline the topography, the "imaginative geography" (Said 1979, 59) of a generic history of Chicano narrative forms, would be complete without a consideration of the most vibrant new development in Chicano literature, the emergence of a significant body of works by women authors in the 1970s and 1980s. While scholars have identified works by male authors dating from the mid-nineteenth century, until recently, texts by nineteenth- and early-twentieth-century women writers have not been readily available. Archival work is now rediscovering a whole body of texts by Chicana writers of the nineteenth century and adding their contributions to the literary history of Chicano literature.[1]

---

1. Groundbreaking work is currently being done by Chicana and Chicano scholars to modify the traditional misperception that Chicanas did not produce significant literatures until the postmovement era. Ongoing research by Clara Lomas, for example, has revealed that "not only were women actively writing [before the Movement years], but they were also publishing their work. Many of the women's writings can be located in the Spanish language newspapers, published in the Southwest from as early as 1870." Lomas adds that "with these findings, we can begin to piece together a first coherent narrative of women's writings from 1870–1970" (1985). In an essay entitled "Mexican Precursors of Chicana Feminist Writing," Lomas identifies five women "who used their fiery pens to write of the ideas of their times" along the Texas-

Reasons for the continued exclusion of women writers from the history of Chicano narrative are as complex as are the reasons for the sexism of any other literary tradition.[2] We will examine the nature of this exclusion as we discuss specific texts. Before we proceed to this discussion, however, it is useful to bring to the forefront the critical and theoretical presuppositions that have guided this study. As crucial as an understanding of these theoretical presuppositions is for

Mexican border (forthcoming). See also Lomas' translation and discussion of a work by one of these writers, Leonor Villegas de Magnon (1989). Juanita Luna-Lawhn notes the presence of late-nineteenth-century Mexican women writers in the important San Antonio Spanish-language newspaper, *La Prensa* (1986).

Archival work by Genaro Padilla (1985) at the Bancroft Library of the University of California, Berkeley, has revealed as many as forty volumes of memoirs, collections of letters, and autobiographical narratives by nineteenth-century Chicana writers, none of which to date have been comprehensively studied. See also, the excellent anthology of essays by Adelaida R. del Castillo, *Between Borders: Essays on Mexicana/Chicana History* (1988). Clearly, the history of Chicana writings has only just been broached.

2. The bibliography of Chicana feminism is now extensive and profound. I cite representative writings that have influenced the course of my own work: Marta Cotera, *Diosa y Hembra* (1976); *Essays on La Mujer*, ed. Rosaura Sánchez and Rosa Martinez Cruz (1977); *This Bridge Called My Back: Writings by Radical Women of Color*, ed. Cherríe Moraga and Gloria Anzaldúa (1983); *Chicana Voices: Intersections of Class, Race, and Gender*, ed. Teresa Córdova et al. (1986); *Chicana Creativity and Criticism: Charting New Frontiers in American Literature*, ed. María Hererra-Sobek and Helena María Viramontes (1988); *Between Borders: Essays on Mexicana/Chicana History*, ed. Adelaida R. del Castillo (1988); Norma Alarcón, "Chicana's Feminist Literature: A Re-vision Through Malintzín/or Malintzín: Putting Flesh Back on the Object" (1983), "Making 'Familia' From Scratch: Split Subjectivities in the Work of Helena María Viramontes and Cherríe Moraga" (1988), and "The Sardonic Powers of the Erotic in the Work of Ana Castillo" (1989); Alvina Quintana, "Women: Prisoners of the Word" (1986), and "Chicana Motifs: Challenge and Counter-Challenge" (1988); Norma Cantú, "Women, Then and Now: An Analysis of the Adelita Image versus the Chicana as Political Writer and Philosopher" (1986); Gloria Anzaldúa, *Borderlands/La Frontera: The New Mestiza* (1987), and "Speaking in Tongues: A Letter to Third World Women Writers" (1983). José David Saldívar, "The Limits of Cultural Studies" (1989), offers a fine discussion of Anzaldúa's feminist cultural critique.

Additionally, Rosaura Sánchez, "Ethnicity, Ideology and Academia" (1987); Tey Diana Rebolledo, "The Politics of Poetics: Or, What Am I, A Critic, Doing in This Text Anyhow?" (1988); Yvonne Yarbro-Bejarano, "Chicana Literature from a Chicana Feminist Perspective" (1988); and Ellen McCracken, "Sandra Cisneros' *The House on Mango Street*: Community-Oriented Introspection and the Demystification of Patriarchal Violence" (1989) are important discussions. Barbara Harlow offers an excellent statement on the place of Chicana writings among Third World women's struggles in "Sites of Struggle: Immigration, Deportation, Prison and Exile" (forthcoming). An especially important comprehensive statement on the status of Chicana feminism is Sonia Saldívar-Hull's, "Feminism on the Border: From Gender Politics to Geopolitics" (forthcoming).

the interpretation of Chicano texts in general, a self-conscious analysis of our own interpretive methods becomes even more important for the male critic as he tries to read texts by women authors.

Contemporary Chicana writers challenge not only the ideologies of oppression of the Anglo-American culture that their Chicano brothers confront, but they also challenge the ideologies of patriarchal oppression evinced by Chicano writers and present within Chicano culture itself. If Chicano narrative is, as we have claimed throughout this study, a perfect case study of the work of ideologies that are not simply counterhegemonic but truly oppositional and revolutionary, then the literature produced by Chicana authors is counterhegemonic to the second power, serving as a critique of critiques of oppression that fail to take into account the full range of domination. This metacritical function of Chicana narrative makes this new body of texts doubly differential and dialectical and of great significance to anyone interested in the literatures of the Americas and in the theories that respond to them. To understand how and why this is so, we must return to the issue of dialectics and how it aids in the construction of socially symbolic acts of resistance to oppressive class, race, and gender structures within contemporary culture.

To this point we have discussed Chicano narrative and the constructed identity of the Chicano subject as a function of the deconstructed "difference" of various binary oppositions. We may begin to approach contemporary Chicana narrative by noting that Adorno begins *Negative Dialectics* (1966), his study of the concept of identity, with the Hegelian idea of identity between subject and object. Adorno's book is marked by the modern experience of the world, an experience that cannot easily ascertain the primacy of the subject or of its romantic desire for identity with the objective world. A *negative* dialectic does not claim that the allure of transcendental unity of subject and object, self and other, in a transfiguring coalescence is no longer desirable. But it does negate the possibility of an ultimate synthesis of subject and object in every conceivable concrete situation that might arise before it.

Adorno sees this transcendental unity of self and other as a contradiction because this identification lifts the conceptualized object into a spiritual idea (a kind of Kantian *ding-an-sich* as intelligible being). "To think is to identify," says Adorno (5). Yet, in thinking, that is to say, in identifying, we necessarily negate what cannot be entirely negated, the objective quality of the conceptualized object.

Identity is a contradiction; it is, in Adorno's terms, "non-identity under the aspect of identity" (5). And it is then the work of dialectics to derive and emphasize the persistence of nonidentity within identity. Within the desire for reconciliations and syntheses, it endeavors to uphold the power and value of multiplicity, diversity, and difference, the instantiation of nonidentity within identity. From this vantage point, subject and object "are not positive, primary states of fact but negative throughout," claims Adorno (174). They constitute one another as much as they differ from each other.

In opposition to a positive identity, fixed, nameable, absolute, and self-satisfied in its stability, the kind of identity that Hegelian or pre-Marxist thought had postulated, Adorno offers a negative dialectic that proposes a critique of "every self-absolutizing particular" (406), even the absolute notion of the self as an autonomous, independent entity. Adorno points out the otherness within the self and the incessant presence of the self in the other. It should now begin to be apparent why I have gone so far afield from my topic of Chicano narrative. The notion of a positive, central identity is the bedrock of hegemonic bourgeois-humanist ideological systems because a fixed identity can be persuaded, coerced, and ultimately, controlled. An unfixed, decentered identity alters the pattern by which a society must position the subject so that "it shall freely submit to its subjection" (Althusser 1969, 182). In various forms, each of the texts we have discussed to this point have offered versions of such a decentered notion of subjectivity and of the ways it resists hegemonic manipulation, as identity is spread out along the collective axis of organic community life.

Identity in Chicano narrative reveals the dialectical tension explained by the work of Adorno. From this perspective, identity in Chicano narrative is not unified and linear; still less is it created along the Hegelian lines of synthesis and reconciliation. Rather—and this is the reason for our digression into Hegel, Marx, and Adorno—subjective identity, as we have seen throughout this study, tends to be complexly dialectical, without coalescence or synthesis. It establishes itself continuously on the unstable borderline of difference between Mexican and American social ideologies and expresses itself as the historical working out of the contradictions implicit in both the Mexican and the American ethical, cultural, and political economies. Chicano subjectivity as represented in the works of fiction we have discussed is both Mexican and American and also neither one nor the other, completely. It remains on that precarious utopian margin between the two, perhaps as the very sign of marginality institu-

tionalized in geopolitical terms by the border between the sovereign
states of Mexico and the United States.

Now in the writings of Chicana authors, dialectics works to undo
not only the presumptive permanence and sovereignty of abstract
binary oppositions, but of decidedly material bodily forms as well.
The writings of Chicana authors advance the resistance to dominant
ideologies initiated by male authors by adding both male/female and
hetero-/homosexual binarisms to the discussion of the social construction of a Chicano identity, insisting with radical poststructuralist feminist theories that an "identity politics" that does not account
for the social construction of gender and sexual orientation merely
reproduces the hierarchies of oppression implicit in bourgeois Anglo-
American society. Chicana writers are thus building an instructive
alternative to the exclusively phallocentric subject of contemporary
Chicano narrative.

The texts by Chicana authors with which I wish to conclude my
study of Chicano narrative bear witness to the "dialectics of difference," to subjectivity in process attempting to resist the absolutiz-
ing tendencies of a racist, classist, patriarchal bourgeois world that
founds itself on the notion of a fixed and positive identity and on
specified gender roles based on this positive fixation. In the cases of
the writers to whom we now turn, the acts of symbolic resistance
that these authors compose are aimed not exclusively at the dominant Anglo culture. They also speak to the harsh oppressiveness,
an oppression within oppression, that women face in the day-to-day
world of male-centered Mexican American society as they live out
between worlds, cultures, and histories what Sonia Saldívar-Hull has
elegantly termed their "feminism on the Border" (1989).

Quite apart from the cultural, racial, and political tensions that
arise in the economy of the subject as represented in the writings
of Chicano male authors, in works such as Isabella Ríos' *Victuum*
(1976), Sandra Cisneros' *The House on Mango Street* (1983), and
Cherríe Moraga's *Loving in the War Years: lo que nunca pasó por
sus labios* (1983), we find the additional clashes precipitated by questions of gender and sexual orientation. For Chicana writers the very
form and nature of "identity" itself is put into question. Allied with
unity, integrity, oneness, and the desire for an organic political collectivity in the writings of male authors, in the texts to which we
now turn the question of the identity of Chicana "identity" (who
constructs it? how is it constructed? to what ends?) reveals multiple
and sometimes contradictory answers.

Victuum

Isabella Ríos' novel *Victuum*[3] is certainly one of the strangest pieces of writing ever done by a Mexican American author, male or female. The novel is not written in the tradition of belles lettres, a finely crafted stylistic masterpiece like Richard Rodriguez's *Hunger of Memory*. In fact, its prose is rough, primitive, certainly naive in its appearance. And yet, the novel is technically a tour de force in its almost total rejection of traditional narrative procedure. We have already seen that narrative experimentation is one of the hallmarks of Chicano fiction. Ríos' novel supports this view with a vengeance. For three hundred and forty-five pages of text the novel avoids diegetic narrative—narration pure and simple where the narrator describes people, places, or settings in indirect voice—in favor of mimetic narrative, where the characters speak for themselves, as themselves, with no narrative interruption or mediation whatsoever (Genette 1980, 162–64). There is virtually no narrative *telling* in this text of almost uninterrupted narrative *showing*, for *Victuum* is a novel of pure dialogue.

Except for the first two pages of the novel, where the main character, Valentina Ballesternos, is describing her own birth as she is in the process of being born, and a few pages at the end of the novel, where Valentina experiences a supernatural tour of time and space, there are no expository sections, no descriptive passages, no narrative commentary whatsoever in the text. We are as if in a disembodied world where only voices exist to denominate the presence of dematerialized minds or spirits. We gradually do come to know the main characters of the novel very well, but oddly enough, we hardly get to know what they look like, since there are few expository passages in the text. Tomás Rivera and Rolando Hinojosa have done something like this in portions of their novels, but not to the extent that Isabella Ríos does. The family of Adolfo and Isabella Ballesternos and their seven children, six daughters and one son, parade before us transparently, present only as incarnate words.

Part 1 of the novel is a "realistic" portrait of the familiar world of small-town Oxnard, California, over the period roughly from 1925 to 1965. The difference between this and the other Chicano novels dealt with thus far is the feminine perspective we are offered in *Victuum*.

3. Isabella Ríos (Diane López), *Victuum* (Ventura: Diana-Etna, 1976). Page references are to this edition of the text. See Lomelí (1980b, 49–61) for an interesting interview with the author and (1985a, 29–46) for a discussion of the novel's narrative procedures. Lomelí claims that with this text the Chicano novel moves away from "a more conscious ideology of culture [to] a concentration on the person."

Whereas in other Chicano novels we face a male-oriented culture from the central point of view of a sensitive son attempting to revalidate the lost world of his father's principles, Ríos gives us that same world from the margins. The boy heroes of other Chicano novels are at the center of their father's and mother's concerns and sometimes, in their enlightened adulthood, become the sympathetic narrators of women's lives. In *Victuum*, the women speak. Valentina is a younger daughter, self-effacing and far removed from the central concerns of the family. She is not especially privileged, as is her brother, or especially talented in any way, as are her older sisters, whose worth is validated by the fact that they are adept in the traditional skills— they sew, cook, and sing with special flair. But Valentina does share a mysteriously spiritual tie with her mother. And therein lies a tale.

Valentina's story is not a classically Freudian one, where identity is fixed in relation to the father's living presence. In fact, almost the opposite is true. Here, the father is conspicuous by his absence. Adolfo is initially absent from the mundane events depicted in the narrated story, that is, in the bulk of the narrative. He is absent simply because his work takes him away from the home during the day, and this is a home-centered story. A passage taken almost at random from the text gives us a sense of the intensely voiced quality of this narrative and of its focus on the work of the home. In this scene, Valentina and her mother discuss the possibility of field work outside the home, picking walnuts. There is no transition to set the scene, nor any out of it to link the scene to the next one. We get only the voices:

> It's summer now, Mama, and you promised we could go with Estella to pick walnuts!
> Estella, are you finished with your work in the packing house.
> Yes, Mama the work ended with Ma, and I feel there's pretty good money with the walnuts . . . Aunt Lucy started and she says there's a bonus if you stick it out until harvest is over . . . she's going to show us how to pick.
> Well, I don't . . . just think, picking walnuts . . . your hands . . . they'll get ruined . . . you don't know the work!
> Yeah, but I'd like a pair of rough hands holding some money for a change!
> Can I go Mama, with Estella . . . Isa and I . . . please Mama . . . I want to buy some clothes for school . . . next September . . . please Mama!
> Alright, Valentina . . . you too, Isa . . . but you girls better not go and just fool around . . . after all, it is a job . . . Wait a minute just how do you intend to get there . . . will they pick up the workers!
> Mama, Lucero said I could borrow a jalopy he had parked there in his garage . . . (*Victuum* 178–79)

I have transcribed the passage exactly as it appears in the text, ellipses and all. The narrative of the entire novel consists almost exclusively of women's voices, speaking the concerns of being in the everyday world, giving expression to the concrete realities of everyday life. When male voices intrude, it is usually through the mediation of Valentina's concerns or of her sisters' concerns, for the story is exclusively theirs.

Later in the novel, Adolfo's death literally removes him from the narrated world of Valentina's present concerns. Isabella's (the mother's) presence fills the vacuum of patriarchal absence. But oddly, after the father's death the conclave of women that is the Ballesternos household does not become a feminist utopia: the utopian vision comes much later and in a drastically different context. In the earlier sections of the novel, after Adolfo's death and when Isabella is attempting to keep her family together, the mother's allegiance to the role of the traditional "mother" deepens their cultural and economic oppression. Having throughout her lifetime accepted without question an ideology of submission and deference to male authority, Isabella cannot even imagine a world capable of accommodating to women's power. In fact, she becomes even more complicit in maintaining the patriarchal family structure once Adolfo is dead than she had been when he lived. Almost as if in attempting to compensate for the male's absence by imaginatively representing male power in their submission to traditional family patterns, Isabella deliberately has her daughters consciously think and act submissively, meekly, and deferentially, even though they now quite capably perform all of the duties formerly performed by the father. Interestingly enough, therefore, the course of the novel's events represents their oppression, as mother and daughters alone in a male-dominated world, less as a natural phenomenon than as a social one, based on specific historical forces of production and reproduction as the mother becomes an agent of the patriarchy. While the title of the novel, *Victuum*, refers to the name of the supernatural visitor with whose prophecies and visions the novel will end, it also puns readily with the word "victim." One might say that this is the story of Valentina's victimization.

The deference, submission, and passivity Isabella imparts to her daughters, and especially to Valentina, perpetuate patriarchy and the denigration of women among the children of these women. Valentina's story is that of a repetition: she too marries and raises a family. The father-absent, mother-centered Ballesternos family thus produces daughters whose identity can be conceived only in terms of the subject position of the traditional mother. It also produces a son whose own subject position prepares him for his future role

as a father in the traditional economy of production and reproduction.[4] And now we have come back to my original point about dialectics: dialectics teaches us that it is in the other that subjectivity
is realized, not internally, biologically, but externally and socially as
a historical event. The mother is a figure for whom, from the child's
perspective, otherness does not exist. Identifying its own image in
the body of the mother, that is, on the ground of nonindividuation,
the child constructs an imaginary possibility of oneness.[5]

In the absence of the father, whom the child does see as a separate
being, the child comes to a bitter realization of its self as otherness.
But as Gayatri Chakravorty Spivak points out, "Whatever the political necessity for holding the position, and whatever the advisability
of attempting to 'identify' (with) the other as subject in order to know
her, knowledge is made possible and is sustained by irreducible difference, not identity" (1987, 254). What Freud once said about dream
analysis might just as well apply to narrative analysis: that is, that
what remains unsaid is often as important as what is said. Ríos'
novel does not talk about the issues of gender formation or subjective identification in theoretical terms. But everywhere in the novel
these issues are represented for us.

Ríos depicts the differential quality of the gendered subject intu-
itively, representing the precritical stage of Chicana writing where,
as in Anaya's *Bless Me, Ultima*, the political remains deeply repressed within the insular confines of the unhistoricized ego and the
fetishized family, which is seen as "the only source of society's labor
force" (Vogel 1983, 142). In *Victuum*, Valentina and Isabella become
almost extensions of one self, especially after Isabella's death when
she actually returns to haunt Valentina's spiritual life. But even before this mysterious unity occurs, the two have had a deeper identification and a more prolonged "symbiosis" than any male-female pair
in the novel seems capable of producing. This symbiosis, literally a
living together of two distinct selves, a dialectic of self and other in

4. See Barbara Johnson, "My Monster / My Self" (1982), Elizabeth L. Berg, "The
Third Woman" (1982), and Coppélia Kahn, "Excavating 'Those Dim Minoan Regions':
Maternal Subtexts in Patriarchal Literature" (1982).

5. Hélène Cixous and Catherine Clément, *The Newly Born Woman* (1986); and
Feminist Theory: A Critique of Ideology, ed. Nannerl O. Keohane et al. (1981). See
also Lise Vogel, *Marxism and the Oppression of Women: Toward a Unitary Theory*
(1983). The crucial counterstatements to the work of traditional American feminism and revisionary French feminism are Gayatri Chakravorty Spivak's discussion
of feminism, Marxism, psychoanalysis and deconstruction in "Feminism and Critical
Theory" (1987), and "Displacement and the Discourse of Woman" (1983).

progress between the mother and the daughter, goes a long way in explaining the more radical dissolution of the boundaries between one ego and another, or indeed between an ego and the cosmos, that is Valentina's special fate in the concluding section of the novel.

In that final section, we find Valentina living in 1950s southern California suburbia, the mother of eight children of her own. Her natural empathy becomes the source of a curious sort of telepathy and ultimately of a kind of supernatural entelechy. Bakhtin has argued that certain kinds of biographical time are intensely specific. Some biographical temporalities do disclose character but do not allow for the "becoming" of character. In these special kinds of biography "character is predetermined and may be disclosed only in a single defined direction" (1981, 141). Historical reality in these cases is deprived of any determining influence on character and becomes instead only the vehicle for the manifestation of character. In works such as Arias' *The Road to Tamazunchale* or in contemporary postcolonial narratives such as Salman Rushdie's *Midnight's Children*, characters often use extraordinary individual magical, spiritual, or telepathic powers as links to the broad realms of transindividual world political history. The trajectory of Valentina's life story, however, leads precisely into *ahistorical* realms, as she cruises time and space in the company of a prototypical Ur-patriarch, the titular character Victuum, who discloses to Valentina the ideal forms of subjectivity. Escaping the grim confines of American life in the 1950s, Valentina finds herself at home in the narcissistic transindividuality of science fiction.

Baudrillard has argued that the concept of the "subject" must be considered in terms of the economic notion of the "individual." "The individual is an ideological structure, a historical form correlative with the commodity form (exchange value), and the object form (use value). The individual is nothing but the subject thought in economic terms, rethought, simplified, and abstracted by the economy. The entire history of consciousness and ethics (all the categories of occidental psycho-metaphysics) is only the history of the political economy of the subject" (1981, 133). Valentina's flight to nowhere in the company of the symbolic Father offers readers, potentially and schematically, if read dialectically and across the grain of its represented terms, a way of reading the Chicano experience in terms that are highly critical of traditional Chicano patriarchal culture. Doubly oppressed within postindustrial American life and traditional Chicano culture of the postwar and premovement era, set up to live within the parameters of class, race, and gender restrictions, Valentina turns away from history, merges with her dead mother, and invents a symbolic paradigm of the male saviour. ??

Victuum offers a dramatic rendition of Baudrillard's critique of the political economy of the subject. Valentina's recognition of the other in her self and of herself in the other begins the disruption of the sovereignty of identity. This economy of the subject then becomes a dialectical play for dispelling the essentialist myth of the unitary subject. *Victuum* represents one character's choice: whether to perpetuate the myths of the present by accepting the given world as "truth," or to employ a dialectical, critical negation to articulate its truth as untruth, applying consciousness, as Benjamin suggests, against the grain of history in order to demystify it and break its spell. That Valentina herself remains bound within the nets of false consciousness that have formed her as a subject by choosing to live her hegemonic dreams is not a sign of the novel's failure. Rather, it signals the coming positive critiques of the dominant society and of the traditional Chicano patriarchy by a whole generation of Mexican American women writers.

The House on Mango Street

Of primary importance among these emerging critiques of the patriarchy in both its Anglo and Chicano forms is Sandra Cisneros' collection of forty-four vignettes narrated from the perspective of a young Chicana named Esperanza. Winner of the Before Columbus Foundation's American Book Award for 1985, *The House on Mango Street* represents from the simplicity of childhood vision the enormously complex process of the construction of the gendered subject.[6] Posing the question of sexual difference within the urban working-class Chicano community, Cisneros' novel also emphasizes the crucial

6. Sandra Cisneros, *The House on Mango Street* (Houston: Arte Público Press, 1983). Page references are to this edition of the text. In an essay entitled "From a Writer's Notebook," (1987), Cisneros notes that her idea for the novel crystalized in a class discussion of Gaston Bachelard's *The Poetics of Space* at the Iowa Writers Workshop. See Julián Olivares' discussion of this aspect of Cisneros' work, "Sandra Cisneros' *The House on Mango Street*, and the Poetics of Space" (1988). See McCracken (1989) for an excellent discussion of patriarchal violence in Cisneros' work. My own discussion touches on both the questions of domestic space and patriarchal violence but is more concerned with the political economy of domestic space as the scene of sexual oppression. Cisneros offers illuminating discussions of her work and her status as a "minority" writer in "Writing Out of Necessity: An Interview with Sandra Cisneros" and in "Living as a Writer: Choice and Circumstance," both in *The Feminist Writers Guild* (1987).

roles of racial and material as well as ideological conditions of oppression. It thus helps establish what over the course of the 1980s
will become a virtual program for writings by Chicanas, namely, a
clear-sighted recognition of the unavoidably mutual overdetermina-
tion of the categories of race and class with that of gender in any
attempted positioning of the Chicana subject.

The title story of the collection places the child Esperanza immediately in the narrativized space and time of a street in one of the
contemporary Chicano barrios of a large American city, presumably
Chicago.

> We didn't always live on Mango Street. Before that we lived on Loomis
> on the third floor; and before that we lived on Keeler. Before Keeler it was
> Paulina, and before that I can't remember. But what I remember most is
> moving a lot.
> . . . We had to leave the flat on Loomis quick. The water pipes broke and
> the landlord wouldn't fix them because the house was too old. We had to
> leave fast. We were using the washroom next door and carrying water over
> in empty milk gallons. (HMS 7)

Like Galarza's first attempts sixty years earlier to fix an identity
for himself by symbolically mapping his new Sacramento surroundings in *Barrio Boy*, Esperanza uses the chronotopes of the house and
the street to denote the ideological and material subject positions
that the characters of her stories will occupy. Each of the episodes
of her tale will refer to these organizing figures, as the child questions the nature of the economy of the domestic, its *oikonomia*, in its
public and private spheres.[7] The chronotope of the house and its met-
onymically linked figure of the street refer, consequently, less to a
poetics of space than to the mutually overdetermining spheres of the
private and the social, for as Gayatri Spivak points out, "The *oikos*
is fully a metaphor for the *polis*" (1987, 252). Having been made to
feel ashamed of her former house on Loomis Street (and thus of her
entire social and subject position) by a nun from her school, the child
yearns for "a real house. One I could point to," all the while realizing
that "the house on Mango Street isn't it" (9). The narratives of identity that follow reveal, however, that the child's dream of a bourgeois

---

7. Etymologically, the meaning of "economy" is derived from the Greek *oikonomia*
and *oikonomos*, "one who manages a household." The wider senses of "economy" as
the practical science of managing the resources of a nation, and as the theoretical science of dealing with the laws that regulate the production and distribution of wealth,
i.e., *political* economy, derive from the original practice of the *domestic* economy.
OED, s.v. "economy."

white house "with trees around it, a great big yard and grass growing without a fence" (8) is not an accession to middle-class values,
but something quite different. In an essay on "Cognitive Mapping,"
Jameson argues that the space of classical or market capitalism may
be described "in terms of a logic of the grid, a reorganization of some
older sacred and heterogeneous space into geometrical and Cartesian
homogeneity" (1988, 349). Here, the spatialized temporalities of barrio life, figured in the tropes of the "house" and the "street," stand
against the attempted institutionalization of the subject into the
"geometrical and Cartesian homogeneity" of contemporary society.

While domestic narratives have traditionally delineated the space
of the house as the preeminent symbol of the privatized, sovereign,
and individual self, plotted and fixed topographically onto a terrain
of white male values, the mapping of the domestic economy in Cisneros' narratives opens the interiorized space of the house and the
private self to the collective world of work and commerce symbolized by the figure of the street. Jameson goes on to suggest in the
same essay that certain "fundamental realities are somehow ultimately unrepresentable or, to use the Althusserian phrase, are something like an absent cause, one that can never emerge into the presence of perception. Yet this absent cause can find figures through
which to express itself in distorted and symbolic ways" (1988, 350).
The absent cause of the desire for a kind of poetic dwelling that cuts
across the positivist distinctions between private and public housing
hinted at in the first story of Cisneros' novel and developed in later
stories like "A House of My Own," "Bums in the Attic," and "Mango
Says Goodbye Sometimes" is the topic of the narratives of identity
that make up *The House on Mango Street*.

In "A House of My Own" Cisneros' narrator echoes the feminist
plea for "a room of one's own" as a site of poetic self-creation: "Not
a man's house. Not a daddy's. A house all my own . . . a house quiet
as snow, a space for myself to go, clean as paper before the poem"
(*HMS* 100). But private self-creation is not the point of the "house"
tropes, as "Bums in the Attic" makes clear. Aside from the personal
requirement of a gendered woman's space, Esperanza recognizes the
collective requirements of the working poor and the homeless as
well. Dreaming of a house on a hill like the ones with the gardens
that her father tends for the ruling classes, Esperanza says:

One day I'll own my own house, but I won't forget who I am or where I
came from. Passing bums will ask, Can I come in? I'll offer them the attic,
ask them to stay, because I know how it is to be without a house.

Some days after dinner, guests and I will sit in front of a fire. Floorboards
will squeak upstairs. The attic grumble.
    Rats? they'll ask.
    Bums, I'll say, and I'll be happy. (*HMS* 81)

Incapable of imagining a house without rats in the attic, and naively
accepting the derogatory epithet "bums" for all street people, the
child innocently combines the features of a cognac advertisement
with a scene from a shelter for the homeless. But as in "A House
of My Own," the trope of the house is a pretext for alluding to the
more fundamental reality of the necessity for a decent living space
that is expansively open to victims and agents of current history.
The three luminous faces depicted on the paper cover of Cisneros'
book, formed by and imbued with the dynamic motion of the trans-
actional cityscape, represent just such an *oikonomia* of mutuality, of
differentially conjoined public and private living spaces, like the one
that Esperanza here suggests.

The concluding chapter of the novel, "Mango Says Goodbye Sometimes," emphasizes even more starkly the child's awareness of the
connections between the privately created self and its public responsibilities:

One day I will pack my bags of books and paper. One day I will say goodbye
to Mango . . .
    Friends and neighbors will say, What happened to that Esperanza? Where
did she go with all those books and paper? . . .
    They will not know I have gone away to come back. For the ones I left
behind. For the ones who cannot get out. (102)

Each of these stories narrates Esperanza's negotiations with the realities of working-class life. They also speak to the link between artistic
creation and a kind of poetic self-creation that is not separated out as
an individual imperative but is conditioned by its ineluctable tie to
the community. Other chapters add to the issue of individual artistry
and collective responsibility the overriding concerns for the woman
artist of gender and sexual power.

In "The Family of Little Feet," for example, Esperanza's mother
gives her and her friends three pairs of old high-heeled shoes. Now
the subject-self that the girls create is one that must transact beyond the domestic *oikos* into the commercial *polis*. But in turning
to the commercial economy of the street and street life outside the
house, the girls come unwittingly face to face with the contours of
their prescribed roles as players in the sexual economy. Wearing the
high heels, the little girls find themselves magically transformed like

Cinderella into elegantly latent sexual beings: "We have legs. Skinny and spotted with satin scars where scabs were picked, but legs, all our own, good to look at, and long" (38). Experimenting with their new roles, they learn to "strut in those magic high heels," to "cross and uncross" their legs, and to "walk down to the corner where the men can't take their eyes off us" (38). The transformation from little girl to seductive child-woman is so successful and alluring that Mr. Benny, the corner grocer, challenges the girls about the shoes, telling them that the shoes are "dangerous." "You girls too young to be wearing shoes like that," he says. Offended by the children's violation of the line separating girlish play from woman's sexuality and ready to marshal the power of the state apparatus to keep sexuality safely leashed, the grocer warns them to "take them shoes off before I call the cops" (38). As the girls "just keep strutting," the grocer's scandalized response to the girls' footwear and role-playing is justified when a passing boy, using another kind of tactic in men's war of position against women's sexuality, calls out lewdly to the girls: "Ladies, lead me to heaven" (38). A "bum man" in front of the tavern stops them and grotesquely combines symptoms of pedophilia with podophilia as he fetishizes their nascent sexuality by framing his desire for them in commodity terms, offering them "a dollar" for "a kiss": "Your little lemon shoes are so beautiful . . . What's your name, pretty girl?" (39).

"Tired of being beautiful" (40), the girls return home and throw away their innocent toys that have turned out to be all too readily the implements of a sexual power structure the girls at this point only dimly perceive. In their short foray down Mango Street, Esperanza and her friends experience the various ways in which female sexuality is defined, constrained, coerced by patriarchal society and the state apparatus, and then plotted into the same narrow "geometrical and Cartesian homogeneity" that determines the social horizon they inhabit.

"Sally" is one of several chapters in a sequence about a "girl with eyes like Egypt and nylons the color of smoke" whose father thinks that "to be this beautiful is trouble" (77). Esperanza wishes to be like Sally, wishes to learn to flick her hair when she laughs, to "paint [her] eyes like Cleopatra," and to wear black suede shoes and matching nylons as Sally does. But as with other beautiful women on Mango Street whose houses are not sanctuaries of private space but rather confining prisons in which they are locked by their fathers or husbands or brothers because their beauty is "dangerous," Sally's most intimate sense of herself is not her own to determine. "And why do you always have to go straight home after school?" asks Esperanza. "You become a different Sally . . . You don't laugh, Sally. You look at your feet and walk fast to the house you can't come out from" (78).

Responding to Sally's dreams of wanting "to love and to love and to love" (79), Esperanza faces the grim reality of male sexual domination in "Red Clowns." Waiting to meet Sally at an amusement park, Esperanza is assaulted by three white boys. "Sally, you lied," cries Esperanza. "They all lied. All the books and magazines, everything told it wrong. Only his dirty fingernails against my skin, only his sour smell again. . . . He wouldn't let me go. He said I love you, I love you, Spanish girl" (94). Esperanza's brutal encounter with male power adds the vulgarity of racial politics to the horror of sexual politics. Esperanza sees that the ideologies of romantic love serve as the propaganda for the maintenance of the sexual economy that makes women like Sally and Esperanza victims merely because they are women. But in the shared experiences with women like Sally, or Rafaela who is locked up because she is too beautiful, or Minerva who writes poems on slips of paper that her husband will not find, or Alicia who stays up late after her family is asleep to study and write, preeminently *economists* all, Cisneros helps create an alternate space for the Chicana subject, one that is not subjected by the geometrical homogeneity of contemporary patriarchal culture.

Put in the overtly political context of women's oppression, Cisneros' children's stories emphasize that living space and writing time are, as Jacqueline Rose suggests, "not marginal issues in relation to the question of political change, but are terms through which the issue *of* marginality—of how a political critique should best place itself in relation to dominant institutions—is being played out" (1987, 10). Their collective histories speak what one character, a *comadre* (a godmother, but literally, a comother) of Esperanza's friend Lucy, will later say to Esperanza: "When you leave you must remember to come back for the others. A circle, you understand? You will always be Mango Street. You can't erase what you know: You can't forget who you are" (98).

Loving in the War Years: lo que nunca pasó por sus labios

If I were abiding strictly by the law of genre, my discussion of Moraga's work would properly take place in the context of the earlier discussion of Chicano autobiography, instead of serving as the concluding piece to a chapter on women's writings. Separating it out to discuss it with other works by Chicana authors has the possible (though unintended) effect of marginalizing Moraga's autobiography, or worse, of seeming to contain her powerful critique of the Anglo patriarchy, of counterhegemonic middle-class feminisms, and of the Chicano sexist oppression of women within the confines of a neu- *yes, well —* tralizing token gesture. It also leaves the earlier discussion of Rodriguez's and Galarza's autobiographical texts untouched by questions addressing the sociohistoric processes involved in the formation of the gendered Chicano subject. While the tracing out of the gaps and silences in Chicano texts concerning men's sexual orientation, their sense of gender roles, and their oppression of women is a subject demanding a book-length analysis in its own right, I have tried to sketch out the preliminary borders of that theoretical terrain within a race and class analysis of Chicano writings.

Moraga's book demands that we make such implicit questions explicit as it everywhere represents the marginalization of Chicanas, rejects a facile and precritical union with men, and works instead to celebrate the alliance of women with women. *Loving in the War Years* raises precisely to the foreground issues alluded to but not theorized in *Victuum* and *The House on Mango Street*. It speaks powerfully to the marginalized issues of sexuality, fills the dehis- *?* cences at the center of texts by male writers, and dares to name, as the subtitle of her autobiography puts it, "what was not uttered by their lips." Representing the absent subject of other texts, Moraga's autobiography seeks to define for Chicanas a conceptual space that is not a priori enmeshed in the ideological systems denoted by white patriarchal culture, by the white feminist opposition to that culture, by the Chicano male resistance to Anglo hegemony, or even by heterosexual Chicana feminists. I have thus felt that placing *Loving in the War Years* too readily in dialogue with male discourses before allowing it to voice its different concerns could belie its singularly refractive spirit.

The combative nature of Moraga's version of resistance acknowledges from the first the difficulty and the costs of the Gramscian "war of position" (1971, 229–39) in which women of color are engaged against the patriarchy during the uncivil "war years" of everyday life in postindustrial capitalism. A prisoner of war in the class, racial, and sexual struggle with and against Chicano men, with and against the dominant Anglo culture, with and against white feminisms, Moraga begins her life story by offering a parable on the politics of love:

Sueño [Dream]
My lover and I are in a prison camp together.
We are in love in wartime.

A young soldier working as a guard has befriended us.
*We ask him honestly—the truth—*are we going to die?

He answers, yes, it's almost certain. I contemplate escaping. Ask him to help us. He blanches. That is impossible, *he says. I regret asking him, fearing recriminations.*

I see the forest through the fence on my right. I think, the place between the trees—I could burrow through there—toward freedom? Two of us would surely be spotted. One of us has a slim chance. I think of leaving my lover, imprisoned. But immediately I understand that we must, at all costs, remain with each other. Even unto death. That it is our being together that makes the pain, even our dying, human.

Loving in the war years.[8]

Covering a span of seven years from 1976 to 1983 and published contemporaneously with Richard Rodriguez's *Hunger of Memory*, Moraga's *Loving in the War Years* is on one level a bilingual chronicle of the author's psycho-sexual debut, her coming "out-to-the-world," as she puts it, about her lesbianism. It is also a heterogeneously patterned text, part political manifesto, part dispatch from the frontlines, and part love poem, that self-consciously breaks the laws of the autobiographical genre as it builds "a kind of emotional/political chronology" (*LWY* i). Unlike Rodriguez's work, which preciously cultivates a private sense of self from the anguish he feels over his separation and difference from the public white world he would serve, Moraga's autobiography disrupts facile conceptions of a private and a public self as she constructs her life story amid the historical conditions, material circumstances, the analytical categories of race, class, and gender that are the crucial mechanisms in the maintenance of power.

The introductory prose poem signals the issues that will form the life about to be narrated. In the forest clearing stands a prison

8. Cherríe Moraga, *Loving in the War Years: lo que nunca pasó por sus labios* (Boston: South End Press, 1983), i. All references are to this edition of the text. Moraga underscores the urgency of the issues she raises when she notes in a recent interview that "writing as an out lesbian in the 1970s was not a good time to be gay in the Chicano movement at large, or in the Chicano literary movement. For instance, in 1983, when *Loving in the War Years* came out, I left the country because I was very frightened of bringing up the issue of being lesbian and Chicana together within the covers of a book. It is only now, because there is such a strong movement of women writers, some of whom are lesbians but taking on feminist themes, that there is now a community, in which to make that voice public" (1989, 54). My thanks to Diana Fuss for showing me this interview.

camp. An inmate of that camp, the narrator, doomed to die, faces the awful choice of a possible flight to freedom alone, or certain death together with her lover. But in truth, there is no choice: the path of private escape is a path away from human essence; to remain in the prison compound with the lover "makes the pain, even our dying, human." Individual survival, by contrast, seems inhuman. The rest of the autobiography makes manifest the latent terms of this initial allegorical dream sequence, filling out the special meanings of what it means to be relationally human, of "loving in the war years," of prison and the impossibility of escape, and of being implicated in the lives of others (women) at all costs. At stake is the very meaning of the notion of an "individual."

Offering a virtual history of Chicana oppression, Moraga's autobiography addresses the iconic representations of Mexican womanhood. We have mentioned earlier how the central cultural symbols of Mexican femininity juxtapose impossible models of purity (the Virgin of Guadalupe) with monstrous images of depravity (la Llorona), or the traitorous la Malinche against the idealized and reified figures of the ever-loyal camp followers of the Mexican Revolution (the Adelitas).[9] Proceeding from the opening prose poem and the proclamation of her lesbianism, Moraga recalls her own first visit to the Mexican basilica that houses the cloth upon which was miraculously revealed the image of Our Lady of Guadalupe after her appearance on December 9, 1531, to the Indian child, Juan Diego. "I was shocked to see that below it [the portrait of the Virgin of Guadalupe] ran a moving escalator." This "moving sidewalk built to keep the traffic going" is an "irreverence imposed by . . . technology." Still, "the most devout of the Mexican women—las pobres [the poor], few much older than me

9. Of many important discussions of these salient icons of Mexican culture, the classic statement is Eric R. Wolf's, "The Virgin of Guadalupe: A Mexican National Symbol" (1958). Wolf notes that "the Guadalupe symbol thus links together family, politics and religion; colonial past and independent present; Indian and Mexican. It reflects the salient social relationships of Mexican life, and embodies the emotions which they generate. It provides a cultural idiom through which the tenor and emotions of these relationships can be expressed. It is, ultimately, a way of talking about Mexico: a 'collective representation' of Mexican society" (39). Chicanas have noted that what gets lost in the heterogeneity of the symbol's function is its role in bolstering the patriarchy. An excellent revisionary, feminist view of the relationships between the symbolic values of the Virgin of Guadalupe and La Malinche figures is Liliana Valenzuela's Mexico's La Malinche: Mother or Whore, Creator or Traitor? (1988). For a related discussion of the "Adelita" image, see, Norma Cantú, "Women, Then and Now: An Analysis of the Adelita Image versus the Chicana as Political Writer and Philosopher" (1986).

—clung to the ends of the handrailing of the moving floor, crossing themselves, gesturing besos al retrato [kisses at the portrait], their hips banging up against the railing over and over again as it tried to force them off and away. They stayed. In spite of the machine. They had come to spend their time with La Virgen" (ii).

Leaving the church in tears, Moraga feels the "passionate pull" of her Catholic faith "that promised no end to the pain," but seeks to justify the meaningfulness of suffering in the world. "I grew white," she says. "Fought to free myself from my culture's claim on me." The pitiful spectacle of young, impoverished Mexican women struggling against "the machine" to bond again with the dark-skinned virgin, mother of all Mexicans, and symbol of salvation for the oppressed mestizo and Indian populace, causes her to step outside herself and her family "to see what we as a people were suffering." For in that moment chaotically blending images of love, faith, and struggle with the irreverance of technology and the inexorable flow of suffering represented by the moving sidewalk, a virtual allegory and *tableau vivant* of the course of Mexican working-class history, Moraga at one and the same time loses and finds herself: "This is my politics. This is my writing," she claims. Sundered from her culture's claim on her, freed from her religion's pull, and distanced from her family's attempts to define her, she attains "consciousness."

In this case, however, consciousness is consciousness of difference, her sense that she was "born into this world with complications," knowing at ten years old that "she was queer" (ii). But consciousness does not produce either the kind of alienation that Rodriguez blames on his education, or the escape from history that Ríos presents as the solution to women's oppression. Rather, it produces the political poem of her life as she embraces and celebrates her multitudinous difference. Still, acceptance of difference does not diminish the pain of separation that difference implies. For, after all, consciousness of difference "is what has made me the outsider so many Chicanos— very near to me in circumstance—fear" (iii).

Exploring the substance of this fear fostered by difference, Moraga returns to a scene from the family romance, a moment of childhood definition. But here, as in *Victuum*, the moral economy of the family romance is the story of the mothers and their daughters.

I am a child. I watch my mamá, mis tías en una procesión cada día lle-gando a la puerta de mi abuela [my mother, my aunts in a procession arriving daily at my grandmother's door]. Needing her, never doing enough for her. I remember lying on my bed midday. The sun streaming through the long window, thin sheer curtains. Next door I can hear them all. Están peleando [They are arguing]. Mi abuela giving the cold shoulder, not giving in. Each daughter vying for a place with her. The cruel gossip. Las mentiras [The lies]. My mother trying to hold onto the truth, her version of the story, su integridad [her integrity]. (iii)

The untold story of the daughters' competition for the grandmother's favor is less important than the effects of that competition on the young girl who reaches into this past moment as she begins to fashion her own identity in difference. While in the previous scene in the basilica the women fight the technology of crowd control to adore the Virgin mother, in the next scene the daughters contend with one another as they arrive in procession, arguing against each other, as they vie for a place with their mother. Just as the holy mother Catholic Church has enforced on Mexican women a cultural model of passivity and guilt figured in the Virgin of Guadalupe to ensure their allegiance to a transcendental, phallocentric Logos, so the grandmother apparently orchestrates a matrix of "gossip" and "mentiras" as her strategy to maintain her control of the daughters. Against the cold-shouldered indifference of literal and symbolic mothers to the separate and different truths of each daughter's life, Moraga's own mother tries "to hold onto the truth, her version of the story, su integridad." The substance of her life is figured here as a history of integrity that refuses to romanticize the line of descent from grandmother to mother to daughter as a sojourn into the motherland of harmony, but that seeks instead to see it as the problematical site of ambiguous struggle among sedimented levels of conflicting ideologies of the self.

The clean dichotomies represented in the traditional politics of racial and gender categories (whites/others, male/female) and pre-critically synthesized under the paradigm of a presumed universal sisterhood (mother/daughter, Woman/women) will not suffice to describe the cross-cutting and overdetermined realities that make up the life of a lesbian woman of color. Mother-daughter nurturing, the sisterhood of women, the idealization of an essential Woman should not be regarded as transhistorical concepts that uniformly liberate women from oppression but as constructions that acquire specific political meanings at different historical moments and under different economic and racial conditions. Over the course of her autobiography, Moraga will name herself by investigating fully the place of lesbianism and identity politics in the current theories of sexual difference and Third World liberation movements.

In the present scene, as the grandmother lies dying, Moraga continues to lay the groundwork for that analysis by asking, "And what goes with her? My claim to an internal dialogue where el gringo does not penetrate?" A few pages later, Moraga will tell us that "I am the daughter of a Chicana and anglo. I am an embarrassment to both groups" (vi). White-skinned and protected by an Anglo name, Moraga admits that she has come to her ethnicity late, as a by-product of her lesbianism. She thus admits that "I sometimes hate the white in me so viciously that I long to forget the commitment my skin has imposed upon my life. To speak two tongues" (vi). The "internal dialogue" with her mother and grandmother, the dialogic pretext of Moraga's present book, is part of that commitment.

This "internal dialogue" turns out to be very like what Bakhtin has called "dialogized heteroglossia," a verbal ideological nexus of competing unitary/normative and disunifying/decentralizing languages, discourses, rhetorics, dialects, and idioms that do not attain dialectical balance but remain in constant differential tension (1981, 272). Moraga's "internal dialogue" seeks to salvage the grandmother's memory of "a time where 'nuestra cultura' [our culture] was not the subject of debate" (*LWY* iii) and to resituate her identity among women of color. Simultaneously, it staves off the imposition of the word of the white father, by defining a gendered racial space into which he cannot "penetrate." Yet, Moraga fully realizes that, in the present, the debate over "nuestra cultura" rages and that she carries the word of her Anglo father hieroglyphically in the very hue of her light-colored skin. As in the thirteenth book of Augustine's *Confessions*, where he reminds us that we carry "the sublime authority" of Scripture "stretched over us like a skin," here the unitary True Word implied in the canonization of Anglo ideological systems and represented by the father cannot be resisted by an oppositional word that is merely different from the father's unitary language. It must be consciously aimed sharply and polemically against the normative, centralizing implications of the word of the father, referring as it does to a white, middle-class, heterosexual world.

As this initial section of her autobiography draws to a close, Moraga narrates two dreams occurring after her grandmother's death. In the first dream, her grandmother "appears outside la iglesia [the church]" and Moraga is elated to see her. But the grandmother's pain from her surgical wound becomes Moraga's as well: "*The wound is like a huge crater in her calf—crusted, open, a gaping wound. I feel her pain so critically.*" In the second dream, Moraga wishes to photograph her grandmother and mother while a woman awaits her in bed:

"The pull and tug present themselves en mis sueños [in my dreams].
Deseo para las mujeres/la familia [Desire for women/the family]"
(iv). Both dreams answer before the fact the questions that open the
second section: "*Can you go home? Do your parents know? Have*
they read your work?" In fact, all of the conflicted issues raised in the
first pages of the autobiography return now to Moraga's first words
concerning consciousness and difference:

> It is difficult for me to separate in my mind whether it is my writing or
> my lesbianism which has made me an outsider to my family. The obvious
> answer is both. For my lesbianism first brought me into writing. My first
> poems were love poems. That's the source—el amor, el deseo [love, desire]
> —that brought me into politics.

The politics of loving prefigured in the initial scenes of the autobiography and mediated by the writing of the book gradually develop into an aesthetics of resistance, as Moraga explores the racial,
sexual, and class parameters of her conflicted self. In this scene, the
dreams return us to the issues raised in the opening dream of the
prison camp, as we see Moraga struggling with the various images
of other's visions of herself: the church as the sign of the one true
word; the grandmother as a sign of a past cultural-historical integrity; the mother as a sign of intermingled devotion and resistance to
that past; the lover in bed as a sign of the conjoined epistemological
and sexual intercourses that a future moment of achieved integrity
might contain. Desire as freedom from cultural oppression must me-
diate among these various dizzyingly chaotic masses of authoritative
discourses, all of which interpret, praise, apply, qualify, resist, and
even deny it in various ways.

In "Feminism, Marxism, Method, and the State," a powerful critique of the failure of leftist ideologies to account for gender-based
oppression, Katherine MacKinnon argues that

> The personal as political is not a simile, not a metaphor, and not an analogy.
> It does not mean that what occurs in personal life is similar to, or comparable
> with, what occurs in the public arena. It is not an application of categories
> from social life to the private world, as when Engels (followed by Bebel) says
> that in the family the husband is the bourgeois and the wife represents the
> proletariat. It means that women's distinctive experience as women occurs
> within that sphere that has been socially lived as the personal—private,
> emotional, interiorized, particular, individuated, intimate—so that what it
> is to *know* the *politics* of woman's situation is to know women's personal
> lives. . . .
> To say that the personal is political means that gender as a division of
> power is discoverable and verifiable through women's intimate experience of

sexual objectification, which is definitive of and synonymous with women's lives as gender female. Thus, to feminism, the personal is epistemologically the political, and its epistemology is its politics. (1981: 20–21)

MacKinnon's analysis identifies the origins of feminist consciousness and politics with the most intimate and quotidian of women's experience and offers a veritable gloss of Moraga's own initial equation of the private and interior worlds of loving and desiring with political action. In a Lukácsian move, both MacKinnon and Moraga thus name the objectification of women itself as the very source of their possible liberation from oppression, for objectification and the self-awareness of objectification become the motivating principles by which a feminist consciousness might arise.

The nature of women's gender consciousness is developed in the concluding section of Moraga's work, "Lo que nunca pasó por sus labios" ("What never passed her lips"), which includes an essay entitled "A Long Line of Vendidas" ("Sell-outs"). Here Moraga steps beyond the privatized interior quality of feminist consciousness that, in MacKinnon's description, privileges the "personal" as the base upon which the superstructures of epistemology and politics are raised. Moraga wishes to expand the parameters of gender politics to the points where it overlaps with the concerns of class and racial politics.

Arguing that in failing to approach feminism from any kind of materialist base, in failing to take race, ethnicity, and class into account in determining women's sexuality, Moraga insists that "many feminists have created an analysis of sexual oppression (often confused with sexuality itself) which is a political dead-end" (*LWY* 129). Essentializing the notion of the gendered "woman" and not accounting for the determining ways that race and class oppression cross-cut with gender oppression, radical feminists are liable to produce an alternative ideology that cannot account for the "simultaneity of oppression" that is the concern of "Third World feminism" (130):

For, if race and class suffer the woman of color as much as her sexual identity, then the Radical Feminist must extend her own "identity" politics to include her "identity" as oppressor as well. (To say nothing of having to acknowledge the fact that there are men who may suffer more than she.) (128)

In contrast to the retreat on the part of bourgeois and radical feminisms from the specific cultural-political contexts that have constructed the gendered subject, Moraga's "Third World feminism" attempts to ground its critique in a dialectical interplay of a material historical consciousness that has not abandoned the "spiritual imperative" of a more privatized feminist consciousness that takes into account the simultaneity of oppression: "To walk a freedom road that is both material and metaphysical. Sexual and spiritual. Third World feminism is about feeding people in all their hungers" (132). Kumari Jayawardena has argued that Third World feminism "goes beyond movements for equality and emancipation . . . [to] tackle such basic issues as women's subordination within the family [and] challenge the existing framework of men-women relations in which the subordination of women is located" (1986, 2). The basic hunger satisfied by this vision is not Richard Rodriguez's personal one, of memory for a privatized past or a bourgeois future, but a broadly collective one encompassing the needs of all women and men, colored and white, in their most fundamental circumstances of existence.

When she begins to specify the qualities that make Chicana feminism one particular form of Third World feminism, and, almost incidentally, that make the author herself one particular gendered, politicized, and inscribed subject of an autobiographical text, Moraga returns to her original metaphor of the committed writer filing her dispatches from the sexual-political "battleground" of contemporary, late-capitalist, postmodern life: "It is our tradition to conceive of the bond between mother and daughter as paramount and essential in our lives. . . . [T]his is what being a Chicana feminist means— making bold and political the love of the women of our race" (LWY 139).

This return to the primacy of the "bond between mother and daughter" may seem to contradict our earlier statement about Moraga's rejection of a "motherland of harmony." It does not. Differently from others' notions of the bonds of nurturance between mothers and daughters, Moraga upholds the bond between mother and daughter as a preeminently political act that vouchsafes the insistence of class and race categories as the underpinnings of a truly radical feminism. Moraga's new version of the mother-daughter bond is different precisely as it insists on *politicizing* the history of that relationship and the history of the family by showing how the struggle about the meaning and production of family life is decisively a class-based issue as much as it is a gender-based one. Likewise, the genealogical imperative that binds "the women of our race" of necessity must allow for the bonding of sexual desire of women for other women or the cultural political work of gender construction within the Chicano community will keep "lesbians and gay men political prisoners among our own people" no less certainly than does the policing of desire carried out by the dominant state apparatus. As a self-consciously theoretical intervention in contemporary American social formations, Moraga's autobiography thus scripts a course for Chicana feminism that sharply resists reductive attempts to assimilate the experiences of all Mexican American women, Mexican origin women, or Chicanas to essentialist or ahistorical expositions of a unitary "Chicana feminism."

It is not surprising, consequently, that Moraga's autobiography ends as it begins, reiterating in poetic discourse the politics of loving. In a final poem, Moraga makes explicit what has been implied throughout her text, namely the imperative to resist the ideological interpellation of our singular subjectivity by the authoritative discourse of the patriarchal, racist, ruling-class order:

> qué puedo decirte [what can I say to you] in return
> stripped of the tongue
> that could claim lives
> de otras perdidas [lost by others]?

> la lengua que necesito [the tongue I need]
> para hablar [in order to speak]
> es la misma que uso [is the same one I use]
> para acariciar [to caress]

> tú sabes [you know/taste].
> you know the feel of woman
> lost en su boca [in her mouth]
>   amordazada [muzzled]

> it has always been like this.

> profundo y sencillo [profound and simple]
> lo que nunca [what never]
> pasó [passed]
> por sus labios [through her lips]

> but was
>   utterly
>   utterly
>   heard.

> (149)

Bakhtin describes the ideological working of hegemonic discourse as that language that speaks someone else's word "internally persuasively" for us, becoming so tightly interwoven with our own word that it seems to speak for us authoritatively.

The authoritative word demands that we acknowledge it, that we make it our own; it binds us, quite independent of any power it might have to persuade us internally; we encounter it with its authority already fused to it. The authoritative word is located in a distanced zone, organically connected with a past that is felt to be hierarchically higher. It is, so to speak, the word of the fathers. (1981, 342)

Not to be profaned or its name taken in vain, the word of the fathers is an a priori discourse that demands our unconditional pledge of allegiance (1981, 342–43). In sharp contrast to the word of the Fathers, the authoritative discourse of the political, religious, moral world that strives to determine the very basis of the subject's interrelationships with the world and other subjects, Moraga offers the word of love as the basis of her autobiography. This loving word is denied all privilege, backed by no authority, and not even acknowledged to be an ideological discourse in its own right.

Hazel Carby, echoing V. N. Volosinov (1973), has argued that language itself "is a terrain of power relations" (1987, 17). Moraga's work represents Carby's claim in practice by showing how the sign is an arena of struggle that is not divorced from the differently oriented social, political, and sexual interests within one and the same community. "Our resistance as a people to looking at the relationships within our families—between husband and wife, lovers, sister and brother, father, son, and daughter, etc.—leads me to believe that the Chicano male does not hold fast to the family unit merely to safeguard it from the death-dealings of the anglo," she says.

Living under Capitalist Patriarchy, what is true for the "man" in terms of misogyny is, to a great extent, true for the Chicano. He too, like any other man, wants to be able to determine how, when, and with whom his women —mother, wife, daughter—are sexual. For without male imposed social and legal control of our reproductive function, reinforced by the Catholic Church, and the social institutionalization of our roles as sexual and domestic servants to men, Chicanas might very freely "choose" to do otherwise, including being sexually independent *from* and/or *with* men. . . . The control of women begins through the institution of heterosexuality. (LWY 110–11)

For Chicanos as well as white men, sexuality is a form of power. Patriarchy divides women and men into the sexes by the social requirements of heterosexuality, which then under capitalism institutionalizes male sexual dominance and female sexual submission (MacKinnon 1981, 19). To counter institutionalized constructions of "male" and "female," the entire construct of the family itself must be thought through again.

Family is *not* by definition the man in a dominant position over women and children. Familia is cross-generational bonding, deep emotional ties between opposite sexes, and within our sex. It is sexuality, which involves, but is not limited to, intercourse or orgasm. It springs forth from touch, constant and daily. The ritual of kissing and the sign of the cross with every coming and going from the home. It is finding familia among friends where blood ties are formed through suffering and celebration shared. (*LWY* 111)

But in understanding the elaborations of structures of oppression in contemporary culture, it is not sufficient to think that because racism and sexism predate capitalism it is not necessary to specify the particular articulation of sex roles and family structures with economic systems of oppression (Carby 1987, 18).[10] Moraga thus revises the borders of sisterhood, of mother-daughter bonding, and of the male-female binarism by reminding that "in the 80s with the increasing conservatism of the country manifested in the reign of Reagan and the rise of the Moral Majority, Third World organizations and organizers can no longer safely espouse the family and, therefore, homophobia, as the righteous *causa* without linking themselves with the most reactionary, and by definition, the most racist political sectors of this country" (*LWY* 131). Refusing to fetishize the "family" as the sole site of subject-formation and in response to the neoconservatives and their reactionary claim to the forces of family, Moraga thus calls for a Third World Feminism that "is about feeding people in all their hungers." Opening her mouth to satisfy all form of hungers, Moraga proclaims: "My mouth cannot be controlled. It will flap in the wind like legs in sex, not driven by the mind. It's as if la boca [the mouth] were centered on el centro del corazón [the center of the heart], not in the head at all. The same place where the cunt beats" (142).

Each uttered word is an arena for the clash and crisscrossing of differently oriented social forces. In the mouth of a particular individual person it provides for the interpenetration of the various social intercourses that help shape material life (Volosinov 1973, 41). Cherríe Moraga's life story intervenes into the matrix of social intercourses by elaborating the ways in which sexual difference and sexual preference figure as instruments in the exercise of power and as the signs of the struggle over meaning. It voices alternative situations from which the traditionally accepted meanings of "woman" might be exposed. "Feminism," writes Biddy Martin, "does, in fact, provide a context out of which we can pluralize meaning by opening apparently fixed constructs onto their social, economic, and political determinacies" (1988, 18). Consistently, Moraga attempts to pluralize

10. See also Norma Alarcón (1988).

meaning by violating the taboos erected by the classist, racist, sexist ruling-order by opening her lips, politicizing the word, and proclaiming its revolutionary force. In doing so, she participates actively with Isabella Ríos, Sandra Cisneros, and other Chicana writers like Gina Valdés, Lorna Dee Cervantes, Gloria Anzaldúa, Denise Chavez, Ana Castillo, and Helena María Viramontes in the ongoing disruption of the absolute fusion of hegemonic ideologies and the status quo.

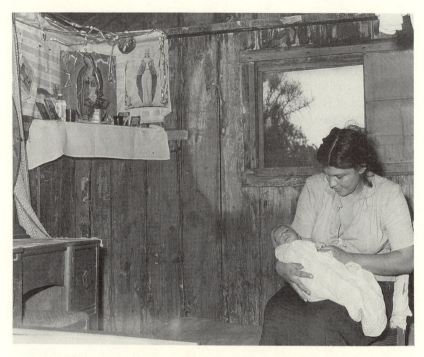

17. Mother and newborn child beside family shrine to the Virgin of Guadalupe, Corpus Christi, Texas, April 1949. (Russell Lee Collection, courtesy of the Eugene C. Barker Texas History Center, University of Texas at Austin)

18. Grandmother and child at their festively decorated family shrine to various saints and icons but with pride of place given to the Virgin of Guadalupe and the Virgin of San Juan, Corpus Christi, Texas, April 1949. (Russell Lee Collection, courtesy of the Eugene C. Barker Texas History Center, University of Texas at Austin)

19. Wistful child of the Chicano urban working class, Corpus Christi, Texas, April 1949. (Russell Lee Collection, courtesy of the Eugene C. Barker Texas History Center, University of Texas at Austin)

20. The realities of everyday life are reflected in the face of this Chicana, Stockdale, Texas, June 1949. (Russell Lee Collection, courtesy of the Eugene C. Barker Texas History Center, University of Texas at Austin)

Conclusion
The Reconstruction of American Literary History

We have reached a point in literary studies where it is no longer fruitful, nor even accurate, for us to assume that we can go to a text without considering the critical presuppositions that we bring to our reading of a text. I hesitate to say this because the importance of the self-critical moment has become at this moment in the history of criticism, almost a commonplace. But perhaps it is not a commonplace when we approach what have come to be called "marginal" or "noncanonic" literatures.

Awareness of critical presuppositions is especially important in the case of Chicano narrative and its literary criticism as they produce texts that, for the various social, political, and historical reasons that we have outlined in the preceding chapters, have been systematically excluded from the traditional framework of American literary history. Works by Mexican American authors are virtually absent from the histories, the anthologies of American literature, and from the syllabi of courses on American literature. Spanish departments in American universities have also participated in this strategy of exclusion. The exclusion is by no means innocent. Its effect has been very similar to that of the exclusion from the American canon of African American art. In that exclusion, as described by Henry Louis Gates, Jr., "logocentrism and ethnocentrism marched together in an attempt to deprive the black human being of even the potential to create art, to imagine a world and to figure it" (1984, 7).

The recent debates over "canons" and "canon formation" have begun to free us from the reification of American Literature as a singular, homogeneous entity. Toni Morrison, for instance, has suggested that questions concerning the presence of "other" traditions in American Literature have beneficially begun to "spring the whole literature of an entire nation from the solitude in which it has been locked." This paradigm shift in American literary studies may finally dispel the misconception that:

There is something called American literature that, according to conventional wisdom, is certainly not Chicano literature, or Afro-American literature, or Asian-American literature, or Native American, or . . . It is somehow separate from them and they from it. . . . Although the terms used, like the vocabulary of earlier canon debates, refer to literary and/or humanistic value, aesthetic criteria, value-free or socially anchored readings, the contemporary battle plain is most often understood to be the claims of others against the whitemale origins and definitions of those values; whether those definitions reflect an eternal, universal and transcending paradigm or whether they constitute a disguise for a temporal, political and culturally specific program. (1989, 1–2)

In the preceding chapters of textual analysis I have suggested a method of interpretation that, while distinguishing among logical, semiotic, and rhetorical notions of the linguistic sign, provides a firm ground for reading Chicano literary texts as works that intentionally exploit their peripheral status to and exclusion from the body of works that we might call "majority literature." This method of reading obliges us to make connections between the findings of narrative analysis and traditional as well as modern approaches to ideology. A critical, dialectical awareness of the process of reading is crucial in the case of a developing literature like contemporary Chicano literature, where literary historians are still involved primarily in the process of establishing a "tradition" and resolving questions concerning the issue of canon formation.

This work is crucial, for as a reflection on the primary texts that constitute a tradition, the dialectical critical work of which I speak both defines "tradition" and helps to shape the direction of an art that is, to paraphrase Gates, in the process of "imagining" and "figuring" a world. It will also tell us much about why English and Spanish departments in American universities have avoided Chicano literature and have disguised this ideological decision under an appeal to the supposedly neutral categories of aesthetic standards and values that turn out to serve, as Morrison suggests, as a "disguise for a temporal, political and culturally specific program."

Narrative and Dialectics

The problem of narrative structure and its relationship to the thematic aspects of texts is currently one of the most vital areas of analysis in literary theory. Contemporary narrative analysis reveals the "dialogic" nature of meaning. Various studies in narratology have shown that since the mid-nineteenth century the assumed homology between the rhetorical and instrumental functions of narrative language to narrative representation has become exceptionally problematic. The language of the late modernist novel and all subsequent novels does more than simply reflect or mirror a "reality." It *produces* that reality by a reconstruction and systematic transformation of the older formations of a previous historical moment.

In *Figural Language in the Novel* (1984) I argued that with its care for authenticating detail and its passion for credibility and intelligibility, the novel expresses a continuing desire for types, for monological readings, for an anachronistic mythos of common understanding and a shared universe of meaning. And yet in the same breath, the novel never ceases to express the dazzling conceptual maneuvering that we all must perform in order to conceive reality, indeed to shape reality, in ways that will make sense to the human mind. The novel allows us to seek to absorb and understand new experiences by discovering new forms and rhythms, "grasping and reconstructing the stuff of social change in the living substance of perceptions and relationships" (Eagleton 1975, 34). This conflict between the contrary tendencies toward monological unifications, single voices, on the one hand, and polyphonic diversity, Bakhtin's choir of voices, on the other, makes the novel, and its allied novelistic discourses, particularly important to Chicano literary forms.

I have argued that interpretation is essentially an allegorical act that consists in reading a text in terms that most rigorously account for its rhetorical and formal strategies (1984). Its aim is not to elaborate some sophisticated précis of a story but to *produce* the text's epistemological and ideological concept of the real world, to reveal the competing systems of ideas and modes of representation that structure the world at a particular place and time.

As narrative productions and "socially symbolic acts," not mere reflections of the ideological formations within which they arise, the texts that we have examined in this book put ideology to work, exposing the framing limits of what we take as the self-evident truths, as the common sense of our times (Eagleton 1976, 155). Narratives by Chicano men and women represent that what appears "natural" in the ways individuals live their lives in society is the result of identifiable cultural matrices. These cultural matrices, the truths that we hold to be self-evident, use the signifier to create truths and set these as norms, coercive texts for meaning, that claim universality.

Dialectical readings can point out the reification of these truths from the constructed domains of a specific history and a particular culture. They allow us to see the production of ideology not as a system of formalized ideas, but as ordinary ways of thinking, as common sense. E. P. Thompson puts it very sensibly in these terms:

> Very rarely in history—and then only for short intervals—does any ruling class exercise authority by direct and unmediated military or even economic force. People are born into a society whose forms and relations seem as fixed and immutable as the overarching sky. The "common sense" of the time is saturated with the deafening propaganda of the *status quo*; but the strongest element in this propaganda is simply the fact that what exists exists. (1978, 254)

As narrative representations, these productive processes are necessarily figurative and cannot be abolished because they allow social formations to persist; but they can be articulated and analyzed. That articulation would have as its object what Jameson has called "ideological analysis" (1981, 12), namely a critical exposition of cultural texts that amounts to a rewriting of the text so that it is seen itself as a rewriting of a prior historical and ideological *sub*text that is no longer present as such (1981, 81).

Narratives, in sum, can be thought to dramatize the ability of knowledge, ideology, subjectivity, and cultural productions in general to create the "ontologically empty but historically full" (Lentricchia 1980, 184) forces that constrain the course of narrative. But narratives persist, nonetheless, in uncovering this coercion by representing it as the irreducibly dialectical clash of the cultural-historical forces that surround a text and the rhetorical and formal dynamics within a text. Narratives are thus preeminently and rigorously dialectical. Like the ideologies that they make concrete, they figure and are determined by their social context (Jameson 1981, 4–10). Insisting upon and employing all the devices of rhetoric, they situate the natural truths of precritical idealism as the local effects of "differential relations, institutions, conventions, histories, practices" and as the deferred results of the "institutionality and spatiality of language" (Ryan 1982, 24). Read dialectically, narratives indicate that language and discourse do affect human life in determining ways, ways that are themselves shaped by social history. Giving rise to questions concerning language itself, the sovereignty of our identity, and the laws that govern our behavior, they reveal the heterogeneous systems that resist the formation of a unitary base of truth.

Ideology and Narrative

Turning to the notion of ideology itself, I follow Jameson's suggestion that narratives in general instantiate ideology as the substance
of our collective thinking and collective fantasies about history and
reality. The concept of ideology to which we have referred in this
study is thus at least in part distinguishable from the three common
versions of the term as identified by Raymond Williams:

> (i) a system of beliefs characteristic of a particular class or group;
> (ii) a system of illusory beliefs—false ideas or false consciousness—which
> can be contrasted with true or scientific knowledge;
> (iii) the general process of the production of meanings and ideas. (1977, 55)

As Stuart Hall points out, the term "ideology" dates from the end
of the eighteenth century, when it was introduced by Destutt de
Tracy to denote the study of the origin and function of "ideas" in
Condillac's sense as psychic operations of all kinds and their relation to language (1977b, 10). The term "ideologues" was then applied to scholars and public men (Destutt, Cabanis, Volney) who
carried on the tradition of the *Encyclopédistes*. Napoleon applied it
to them in the pejorative sense of "political dreamers." The Hegeli-
ans used "ideology" to denote the subjective aspect of the cognitive
process (Kolakowski 1978, 56; Hall 1977b, 11–13; Williams, 1983,
153–54). Stendhal even used it in his scientific study of passion in
De L'amour (1822). These early uses of the term tend to lend it the
decidedly suspect sense of thought that has been led astray from its
proper course. They turn attention away from the role that ideologies play, as Clifford Geertz says, in "defining (or obscuring) social
categories, stabilizing (or upsetting) social expectations, maintaining
(or undermining) social norms, strengthening (or weakening) social
consensus, relieving (or exacerbating) social tensions" (1973, 203).

Certainly the most important early use of the term is that of Marx
and Engels in *The German Ideology*, where it is used primarily in
sense (ii) above—that is, as "false consciousness." False consciousness is the obfuscated mental process in which men and women
do not understand the factors that guide their thinking, but rather
imagine thinking to be governed by logic and intellectual influences
alone. This is to forget, according to Marx and Engels, that

> the individuals composing the ruling class possess . . . consciousness, and
> therefore think. Insofar . . . as they rule as a class and determine the extent
> and compass of an epoch [expressed in the language of politics, laws, mo-

rality, religion, metaphysics, aesthetics, etc.], it is self-evident that they . . .
rule also as thinkers, as producers of ideas, and regulate the production and
distribution of the ideas of their age: thus their ideas are the ruling ideas of
the epoch (1978, 173).

The deluded thinker in this sense of the term is unaware that all
thought is subject to extra-intellectual social conditions, which are
expressed in distorted forms (Hall 1977a, 315–17).

"Ideology" has sometimes been generalized in sense (iii) to denote
the very process of meaning-creation as a sociohistorical, transindividual process. Thus, according to Volosinov, "Every sign is subject
to criteria of ideological evaluation. . . . The domain of ideology co-
incides with the domain of signs. They equate with one another.
Wherever a sign is present, ideology is present, too. *Everything ideological possesses semiotic value*" (1973, 10). In our own time, "ideology" has sometimes been generalized to denote *all* forms of social
consciousness, including those that are aware of their social base,
encompassing both senses (i) and (iii). The "ideological" has come to
be seen as "programs" that "provide a template or blueprint for the
organization of social and psychological processes, much as genetic
systems provide such a template for the organization of organic processes. . . . Through the construction of ideologies, schematic images
of social order, man makes himself for better or worse a political
animal," according to Geertz (1973, 216, 218).

One particularly salient way of conceiving ideology is to think of
it as the ways that a culture links social action with fundamental
beliefs, a collective identity with the course of history. Basically, ideology functions as a unifying social force (Higham 1974, 10–18). In
this sense, according to Sacvan Bercovitch, ideology is "the system
of interlinked ideas, symbols, and beliefs by which a culture . . .
seeks to justify and perpetuate itself; the web of rhetoric, ritual, and
assumption through which society coerces, persuades, and coheres"
(1986b, 8). In an essay on American literary history, Bercovitch points
out that ideology is at work when it becomes the "network of ideas
through which the culture justifies itself" and when it is "internalized rather than imposed, and embraced by society at large as a system of belief" (1986a, 9). The beauty of the hegemonic power of what
Bercovitch calls "the American ideological consensus" (1981, 20–21)
is that, in addition to possessing the status of "common sense," it
also already has built into it a way of dealing with, and thus neu-
tralizing, "alternative and oppositional forms" of social formation
(1986b, 9).

In literary and historical terms, this American ideological consensus has involved "the legitimation of a certain canon," a canon based on the works of the Puritan forefathers. It has also involved consensus about "the meaning of the term history that was legitimated by a certain vision of America" (1986b, vii), as a land of men of independent mind and independent means, developing through "initiative, individualism, self-reliance, and demands for freedom" (1986b, 3). Bercovitch goes on to say:

An ideology . . . arises out of historical circumstances, and then re-presents these, symbolically and conceptually, as though they were natural, universal, and right; as if the ideals promulgated by a certain group or class (. . . individualism, mobility, self-reliance, free enterprise) were not the product of history but the expression of self-evident truth. The act of re-presentation thus serves to consecrate a set of cultural limitations, to recast a particular society as Society, a particular way of life as the pursuit of happiness. (1986b, 10)

An ideology as such is not necessarily good or evil, true or false. We can set aside crude notions of "false consciousness." But it is a system of ideas underlying a certain social order. That is to say, ideology connects what we say and believe with the power structure and power relations of the society we live in (Eagleton 1983, 14). Ideology is thus much more than the unconscious beliefs a people may hold; it is more particularly "those modes of feeling, valuing, perceiving, and believing which have some kind of relation to the maintenance and reproduction of social power" (Eagleton 1983, 15). An ideology will thus repress alternative or oppositional forms when these arise. The ideology of the Puritan colonies, for example, did not simply exclude Native Americans from the colonists' consensus about the new world being fashioned from the wilderness. The native inhabitants were seen as the very embodiments of the evils most threatening to the creation of the New Jerusalem. This ideology of exclusion remained central to the American creed throughout the nineteenth century. And we see its effects in other historical and literary moments.

While I employ these general senses of "ideology" in the course of this study, I rely mainly on Althusser's provisional definition of the ideological as "a 'representation' of the Imaginary relationship of individuals to their real conditions of existence" (1969, 162). For our purposes, we need retain but two features from this somewhat cryptic definition.

First, ideology must always be necessarily narrative in its structure because it involves a mapping of the real. That is, it underwrites the stories about what we conceive of as real. Ideology also involves the essentially narrative, or fabulous, attempt of the subject to inscribe a place for itself in a collective and historical process. But I must also add that, as Paul Hirst reminds us, except as a part of a totality, an entity governed by a principle, these relations exhibit no *necessary* homogeneity. This means that the "cognitive mapping" of the imaginative geography of the real cannot exhibit a singular "ideological instance." It must insist instead on the "heterogeneity of ideological social relations and their effects" (1979, 2). Ideology thus refers to "a non-unitary complex of social practices and systems of representations which have political significances and consequences" (1979, 54). As our textual discussions have shown, for Chicano narrative the mapping of the "imaginary relationship" of political significances and consequences cannot be limited to issues of class ideology alone. Questions concerning race and gender are no less important and will not allow us to subordinate them to one single structure. No single map will suffice for an understanding of the "Real"; and its features cannot be predicated in advance.

Second, we also need to retain the notion that the "Real" is an outer limit that the subject approaches in the anxiety of moments of truth—moments of personal crisis, of the loss of identity, or of the agonizing political polarizations of revolutionary situations such as those experienced by the subjects of contemporary Chicano narrative. The make-up of "history" as such, then, is not so much the empirical events of the world as the self-inscription and symbolization in texts of those events and in our thinking about them. In other words, our approach to the "Real" must always pass through its textualization, or what Jameson calls its "narrativization in the political unconscious" (1981, 35).

Althusser's notion of ideology offers "a representational structure which allows the individual subject to conceive or imagine his or her lived relationship to transpersonal realities such as the social structure or the collective logic of History" (Jameson 1981, 30). In this sense, the "Real" is not to be considered as a knowable "thing-in-itself." Nor is it a string of facts that one can know directly in the positive form of some "true" representation of consciousness. It is instead a cultural-historical and subjective invention, projected by an ideologically riddled consciousness. Now if the "real" is what "resists symbolization absolutely" (Jameson 1981, 35), then "the text takes as its object, not the real, but certain significations by which the real lives itself—significations which are themselves the product of its partial abolition," claims Eagleton (1975, 72). This narrativized real is not a reproduction, a reflection, or a mirroring of the historical real. Althusser thus argues that rather than conceiving it as an imaginary transposition or concretization of the historical real, the textual real should be conceived as the product of signifying practices whose source is history itself (1969, 222–25).

What all this means, basically, is that reality can be known in experience only if it is first *imagined* as a formed product of the subjects who recognize it or misrecognize it and express it in symbolic forms. The "imaginary" is thus both an image and a spectral reality through the recognition of which the subject becomes a subject (Hirst 1979, 57). As Paul de Man argues, ideology, like metaphysics, may be conceived preeminently as a precritical stage of knowledge (1984, 132).

And yet the narrative apparatus that informs ideological representations is not mere "false consciousness." Ideology is much more than that. It is an authentic way of grappling with a Real that must always transcend it, a Real into which the subject seeks to enter, all the while painfully learning the lesson of its own ideological closure and of history's resistance to the fantasy structures in which it is itself locked. A text can thus be said to refer not to concrete situations so much as to the ideological formations that concrete situations have produced.

For literary studies, one particularly important result of this way of conceiving the work of ideology is that it allows us to understand the radical "decentering" of the subject, and the consequent emphasis on the collective and the political, that occurs in a contemporary literature like Chicano literature. There are no given, constitutive subjects with an experience of the real. "Subjects are not essential but are constituted" (Hirst 1979, 41). Or, in Althusser's words, "Ideology interpellates individuals as subjects" (1971, 170). Appropriating Jacques Lacan's concept of the "mirror phase" (1968) as a "speculary, i.e., a mirror-structure" phenomenon, Althusser argues that the subject exists as a mirror reflection of an *other* subject and becomes a subject itself in its recognition and reflection of and in the other (1969, 180, 195–219; Hirst 1979, 57).

Individuals are always "subjected" to and by certain principles and directives of ideology so that they will be "happy, useful, and safe subjects, in the political sense of the term" (Lentricchia 1983, 1). To conceive of a text as ideology is thus to focus on the way that ideology affects the formation and transformation of human subjectivity (Therborn 1980, 2). Ideology is socially conditioned consciousness, allowing men and women to live what Geertz has called "lives of patterned desperation" (1973, 204). From this perspective, human thought comes to be seen as a public and not fundamentally a private activity.

No culture is ideology-free. Chicano narrative presents subjects acting according to variant and competing ideologies, ideologies in active resistance to the existing material apparatus of American society, prescribing as Althusser says, "material practices governed by a material ritual" (1969, 170). The narrative writings of Chicano men and women thus produce clashes or textual aporias that demarcate the limits of ideology itself. These writings carry out a metacritical resistance to the dominant ideology at the level of various symbolic languages, attempting to figure what we might call, echoing Göran Therborn, an "alter-ideology" (1980, 28). It is worth repeating that the work of this "alter-ideology" is conflictual rather than consensual or integrative. The great ethnographic work of Américo Paredes on the corrido and the more recent writings of Chicanas like Sandra Cisneros and Cherríe Moraga can serve as models for understanding Chicano narrative as just such an "alter-ideological" resistance formation.

From this perspective, the utopian vision of a moment when the individual subject would be completely aware of his or her determination by class ideology and would be able to step outside of this determination by sheer lucidity and clarity of thought is a myth (Jameson 1981, 283). But it is precisely at this point that the value of art emerges. If men's and women's conditions of existence cannot be present to them as experience, and if in consequence they live their relation to these conditions in an imaginary mode as if they were given, then art, with its ability to produce the individual's imaginary relationship to conditions of existence, is a vital element of ideological analysis. Great art distances ideology by the way in which, endowing ideology with figurative and narrative articulations, the text frees its ideological content to demonstrate the contradictions within which ideologies are created. Great art is thus speculative in the most fundamental of senses: it allows us to see.

This is not to say that art itself is therefore ideology-free. On the contrary, as Jameson suggests, "ideology is not something that informs or invests symbolic production; rather the aesthetic act is itself ideological, and the production of aesthetic or narrative form is to be seen as an ideological act in its own right, with the function of inventing imaginary or formal 'solutions' to unresolvable social contradictions" (1981, 79). Resorting for the sake of exposition to a Hegelian formulation, we might argue that one rationale for studying "ethnic" literatures as part and parcel of the general problematic of American literature as a whole (rather than seeing them as merely "regional" or "marginal" phenomena of interest only to a specialized literary fringe) is that the masterworks of the dominant literary culture are the dialogical negations of the marginal texts not sanctioned by the hegemonic culture. As the silenced voices of opposition, these other marginal texts serve to highlight the ideological background of the traditional canon, to bring to the surface that repressed formation that Jameson has called the "political unconscious." This is one reason for the sudden interest on the part of some mainstream scholars in African American and ethnic, as well as feminist, lesbian, and gay literatures in general. The writings of these oppressed groups can be read as the manifest expression of the latent contradictions of the dominant social formation.

The difficult task of textual interpretation as of dream interpretation lies, as Jameson claims, "in detecting the traces of that uninterrupted narrative [of class struggle and oppression], in restoring to the surface of the text the repressed and buried reality of this fundamental history. . . . The assertion of a political unconscious proposes that we undertake just such a final analysis and explore the multiple paths that lead to the unmasking of cultural artifacts as socially symbolic acts" (1981, 20). Pierre Macherey describes this "unconscious" level as the very site of ideological work:

[T]he ideological background, which constitutes the real support of all forms of expression and all ideological manifestations, is fundamentally silent— one might say unconscious. But it must be emphasised that this unconscious is not a silent knowledge, but a total misrecognition of itself. If it is silent, it is silent on that about which it has nothing to say. We should therefore preserve the expression in all its ambiguity: it refers to that ideological horizon which conceals only because it is interminable, because there is always something more, but it refers also to that abyss over which ideology is built. Like a planet revolving round an absent sun, an ideology is made of what it does not mention; it exists because there are things which must not be spoken of. (1978, 131–32)

What I have referred to as the "difference" of Chicano narrative is precisely a function of its relation to ideology. Like African American and other marginalized literatures, Chicano narrative exists precisely because "there are things which must not be spoken of." Ideological analysis of its forms necessarily involves confronting the political consequences of particular social relations and representations. In articulating the space of that "ideological horizon" and the "abyss over which ideology is built," Chicano narrative fills the gaps and names the silences that are the limits of the ideological consensus of American literary history, daring to "speak the unspeakable" (Morrison 1989, 3) and utter, as Cherríe Moraga has phrased it, "lo que nunca pasó por sus labios." As oppositional articulations of those gaps and silences, narratives by Chicano women and men serve as vital correctives to impoverished traditional notions of what today constitutes "American" literature.

Reconstructing American Literary History

A radical reconstruction of American literary history is currently underway in the works of scholars like Paul Lauter (1985), Houston Baker, Jr. (1984, 1987), Henry Louis Gates, Jr. (1987, 1988), Hazel Carby (1987), Toni Morrison (1989) and Cary Nelson (1989). Baker, for example, notes that

> in recent years there have been dramatic shifts in both the elements and ideological ordering principles deemed essential for American historical and American literary historical discourse. At the level of practical criticism, such shifts have offered conditions for revised readings of traditional texts. At a more global level, however, reconceptualizations of historical discourse have led to the laying bare, the surfacing and re-cognition, of myriad unofficial American histories. (1984, 60–61)

Chicano narrative should be seen as an active participant in this reconceptualization of American literary discourse. With African American, feminist, and other formerly ignored American discourses, Chicano narrative is one aspect of what Baker has termed the "figuration for a new American literary history" (1984, 15).

Together, these new alternative versions of American literary history might well stand against the work of more traditional Americanists who are also engaged in revisionary projects with works such as the new edition of the *Cambridge History of American Literature*, in volumes such as Bercovitch's *Reconstructing American Literary History* (1986), and Werner Sollors' *Beyond Ethnicity* (1986). Against the power of the old American ideological consensus as to which texts could be considered literary and historical, this latter group of scholars will, according to Bercovitch, make "a virtue of *dissensus*" (1986b, viii). This dissensus, a dialogue of "conflicting views and interests" (1986b, 5), will serve as the revisionary model for the new American literary history. Against the older consensus, this new dissensus is *integrative:* not "eclectic, synthetic, or indeterminate" but rather "dialogic" (1986b, ix).

Werner Sollors' enterprise "to look at American culture anew"

(1986, 6) by focusing on the notions of *consent* and *descent* as terms which allow us "to approach and question the whole maze of American ethnicity and culture" (1986, 6), follows very much in the reforming spirit of Bercovitch's new literary history. The conflict in American literature between consent and consensus on the one hand and descent and legitimacy on the other, Sollors claims, "can tell us much about the creation of *an* American culture out of diverse pre-American pasts" (1986, 6; my emphasis). Similarly, Sollors' newly edited collection of essays, *The Invention of Ethnicity*, promises to "chart *the* cultural construction of 'ethnicity' as embodied in American ethnic literature" and to provide "*a* new critical framework for understanding not only ethnic literature, but also the underlying psychological, historical, social, and cultural forces" (1989; my emphases).

This sounds wonderful, perhaps even after we notice that both Bercovitch's and Sollors' key words, "consensus" and "consent", "dissensus" and "dissent", "integrative" and "integration", "legitimacy" and "privilege" themselves ring with the unmistakable clarity of their origins in the liberal-democratic bourgeois political theories that form the foundations of the hegemonic American ideological consensus.

The crucial factor here is that, often, these terms refer to consensus and dissent among the ruling groups alone and to their legitimacy as members of the ruling elite state apparatus (Therborn, 109). That is, consensus and dissensus do not apply to those *outside* the ruling group or their educational, cultural, and political state apparatuses: working-class people, people of color, gays and lesbians, women.

In short, even this new integrative model can in practice turn out to be a counterhegemonic move to renew, defend, and modify, but not to *undo*, the earlier forms of dominance (Williams 1977, 113). We might well ask, therefore, *how* the voices of those traditionally excluded from American literary history are to be "integrated" into that history.

The American ideological consensus that I have referred to takes on a very different quality when we take into account the ways that class origins, and racial and gender differences affect literary and social history. At the very least, people of different classes, races, and gender will feel the effects of that consensus and its hegemony differently. And if Jameson's notion of expressive causality is to be taken seriously as a way of regarding history as the "absent cause" accessible to us only through its "narrativization in the political unconscious" (1981, 35), then we must not easily dismiss the real power of difference to resist the reifying tendencies of studies such as Sollors' with their presumptuous claims to chart the construction of a monolithic American "ethnicity" within a single critical framework which will then move us "beyond ethnicity" toward the formation of a unitary American culture.

Baker has noted that the discourse of American social and literary history has tended to be Providential and has readily assumed that

God's divine plan is . . . to reveal (and, ultimately, to fulfill) itself only through the endeavors of religious, European men. And just as such men are considered sole builders of the New Jerusalem, so, too, they are considered exclusive chroniclers of their achievments in the evolutionary phases of an American national literature. (1984, 20)

It might be well to notice that what are usually omitted from such unitary models of an American culture or an American ideological consensus arising from a Puritan, New England, middle-class perspective of the origins of American literary history are the heterogeneous literary traditions of the Southwest. These other stories tell of the extermination of Native Americans, the enslavement of African Americans, the subjugation of Mexican Americans, the oppression of the working class, and the enforcement of the patriarchy.

Because of the decisive connections that are always being made in the writings of Chicano women and men between historical and aesthetic concerns, interest in this "marginal" group of literary texts is by no means unjustifiable. It is certainly the case that the critical project of many Mexican American authors has been to offer a different perspective on the volatile configurations of literary and social history that crystallize in twentieth-century American society, in order that we may better understand the workings of that developing postmodern world. This critical understanding takes the form of what I call "the dialectics of difference."

F. O. Matthiessen's great book, *American Renaissance*, set the terms for the study of American literature: according to Matthiessen, his authors, Thoreau, Emerson, Hawthorne, Whitman, "felt that it was incumbent upon their generation to give fulfillment to the potentialities freed by the Revolution, to provide a culture commensurate with America's political opportunity" (1941, xv). The resistance literature of twentieth-century Chicano men and women challenges American literature to live up to its potentialities and provide a culture commensurate with its political opportunity. To date, the ideas inherent in "America's political opportunity" have served only to rationalize the colonized oppression of the native people of the Southwest and to exclude their writings from the formation of American literature.

The current radical reconstruction of American literary history

seeks to recapture those writings and use them to construct a dialogical system that might help us better understand both the canoni-
cal master works that were sanctioned by the American ideological
consensus and the antagonistic resistance literatures, like Chicano
narrative, that were not sanctioned. By placing the masterworks in
different frameworks that include the voices to which the master
texts were covertly opposed, voices that were and continue to be silenced by the hegemonic culture, we might indeed formulate a new
literary history of a truly integrated American literature.

With their special ties to the borderlines demarcating the differential
structures of contemporary American life, Chicano narrative texts
might well serve as the patterns of that dialogical model of a new
American literary history.

The U.S.–Mexico border *es una herida abierta* (is an open wound) where
the Third World grates against the first and bleeds. And before a scab forms
it hemorrhages again, the lifeblood of two worlds merging to form a third
country—a border culture. Borders are set up to define the places that are
safe and unsafe, to distinguish us from *them*. A border is a dividing line, a
narrow strip along a steep edge. A borderland is a vague and undetermined
place created by the emotional residue of an unnatural boundary. It is in a
constant state of transition. The prohibited and forbidden are its inhabitants.

So begins Gloria Anzaldúa's *Borderlands/La Frontera* (1987, 3). What
it means to construct a life in the liminal chronotopes defined by the
cognitive mappings imposed on the subject by the imaginary political lines drawn between Mexico and the United States is the substance of her autobiography. But as in the works of Paredes, Rivera,
Acosta, Hinojosa, Galarza, Moraga, Cisneros, and other authors, the
life story of the subject takes on an entirely new ideological dimension in Anzaldúa's writings once it traverses these bordered spaces.
We might well thus extend Anzaldúa's guiding figure of the border
as the primary metaphor of the particularly dialectical subject position articulated by each of the texts that we have discussed. The
trajectories of the lives of these subjects take them across borderlines
precisely into the prohibited and forbidden zones that contain the
residue of the unnatural boundaries forged by the unfulfilled potentialities of contemporary American culture. For Anzaldúa, as for the
other Chicano and Chicana authors with whom we have dealt, to
write is preeminently a political act seeking to fulfill the potentialities of contemporary life. It is also, ultimately, an attempt to recall
the originary myths of life on the borders of power in order to fashion
triumphantly a new, heterogeneous American consciousness, within
the dialectics of difference.

Works Cited
Index

Works Cited

Acosta, Oscar Zeta. 1972. *The Autobiography of a Brown Buffalo.* San Francisco: Straight Arrow Books. Rpt. New York: Popular Library, 1972; Penguin, 1989.

Acosta, Oscar Zeta. 1973. *The Revolt of the Cockroach People.* San Francisco: Straight Arrow Books. Rpt. New York: Bantam Books, 1974; Penguin, 1989.

Acuña, Rodolfo. 1981. *Occupied America: A History of Chicanos.* 2d ed. New York: Harper & Row.

Adorno, Theodor. [1966] 1973. *Negative Dialectics.* Trans. E. B. Ashton. New York: Seabury P.

Adorno, Theodor. [1938] 1982. "On the Fetish-Character in Music and the Regression of Listening." Rpt. in *The Essential Frankfurt School Reader,* ed. Andrew Arato and Eike Gebhardt, 270–99. New York: Continuum.

Ahmad, Aijaz. 1987. "Jameson's Rhetoric of Otherness and the 'National Allegory.'" *Social Text* 17: 3–25.

Alarcón, Norma. 1983. "Chicana's Feminist Literature: A Re-vision Through Malintzín/or Malintzín: Putting Flesh Back on the Object." In *This Bridge Called My Back: Writings by Radical Women of Color.* 2d ed., ed. Cherríe Moraga and Gloria Anzaldúa, 182–90. Rpt. New York: Kitchen Table: Women of Color Press.

Alarcón, Norma. 1988. "Making 'Familia' From Scratch: Split Subjectivities in the Work of Helena María Viramontes and Cherríe Moraga." In *Chicana Creativity and Criticism: Charting New Frontiers in American Literature,* ed. María Hererra-Sobek and Helena María Viramontes, 147–59. Houston: Arte Público Press.

Alarcón, Norma. 1989. "The Sardonic Powers of the Erotic in the Work of Ana Castillo." In *Breaking Boundaries: Latina Writings and Critical Readings,* ed. Asunción Horno-Delgado et al., 94–107. Amherst: U of Massachussetts P.

Althusser, Louis. 1969. "Ideology and Ideological State Apparatuses (Notes towards an Investigation)." Rpt. in *Lenin and Philosophy and Other Essays,* trans. Ben Brewster. New York and London: Monthly Review Press, 1971.

Alvarez, Rodolfo. 1973. "The Psycho-Historical and Socioeconomic Development of the Chicano Community in the United States." *Social Science Quarterly* 53: 920–42. Rpt. in *The Mexican American Experience: An Interdisciplinary Anthology*, ed. Rodolfo O. de la Garza et al., 33–56. Austin: U of Texas P, 1985.

Anaya, Rudolfo A. 1972. *Bless Me, Ultima*. Berkeley: Quinto Sol Publications.

Anaya, Rudolfo A. 1977. "The Writer's Landscape: Epiphany in Literature." *Latin American Literary Review* 5, no. 10: 98–102.

Anderson, Benedict. [1983] 1987. *Imagined Communities: Reflections on the Origin and Spread of Nationalism*. Rpt. London and New York: Verso.

Anzaldúa, Gloria. 1983. "Speaking in Tongues: A Letter to Third World Women Writers." In *This Bridge Called My Back: Writings by Radical Women of Color*. 2d ed., ed. Cherríe Moraga and Gloria Anzaldúa, 165–74. New York: Kitchen Table: Women of Color Press.

Anzaldúa, Gloria. 1987. *Borderlands/La Frontera: The New Mestiza*. San Francisco: Spinsters/Aunt Lute.

Arce, Julio G. (Jorge Ulica). 1982. *Crónicas diabólicas (1916–1926)*. Ed. Juan Rodriguez. San Diego: Maize Press.

Arias, Ron. 1975. *The Road to Tamazunchale*. Reno, Nev.: West Coast Poetry Review.

Austin, J. L. [1958] 1971. "Performative-Constative." In *The Philosophy of Language*, ed. John R. Searle. 13–21. New York: Oxford U P.

Austin, J. L. [1961] 1970. "Performative Utterances." In *Philosophical Papers*, 2d ed., ed. J. O. Urmson and G. J. Warnock, 233–52. New York: Oxford U P.

Baker, Houston A., Jr. 1984. *Blues, Ideology, and Afro-American Literature: A Vernacular Theory*. Chicago: U of Chicago P.

Baker, Houston A., Jr. 1985. "Caliban's Triple Play." In *"Race", Writing, and Difference*. ed. Henry Louis Gates, Jr., 381–95. Chicago: U of Chicago P.

Baker, Houston A., Jr. 1987. *Modernism and the Harlem Renaissance*. Chicago: U of Chicago P.

Bakhtin, M. M. 1981. *The Dialogic Imagination: Four Essays*. Trans. Caryl Emerson. Ed. Michael Holquist. Austin: U of Texas P.

Barrera, Mario. 1979. *Race and Class in the Southwest: A Theory of Racial Inequality*. Notre Dame: U of Notre Dame P.

Barrett, Michelle. 1985. "Ideology and the Cultural Production of Gender." In *Feminist Criticism and Social Change: Sex, Class and Race in Literature and Culture*. Ed. Judith Newton and Deborah Rosenfelt, 65–85. London and New York: Methuen.

Baudrillard, Jean. 1981. *For a Critique of the Political Economy of the Sign*. St. Louis: Telos Press.

Benjamin, Walter. [1959] 1973. "The Storyteller." *Illuminations*. Trans. Harry Zohn. New York: Schocken Books.

Bercovitch, Sacvan. 1981. "The Rites of Assent: Rhetoric, Ritual, and the Ideology of American Consensus." In *The American Self: Myth, Ideology, and Popular Culture*, ed. Sam Girgus, 5–42. Albuquerque: U of New Mexico P.

Bercovitch, Sacvan. 1986a. "The Problem of Ideology in American Literary History." Paper delivered at the Graduate Conference on Literary History and Ideology, the University of Texas at Austin, February 4.

Bercovitch, Sacvan, ed. 1986b. *Reconstructing American Literary History.* Cambridge: Harvard U P.

Berg, Elizabeth. 1982. "The Third Woman." *Diacritics* 12: 11–20.

Bernstein, J. M. 1984. *The Philosophy of the Novel: Lukács, Marxism and the Dialectics of Form.* Minneapolis: U of Minnesota P.

Bloom, Harold. 1973. *The Anxiety of Influence: A Theory of Poetry.* New York: Oxford U P.

Bruce-Novoa, Juan. 1975. "The Space of Chicano Literature." *De Colores* 1: 22–42.

Bruce-Novoa. 1980. *Chicano Authors: Inquiry by Interview.* Austin: U of Texas P.

Bruss, Elizabeth W. 1976. *Autobiographical Acts: The Changing Situation of a Literary Genre.* Baltimore: Johns Hopkins U P.

Calderón, Héctor. 1982. "To Read Chicano Narrative: Commentary and Metacommentary." *Mester* 11, no. 2: 3–14.

Calderón, Héctor. 1986. "Rudolfo Anaya's *Bless Me, Ultima*: A Chicano Romance of the Southwest." *Crítica* 1, no. 3: 21–47.

Camarillo, Albert. 1979. *Chicanos In A Changing Society.* Cambridge: Harvard U P.

Cantú, Norma. 1986. "Women, Then and Now: An Analysis of the Adelita Image versus the Chicana as Political Writer and Philosopher." In *Chicana Voices: Intersections of Class, Race, and Gender*, ed. Teresa Córdova et al., 8–10. Austin: U of Texas P and the Center for Mexican American Studies.

Cantú, Roberto. 1973. Review of "*Bless Me, Ultima.*" *Mester* 4 no. 1: 66–68.

Cantú, Roberto. 1974. "Estructura y sentido de lo onírico en *Bless Me, Ultima.*" *Mester* 5, no. 1: 27–41.

Cantú, Roberto. 1979. "Degradación y regeneración en *Bless Me, Ultima*: el chicano y la vida nueva." In *The Identification and Analysis of Chicano Literature*, ed. Francisco Jiménez, 374–88. New York: Bilingual P.

Carby, Hazel V. 1987. *Reconstructing Womanhood: The Emergence of the Afro-American Woman Novelist.* New York: Oxford U P.

Carrasco, David. 1982. "A Perspective for a Study of Religious Dimensions in Chicano Experience: *Bless Me, Ultima* as a Religious Text." *Aztlán* 13, nos. 1–2: 195–221.

Castillo, Adelaida R. del, ed. 1988. *Between Borders: Essays On Mexican/Chicana History.* Encino, Calif.: Floricanto P.

Cisneros, Sandra. 1983. *The House on Mango Street.* Houston: Arte Público Press, 1983.

Cisneros, Sandra. 1987. "From a Writer's Notebook." *The America's Review* 15: 69–73.

Cisneros, Sandra. 1987. "'Writing Out of Necessity': An Interview with

Sandra Cisneros." Beatriz Badikian. Also, "Living as a Writer: Choice and Circumstance." *The Feminist Writers Guild* 10, no. 1 (February): 1, 6–8, 8–9.

Cixous, Hélène, and Catherine Clément. 1986. *The Newly Born Woman.* 1975. Trans. Betsy Wing. Minneapolis: U of Minnesota P.

Córdova, Teresa, et al. 1986. *Chicana Voices: Intersections of Class, Race, and Gender.* Austin: U of Texas P and the Center for Mexican American Studies.

Cortez v. State of Texas. Court of Criminal Appeals of Texas, January 15, 1902 (66 *Southwestern Reporter* 453–60).

Cortez v. State of Texas. Court of Criminal Appeals of Texas, June 15, 1904 (83 *Southwestern Reporter* 812–16).

Cotera, Marta. 1976. *Diosa y Hembra.* Austin: Information Systems Publications.

Coward, Rosalind, and John Ellis. 1977. *Language and Materialism: Developments in Semiology and the Theory of the Subject.* London: Routledge & Kegan Paul.

Dasenbrock, Reed Way. 1987. "Intelligibility and Meaningfulness in Multicultural Literature in English." *PMLA* 102, no. 1: 10–19.

De la Fuente, Patricia. 1985. "Invisible Women in the Narrative of Tomás Rivera." In *International Studies in Honor of Tomás Rivera,* ed. Julián Olivares. *Revista-Chicano Riqueña* 13, nos. 3–4: 81–89.

De Man, Paul. 1971. *Blindness and Insight: Essays in the Rhetoric of Modern Criticism.* New York: Oxford U P.

De Man, Paul. 1979. "Autobiography as De-facement." *MLN* 94: 919–30.

De Man, Paul. 1984. "Phenomenality and Materiality in Kant." In *Hermeneutics: Questions and Prospects,* ed. Gary Shapiro and Alan Sica, 121–44. Amherst: U of Massachusetts P.

Derrida, Jacques. 1973. "Differance." *Speech and Phenomena and Other Essays on Husserl's Theory of Signs.* Trans. David Allison. Evanston: Northwestern U P.

Derrida, Jacques. 1976. *Of Grammatology.* Trans. Gayatri Chakravorty Spivak. Baltimore: Johns Hopkins U P.

Derrida, Jacques. 1985. "Racism's Last Word." In *"Race," Writing, and Difference,* ed. Henry Louis Gates, Jr., 329–38. Chicago: U of Chicago P.

Donnelly, Dyan. 1974. "Finding a Home in the World." *Bilingual Review* 1, no. 1: 112–18.

Duban, James. 1988. "From Emerson to Edwards: Henry Whitney Bellows and an 'Ideal' Metaphysics of Sovereignty." *Harvard Theological Review* 81, no. 4: 389–411.

Eagleton, Terry. 1976. *Criticism and Ideology.* London: NLB, Verso Editions.

Eagleton, Terry. 1983. *Literary Theory: An Introduction.* Minneapolis: U of Minnesota P.

Eagleton, Terry. 1985. "Marxism, Structuralism, and Poststructuralism." *Diacritics* 15, no. 4: 2–12.

Eger, Ernestina, ed. 1982. *A Bibliography of Criticism of Contemporary Chicano Literature*. Berkeley: Chicano Studies Library Publications, University of California.

Fanon, Franz. [1961] 1982. *The Wretched of the Earth*. Trans. Constance Farrington. Harmondworth: Penguin.

Fischer, Michael M. J. 1986. "Ethnicity and the Post-Modern Arts of Memory." In *Writing Culture: The Poetics and Politics of Ethnography*, ed. James Clifford and George E. Marcus, 192–233. Berkeley: U of California P.

Flores, Lauro. 1985. "The Discourse of Silence in the Narrative of Tomás Rivera." In *International Studies in Honor of Tomás Rivera*, ed. Julián Olivares. *Revista Chicano-Riqueña* 13, nos. 3–4: 96–106.

Flores, Richard R. 1987. "Revolution, Folklore, and the Political Unconscious: "Los Sediciosos" as a Socially Symbolic Text." Paper presented at the annual meeting of the American Folklore Society, Albuquerque, October 23.

Galarza, Ernesto. [1971] 1980. *Barrio Boy: The Story of a Boy's Acculturation*. Notre Dame: Notre Dame U P.

Galarza, Ernesto. 1972. "Mexicans in the Southwest: A Culture in Process." In *On Plural Society in the Southwest*, ed. E. Spicer and R. Thompson, 261–98. New York: Interbook.

García, John A. 1981. "Yo Soy Mexicano . . .: Self-Identity and Sociodemographic Correlates." *Social Science Quarterly* 62: 88–98.

García, Mario T. 1980. "The Chicana in American History: The Mexican Women of El Paso, 1880–1920—A Case Study." *Pacific Historical Review* 49, no. 2: 315–37.

García, Mario T. 1981. *Desert Immigrants: The Mexicans of El Paso, 1880–1920*. New Haven: Yale U P.

Gates, Henry Louis, Jr. 1984. *Black Literature and Literary Theory*. London: Methuen.

Gates, Henry Louis, Jr. 1985. "Introduction: Writing 'Race' and the Difference It Makes." In *"Race," Writing and Difference*, ed. Henry Louis Gates, Jr., 1–20. Chicago: U of Chicago P.

Gates, Henry Louis, Jr. 1987. *Figures in Black: Words, Signs, and the "Racial" Self*. New York: Oxford U P.

Gates, Henry Louis, Jr. 1988. *The Signifying Monkey: A Theory of Afro-American Literary Criticism*. New York: Oxford U P.

Geertz, Clifford. 1973. *The Interpretation of Cultures*. New York: Basic Books.

Genette, Gérard. [1972] 1980. *Narrative Discourse: An Essay on Method*. Trans. Jane E. Lewin. Ithaca: Cornell U P.

González, Rosalinda M. 1983. "Chicanas and Mexican Immigrant Families, 1920–1940: Women's Subordination and Family Exploitation." In *Decades of Discontent: The Women's Movement, 1920–1940*, ed. Lois Scharf and Joan M. Jensen, 59–84. Westport, Conn.: Greenwood P.

González-Berry, Erlinda, and Tey Diana Rebolledo. "Growing Up Chicano:

Tomás Rivera and Sandra Cisneros." In *International Studies in Honor of Tomás Rivera*, ed. Julián Olivares. *Revista Chicano-Riqueña* 13, nos. 3–4: 109–19.

Goulden, Joseph C. 1982. *Korea: The Untold Story of the War*. New York: New York Times Books.

Grajeda, Ralph. 1979. "Tomás Rivera's Appropriation of the Chicano Past." In *Modern Chicano Writers: A Collection of Critical Essays*, ed. Joseph Sommers and Tomás Ybarra-Frausto, 74–85. Englewood Cliffs, N.J.: Prentice-Hall.

Gramsci, Antonio. 1971. *Selections from the Prison Notebooks*. Ed. and trans. Quintin Hoare and Geoffrey Nowell Smith. New York: International Publishers.

Gramsci, Antonio. 1985. *Selections from Cultural Writings*. Ed. David Forgacs and Geoffrey Nowell-Smith. Trans. William Boelhower. Cambridge: Harvard U P.

Greimas, A. J. 1970. *Du sens*. Paris: Seuil.

Griswold del Castillo, Richard Allan. 1975. "La Familia Chicana: Social Changes in the Chicano Family of Los Angeles, 1850–1880." *Journal of Ethnic Studies* 3, no. 1 (Spring): 41–58.

Griswold del Castillo, Richard Allan. 1984. *La Familia: Chicano Families in the Urban Southwest, 1848 to the Present*. Notre Dame: U of Notre Dame P.

Hall, Stuart. 1977a. "Culture, the Media and the 'Ideological Effect.'" In *Mass Communications and Society*, ed. James Curran et al., 315–48. London: Edward Arnold.

Hall, Stuart. 1977b. "The Hinterland of Science: Ideology and The 'Sociology of Knowledge.'" In *On Ideology*, Ed. Bill Schwarz et al., 9–32. London: Hutchinson.

Hall, Stuart. 1986. "Gramsci's Relevance for the Study of Race and Ethnicity." *Journal of Communication Inquiry* 10, no. 2 (Summer): 5–28.

Harlow, Barbara. 1987. *Resistance Literature*. New York and London: Methuen.

Harlow, Barbara. Forthcoming. "Sites of Struggle: Immigration, Deportation, Prison and Exile." In *Chicano Criticism in a Social Context*, ed. Héctor Calderón and José David Saldívar. Durham: Duke U P.

Hebdige, Dick. [1979] 1988. *Subculture: The Meaning of Style*. London: Methuen.

Hegel, G. W. F. [1835–38] 1975. *Hegel's Aesthetics: Lectures on Fine Art*. 2 vols. Trans. T. M. Knox. Oxford: Oxford U P.

Heinzelman, Susan Sage. 1988. "Hard Cases, Easy Cases and Weird Cases: Canon Formation in Law and Literature." *Mosaic* 21: 59–72.

Hernández, Guillermo E. Forthcoming. *Chicano Satire: A Study of Valdez, Hinojosa and Montoya*. Austin: U of Texas P.

Hererra-Sobek, María, and Helena María Viramontes, eds. 1988. *Chicana Creativity and Criticism: Charting New Frontiers in American Literature*. Houston: Arte Público Press.

Higham, John. 1974. "Hanging Together: Divergent Unities in American History." *Journal of American History* 61: 10–18.

Hinojosa, Rolando. 1973. *Estampas del Valle y otras obras*. Berkeley: Quinto Sol Publications.

Hinojosa, Rolando. 1977. *Klail City y sus alrededores*. Havana: Casa de las Américas, 1976. Published in the United States as *Generaciones y semblanzas*. Berkeley: Justa Publications.

Hinojosa, Rolando. 1978. *Korean Love Songs: From Klail City Death Trip*. Berkeley: Editorial Justa.

Hinojosa, Rolando. 1981. *Mi Querido Rafa*. Houston: Arte Público Press.

Hinojosa, Rolando. 1982. *Rites and Witnesses*. Houston: Arte Público Press.

Hinojosa, Rolando. 1983. *The Valley*. Author's recreation in English of *Estampas del Valle*. Ypsilanti, Mich.: Bilingual Press.

Hinojosa, Rolando. 1983. "This Writer's Sense of Place." In *The Texas Literary Tradition: Fiction, Folklore, History*, ed. Don Graham et al., 120–24. Austin: The College of Liberal Arts, The University of Texas at Austin and the Texas State Historical Association.

Hinojosa, Rolando. 1985. *Dear Rafe*. Author's recreation in English of *Mi Querido Rafa*. Houston: Arte Público Press.

Hinojosa, Rolando. 1985. *Partners in Crime: A Rafe Buenrostro Mystery*. Houston: Arte Público Press.

Hinojosa, Rolando. 1986. *Claros Varones de Belken / Fair Gentlemen of Belken County*. Tempe, Ariz.: Bilingual Press.

Hinojosa, Rolando. 1987. *Klail City*. Author's recreation in English of *Klail City y sus alrededores*. Houston: Arte Público Press.

Hinojosa, Rolando. 1987. *This Migrant Earth*. Author's rendition in English of Tomás Rivera's . . . *Y no se lo tragó la tierra*. Houston: Arte Público Press.

Hirst, Paul. 1979. *On Law and Ideology*. London: Humanities Press.

Hobsbawm, Eric J. 1965. *Primitive Rebels: Studies in Archaic Forms of Social Movement in the 19th and 20th Centuries*. New York: Norton.

Horkheimer, Max, and Theodor W. Adorno. 1972. "The Culture Industry: Enlightenment as Mass Deception." *Dialectic of Enlightenment*, trans. John Cumming, 120–67. New York: Continuum.

Jameson, Fredric. 1971. *Marxism and Form: Twentieth-Century Dialectical Theories of Literature*. Princeton: Princeton U P.

Jameson, Fredric. 1972. *The Prison-House of Language: A Critical Account of Structuralism and Russian Formalism*. Princeton: Princeton U P.

Jameson, Fredric. 1976. "Collective Art in the Age of Cultural Imperialism," *Alcheringa* 2, no. 2: 108–12.

Jameson, Fredric. 1979. "Reification and Utopia in Mass Culture," *Social Text* 1: 130–48.

Jameson, Fredric. 1981. *The Political Unconscious: Narrative as a Socially Symbolic Act*. Ithaca, N.Y.: Cornell U P.

Jameson, Fredric. 1986. "Third-World Literature in the Era of Multinational Capitalism." *Social Text* 15: 65–88.

Jameson, Fredric. 1988. "Cognitive Mapping." In *Marxism and the Inter-pretation of Culture,* ed. Cary Nelson and Lawrence Grossberg, 347–57. Urbana and Chicago: U of Illinois P.

JanMohamed, Abdul. 1985. "The Economy of Manichean Allegory: The Function of Racial Difference in Colonialist Literature." In *"Race", Writing and Difference,* ed. Henry Louis Gates, Jr., 78–106. Chicago: U of Chicago P.

Jay, Paul. 1984. *Being in the Text: Self-Representation from Wordsworth to Roland Barthes.* Ithaca, N.Y.: Cornell U P.

Jayawardena, Kumari. 1986. *Feminism and Nationalism in the Third World.* London: Zed Books.

Johnson, Barbara. 1982. "My Monster/My Self." *Diacritics* 12: 2–10.

Johnson, Barbara. 1985. "Thresholds of Difference: Structures of Address in Zora Neale Hurston." In *"Race," Writing, and Difference,* ed. Henry Louis Gates, Jr., 317–28. Chicago: U of Chicago P.

Johnson, Elaine D. 1978. "A Thematic Study of Three Chicano Narratives: *Estampas del valle y otras obras, Bless Me, Ultima,* and *Peregrinos de Aztlán.*" Ph.D. diss., University of Wisconsin, Madison.

Kahn, Coppélia. 1982. "Excavating 'Those Dim Minoan Regions': Maternal Subtexts in Patriarchal Literature." *Diacritics* 12: 32–41.

Keohane, Nannerl O., et al., eds. 1981. *Feminist Theory: A Critique of Ideology.* Chicago: U of Chicago P.

Kolakowski, Leszek. 1978. *Main Currents of Marxism: The Founders.* Trans. P. S. Falla. New York: Oxford U P.

Lacan, Jacques. 1968. *Ecrits.* Paris: Seuil.

Lattin, Vernon E. 1979. "The Quest for Mythic Vision in Contemporary Native American and Chicano Fiction." *American Literature* 50, no. 4: 625–46.

Lauter, Paul. 1985. "Race and Gender in the Shaping of the American Literary Canon: A Case Study from the Twenties." In *Feminist Criticism and Social Change: Sex, Class and Race in Literature and Culture,* ed. Judith Newton and Deborah Rosenfelt, 19–44. New York and London: Methuen.

Leal, Luis. 1979. "Mexican American Literature: A Historical Perspective." In *Modern Chicano Writers: A Collection of Critical Essays,* ed. Joseph Sommers and Tomás Ybarra-Frausto, 18–30. Englewood Cliffs, N.J.: Prentice-Hall.

Leal, Luis, and Pepe Barrón. 1982. "Chicano Literature: An Overview." In *Three American Literatures: Essays in Chicano, Native-American, and Asian-American Literature for Teachers of American Literature,* ed. Houston A. Baker, Jr., 9–32. New York: Modern Language Association of America.

Lentricchia, Frank. 1980. *After the New Criticism.* Chicago: U of Chicago P.

Lentricchia, Frank. 1983. *Criticism and Social Change.* Chicago: U of Chicago P.

Limón, José E. 1974. *"El Primer Congreso Mexicanista* de 1911: A Precursor to Contemporary Chicanismo." *Aztlán* 5: 85–117.

Limón, José E. 1980. "Américo Paredes: A Man From the Border." *Revista Chicano-Riqueña* 7, no. 3: 1–5.

Limón, José E. 1981. "The Folk Performance of '*Chicano*' and the Cultural Limits of Political Ideology." In *"And Other Neighborly Names": Social Process and Cultural Image in Texas Folklore*, ed. Richard Bauman and Roger D. Abrahams, 197–225. Austin: U of Texas P.

Limón, José E. 1983a. "Folklore, Social Conflict, and the United States-Mexico Border." In *Handbook of American Folklore*, ed. Richard Dorson, 216–26. Bloomington: Indiana U P.

Limón, José E. 1983b. "The Greater Mexican *Corrido* and Don Américo Paredes as Poet: Oral Tradition, Poetic Influence, and Cultural History." A paper presented at the *Symposium on Chicano Popular Art and Literature*, University of California, Santa Barbara.

Limón, José E. 1983c. "The Rise, Fall and 'Revival' of the Mexican-American Ballad: A Review Essay." *Studies in Latin American Popular Culture* 2: 202–7.

Limón, José E. 1984. "Mexican Ballads, Chicano Epic: History, Influence and Self in Mexican-American Social Poetics." A paper presented at a special session, "Persuasions and Performances: The Poetics of Self and Society," in memory of Victor Turner, American Anthropological Association Annual Meetings, Denver, November 15.

Limón, José E. 1986. "The Return of the Mexican Ballad: Américo Paredes and His Anthropological Text as Persuasive Performance." Unpublished manuscript.

Lipsitz, George. 1987. "Cruising Around the Historical Bloc—Postmodernism and Popular Music in East Los Angeles." *Cultural Critique* 5 (Winter): 157–77.

Lizárraga, Sylvia S. 1985. "The Patriarchal Ideology in 'La noche que se apagaron las luces.'" In *International Studies in Honor of Tomás Rivera*, ed. Julián Olivares. *Revista Chicano-Riqueña* 13, nos. 3–4: 90–95.

Lomas, Clara. 1985. "Development of a Revolutionary Feminist Consciousness: From Exploration of the Self to Political Discourse, 1870–1970." Paper.

Lomas, Clara. Forthcoming. "Mexican Precursors of Chicana Feminist Writing." In *'Wild Zone': Essays on Multi-Ethnic American Literature*, ed. Cordelia Candelaria.

Lomas, Clara. 1989. "Leonor Villegas de Magnon." In *Longman Anthology of World Literature by Women, 1875–1975*, ed. Marian Arkin and Barbara Shollar, 181–84. New York & London: Longman.

Lomelí, Francisco A. 1980a. "Eusebio Chacón: Eslabón temprano de la novela chicana." *La Palabra* 2, no. 1: 47–55.

Lomelí, Francisco A. 1980b. "Isabella Ríos and the Chicano Psychic Novel." In *Minority Voices: An Interdisciplinary Journal of Literature and the Arts* 4, no. 1: 49–61.

Lomelí, Francisco A. 1985a. "Chicana Novelists in the Process of Creating Fictive Voices." In *Beyond Stereotypes: The Critical Analysis of Chi-*

cana Literature, ed. María Herrera-Sobek, 29–46. Binghamton, N.Y.: Bilingual P.

Lomelí, Francisco A. 1985b. "Eusebio Chacón." In *Chicano Literature: A Reference Guide,* ed. Julio A. Martínez and Francisco A. Lomelí, 91–97. Westport, Conn.: Greenwood P.

Lukács, Georg. 1968. "Reification and the Consciousness of the Proletariat." *History and Class Consciousness: Studies in Marxist Dialectics,* trans. Rodney Livingstone, 83–222. Cambridge: MIT P.

Lukács, Georg. [1920] 1971. *The Theory of the Novel: A Historico-Philosophical Essay on the Forms of Great Epic Literature,* trans. Anna Bostock. Cambridge: MIT P.

Lukács, Georg. [1955] 1972. "The Ideology of Modernism" *The Meaning of Contemporary Realism.* In *20th Century Literary Criticism,* ed. David Lodge, 474–87. London: Longman.

Luna-Lawhn, Juanita. 1986. "Victorian Attitudes Affecting the Mexican Woman Writing in *La Prensa* During the Early 1900s and the Chicanas of the 1980s." In *Missions in Conflict: Essays on U.S.-Mexican Relations and Chicano Culture,* ed. Renate von Bardeleben et al. 65–74. Tübingen: Gunter Narr Verlag.

Macherey, Pierre. 1978. *A Theory of Literary Production,* trans. Geoffrey Wall. London: Routledge & Kegan Paul.

McCracken, Ellen. 1989. "Sandra Cisneros' *The House on Mango Street*: Community-Oriented Introspection and the Demystification of Patriarchal Violence." In *Breaking Boundaries: Latina Writings and Critical Readings,* ed. Asunción Horno-Delgado et al., 62–71. Amherst: U of Massachussetts P.

McDowell, John Holmes. 1981. "The *Corrido* of Greater Mexico as Discourse, Music, and Event." In *"And Other Neighborly Names": Social Process and Cultural Image in Texas Folklore,* ed. Richard Bauman and Roger D. Abrahams, 44–75. Austin: U of Texas P.

MacKinnon, Catherine A. 1981. "Feminism, Marxism, Method, and the State: An Agenda for Theory." *Feminist Theory: A Critique of Ideology,* 1–30. Chicago: U of Chicago P.

McLemore, Dale S., and Ricardo Romo. 1985. "The Origins and Development of the Mexican American People." In *The Mexican American Experience: An Interdisciplinary Anthology,* ed. Rodolfo O. de la Garza et al. 3–32. Austin: U of Texas P.

McNeil, Norman Laird. 1946. "*Corridos* of the Mexican Border." In *Mexican Border Ballads and Other Lore,* ed. Mody C. Boatright, 1–34. Austin: Texas Folklore Society Publication, no. 21.

McWilliams, Carey. 1973. *North from Mexico.* New York: Greenwood P.

Marcuse, Herbert. 1972. "The Foundation of Historical Materialism." *From Luther to Popper,* trans. Joris de Bres, 1–48. London: NLB, Verso Editions; rpt. 1983.

Martin, Biddy. 1988. "Feminism, Criticism, and Foucault." In *Feminism &*

Foucault: Reflections on Resistance, ed. Irene Diamond and Lee Quinby, 3–19. Boston: Northeastern U P.

Martínez, Eliud. 1986. "Ron Arias' *The Road to Tamazunchale*: A Chicano Novel of the New Reality." In *Contemporary Chicano Fiction: A Critical Survey*, ed. Vernon E. Lattin, 226–38. Binghamton, N.Y.: Bilingual P.

Martínez, Julio A., and Francisco A. Lomelí, eds. 1985. *Chicano Literature: A Reference Guide*. Westport, Conn.: Greenwood P.

Marx, Karl. "Theses on Feuerbach." [1888] 1978. *The Marx-Engels Reader*. 2d ed., ed. Robert C. Tucker, 143–45. New York: Norton.

Marx, Karl, and Friedrich Engels. [1845–46] 1978. *The German Ideology*. *The Marx-Engels Reader*. 2d ed., ed. Robert C. Tucker. New York: Norton.

Marzán, Julio. 1982. "Richard Rodriguez Talks to Himself." Review of *Hunger of Memory: The Education of Richard Rodriguez*. *The Village Voice* April 27: 46–47.

Matthiessen, F. O. 1941. *American Renaissance: Art and Expression in the Age of Emerson and Whitman*. Oxford: Oxford U P.

Mehlman, Jeffrey. 1974. *A Structural Study of Autobiography: Proust, Leiris, Sartre, Lévi-Strauss*. Ithaca, N.Y.: Cornell U P.

Melville, Margarita, ed. 1980. *Twice A Minority: Mexican American Women*. St. Louis: Mosby Press.

Mendoza, Vicente T. 1954. *El corrido mexicano: Antología*. Mexico: Fondo de Cultura Económica.

Miles, Jack. 1982. Review of *Hunger of Memory: The Education of Richard Rodriguez*. *Los Angeles Times* February 28: 3.

Mirandé, Alfredo, and Evangelina Enríquez. 1977. *La Chicana: The Mexican American Woman*. Chicago: U of Chicago P.

Mirandé, Alfredo, and Evangelina Enríquez. 1979. "Chicanas in the History of the Southwest." In *Introduction to Chicano Studies*, 2d ed, ed. Livie Isauro Duran and H. Russell Bernard, 156–79. New York: Macmillan.

Modleski, Tania. 1988. *The Women Who Knew Too Much: Hitchcock and Feminist Theory*. London: Methuen, 1988.

Monleón, José A. 1986. "Ilusión y realidad en la obra de Rudolfo Anaya." In *Contemporary Chicano Fiction: A Critical Survey*, ed. Vernon E. Lattin, 171–99. Binghamton, N.Y.: Bilingual P.

Monsiváis, Carlos. 1973. "Literatura comparada: Literatura chicana." *Fomento Literario* 1 (January): 42–48.

Montejano, David. 1979. "Frustrated Apartheid: Race, Repression, and Capitalist Agriculture in South Texas, 1920–1930." In *The World-System of Capitalism: Past & Present*, ed. Walter L. Goldfrank. Vol. 2, Political Economy of the World-System Annuals, 131–68. Beverly Hills and London: Sage Publications.

Montejano, David. 1987. *Anglos and Mexicans in the Making of Texas, 1836–1986*. Austin: U of Texas P.

Moquin, Wayne, and Charles Van Doren, ed. 1971. *A Documentary History of the Mexican Americans*. New York: Bantam.

Moraga, Cherríe. 1983. *Loving in the War Years: lo que nunca pasó por sus labios*. Boston: South End Press.

Moraga, Cherríe. 1989. "Writing Is the Measure of My Life . . ." An Interview with Cherríe Moraga. Dorothy Allison, Tomás Almaguer, and Jackie Goldsby. *OUT / LOOK: National Lesbian & Gay Quarterly* 1, no. 4 (Winter): 53–57.

Moraga, Cherríe, and Gloria Anzaldúa, ed. 1983. *This Bridge Called My Back: Writings by Radical Women of Color*. 2d ed. New York: Kitchen Table: Women of Color Press.

Morrison, Toni. 1989. "Unspeakable Things Unspoken: The Afro-American Presence in American Literature." *Michigan Quarterly Review* 28, no. 1 (Winter): 1–34.

Nelson, Cary. 1989. *Repression and Recovery: Modern American Poetry and the Politics of Cultural Memory, 1910–1945*. Madison: U of Wisconsin P.

Nieto, Eva Margarita. 1986. "The Dialectics of Textual Interpolation in Ron Arias' *The Road to Tamazunchale*." In *Contemporary Chicano Fiction: A Critical Survey*, ed. Vernon E. Lattin, 239–46. Binghamton, N.Y.: Bilingual P.

Nostrand, Richard L. 1973. " 'Mexican American' and 'Chicano': Emerging Terms for a People Coming of Age." *Pacific Historical Review* 62: 389–406.

Olivares, Julián. 1988. "Sandra Cisneros' *The House on Mango Street*, and the Poetics of Space." In *Chicana Creativity and Criticism: Charting New Frontiers in American Literature*, ed. María Hererra-Sobek and Helena María Viramontes, 160–69. Houston: Arte Público Press.

Olivares, Julián, ed. 1985. *International Studies in Honor of Tomás Rivera*. *Revista Chicana-Riqueña* 13, nos. 3–4.

Olney, James. 1972. *Metaphors of Self: The Meaning of Autobiography*. Princeton: Princeton U P.

Olney, James, ed. 1980. *Autobiography: Essays Theoretical and Critical*. Princeton: Princeton U P.

Padilla, Genaro. 1985. "Yo sola aprendí: Contra Patriarchal Containment in 19th Century California Personal Narratives." Stanford University, Center for Research on Women. Proceedings of the Conference on Autobiography and Biography: Gender, Text, and Context.

Paredes, Américo. Circa 1939. "The Hammon and the Beans." *The Texas Observer*. April 18, 1963. Rpt. *The Chicano: From Caricature to Self-Portrait*, ed. Edward Simmen, 274–78. New York: New American Library, Mentor Books, 1971.

Paredes, Américo. Circa 1948. "Over the Waves is Out." *New Mexico Review* 23, no. 2 (Summer 1953): 177–87.

Paredes, Américo. 1958a. *"With His Pistol in His Hand": A Border Ballad and Its Hero*. Austin: U of Texas P.

Paredes, Américo. 1958b. "The Mexican *Corrido*: Its Rise and Fall." In *Madstones and Twisters*, ed. Mody C. Boatright, 91–105. Dallas: Southern Methodist U P.

Paredes, Américo. 1970. *Folktales of Mexico*. Chicago: U of Chicago P.

Paredes, Américo. 1976. *A Texas-Mexican "Cancionero": Folksongs of the Lower Border*. Urbana: U of Illinois P.

Paredes, Américo. 1978. "The Problem of Identity in a Changing Culture: Popular Expressions of Culture Conflict Along the Lower Rio Grande Border." In *Views Across the Border: The United States and Mexico*, ed. Stanley R. Ross, 68–94. Albuquerque: U of New Mexico P.

Paredes, Américo. 1979. "The Folk Base of Chicano Literature." In *Modern Chicano Writers: A Collection of Critical Essays*, ed. Joseph Sommers and Tomás Ybarra-Frausto, 4–17. Englewood Cliffs, N.J.: Prentice-Hall.

Paredes, Raymund A. 1982. "The Evolution of Chicano Literature." In *Three American Literatures: Essays in Chicano, Native-American, and Asian-American Literature*, ed. Houston A. Baker, Jr., 33–79. New York: Modern Language Association of America.

Peña, Manuel. 1985. *The Texas-Mexican Conjunto: History of a Working Class Music*. Austin: U of Texas P and the Center for Mexican American Studies.

Pierce, Frank Cushman. 1917. *A Brief History of the Lower Rio Grande Valley*. Menasha, Wis.: George Banta.

Quintana, Alvina E. 1986. "Women: Prisoners of the Word." In *Chicana Voices: Intersections of Class, Race, and Gender*. Ed. Teresa Córdova et al., 208–19. Austin: U of Texas P and the Center for Mexican American Studies.

Quintana, Alvina E. 1988. "Chicana Motifs: Challenge and Counter-Challenge." In *Intersections: Studies in Ethnicity, Gender and Inequality*, 197–217. Pullam: Washington State U P.

Radhakrishnan, R. 1987. "Ethnic Identity and Post-Structuralist Differance." *Cultural Critique* 6: 199–220.

Rebolledo, Tey Diana. 1988. "The Politics of Poetics: Or, What Am I, A Critic, Doing in This Text Anyhow?" In *Chicana Creativity and Criticism: Charting New Frontiers in American Literature*, ed. María Hererra-Sobek and Helena María Viramontes, 129–38. Houston: Arte Público Press.

Retamar, Roberto Fernández. [1971] 1979. "Calibán; apuntes sobre la cultura en nuestra América." *Casa de las Américas* (Havana) 68 (Sept.–Oct. 1971). Rpt. *Calibán y otros ensayos*, 10–102. La Habana: Editorial Arte y Literatura.

Retamar, Roberto Fernández. 1974. "Caliban: Notes Towards a Discussion of Culture in Our America." *Massachusetts Review* 15, nos. 1–2: 7–72.

Ricouer, Paul. 1970. *Freud and Philosophy*, trans. D. Savage. New Haven: Yale U P.

Ricoeur, Paul. 1985. *Time and Narrative*. Vol. 2. Trans. Kathleen McLaughlin and David Pellauer. Chicago: U of Chicago P.

Ríos, Isabella (Diane López). 1976. *Victuum*. Ventura: Diana-Etna.

Rivera, Tomás. 1971. "Into the Labyrinth: The Chicano in Literature." In

New Voices in Literature: The Mexican American, ed. Edward Simmen, 18–25. Edinburg, Tex.: Pan American University.

Rivera, Tomás. 1971. . . . *Y no se lo tragó la tierra / And the Earth Did Not Part*. Berkeley: Quinto Sol Publications; reissued by Justa Publications, 1976.

Robinson, Cecil. 1977. *Mexico and the Hispanic Southwest in American Literature*. Tucson: U of Arizona P.

Rodríguez, Juan. 1967. "The Problematic in Tomás Rivera." *Revista Chicano-Riqueña* 6, no. 3: 42–50.

Rodríguez, Juan. 1979a. "La búsqueda de identidad y sus motivos en la literatura chicana." In *The Identification and Analysis of Chicano Literature*, ed. Francisco Jiménez, 170–78. New York: Bilingual P.

Rodríguez, Juan. 1979b. "Notes on the Evolution of Chicano Prose Fiction." In *Modern Chicano Writers: A Collection of Critical Essays*, ed. Joseph Sommers and Tomás Ybarra-Frausto, 67–73. Englewood Cliffs, N.J.: Prentice-Hall.

Rodriguez, Richard. 1982. *Hunger of Memory: The Education of Richard Rodriguez*. New York: Godine; rpt. Bantam Books, 1983.

Rogers, Jane. 1986. "The Function of the La Llorona Motif in Anaya's *Bless Me, Ultima*." In *Contemporary Chicano Fiction: A Critical Survey*, ed. Vernon E. Lattin, 200–205. Binghamton, N.Y.: Bilingual P.

Rogin, Paul. 1979. *Subversive Genealogy: The Politics and Art of Herman Melville*. Berkeley: U of California P.

Romo, Ricardo. 1983. *East Los Angeles: History of a Barrio*. Austin: U of Texas P.

Rosaldo, Renato. 1987. "Politics, Patriarchs, and Laughter." *Cultural Critique* 6: 65–86.

Rose, Jacqueline. 1987. "The State of the Subject (II): The Institution of Feminism." *Critical Quarterly* 29, no. 4: 9–15.

Rosenbaum, Robert J. 1981. *Mexicano Resistance in the Southwest: "The Sacred Right of Self-Preservation."* Austin: U of Texas P.

Ruiz, Vicki. 1987. *Cannery Women, Cannery Lives: Mexican Women, Unionization, and the California Food Processing Industry, 1930–1950*. Albuquerque: U of New Mexico P.

Ruiz, Vicki. 1989. "From Out of the Shadows: A History of Mexican Women in the Southwest, 1540–1900." A paper presented at the *Latino Graduate Student Training Seminar*, the University of Texas at Austin, July 6.

Ryan, Michael. 1982. *Marxism and Deconstruction: A Critical Articulation*. Baltimore: Johns Hopkins U P.

Said, Edward W. 1975. *Beginnings: Intention and Method*. Baltimore: Johns Hopkins U P.

Said, Edward W. 1979. *Orientalism*. New York: Random House, Vintage Books.

Saldívar, Gabriel. 1943. *Documentos de la rebelión de Catarino E. Garza*. Mexico: Secretaría de Agricultura y Fomento.

Saldívar, José D. 1985. "The Ideological and Utopian in Tomás Rivera's *Y no*

se lo tragó la tierra and Ron Arias' *The Road to Tamazunchale.*" *Critica* 1,
no. 2: 100–114.

Saldívar, José David. 1989. "The Limits of Cultural Studies." Paper presented
to the Program in American Culture, the University of Michigan, Ann
Arbor, January.

Saldívar, José David, ed. 1985. *The Rolando Hinojosa Reader: Essays Historical and Critical.* Houston: Arte Público Press.

Saldívar, Ramón. 1984. *Figural Language in the Novel: The Flowers of Speech
from Cervantes to Joyce.* Princeton: Princeton U P.

Saldívar-Hull, Sonia. Forthcoming. "Feminism on the Border: From Gender
Politics to Geopolitics." In *Chicano Criticism in a Social Context,* ed.
Héctor Calderón and José David Saldívar. Durham: Duke U P.

Sánchez, George. 1961–62. "The American of Mexican Descent." *Chicago
Jewish Forum* 20: 120–24.

Sánchez, Rosaura. 1977. "The Chicana Labor Force." In *Essays on La Mujer,*
ed. Rosaura Sánchez and Rosa Martinez Cruz, 3–15. Los Angeles: Chicano
Studies Center Publications, University of California.

Sánchez, Rosaura. 1985. "From Heterogeneity to Contradiction: Hinojosa's
Novel." In *The Rolando Hinojosa Reader: Essays Historical and Critical,*
ed. José David Saldívar, 76–100. Houston: Arte Público Press.

Sánchez, Rosaura. 1987. "Ethnicity, Ideology and Academia." *The Americas
Review* 15: 80–88.

Sánchez, Rosaura, and Rosa Martinez Cruz, eds. 1977. *Essays on La Mujer.*
Los Angeles: Chicano Studies Center Publications, University of California.

Sánchez, Saúl. 1978. "Tres dimensiones en la narrativa chicana contempo-
ránea." Paper presented at Canto al Pueblo Conference, Corpus Christi,
Tex., June 5.

San Miguel, Guadalupe, Jr. 1987. *"Let All of Them Take Heed": Mexican
Americans and the Campaign for Educational Equality in Texas, 1910–
1981.* Austin: Center for Mexican American Studies Publications, mono-
graph no. 11, U of Texas P.

Slotkin, Richard. 1973. *Regeneration Through Violence.* Middletown,
Conn.: Wesleyan U P.

Sollors, Werner. 1986. *Beyond Ethnicity: Consent and Descent in American
Culture.* New York: Oxford U P.

Sollors, Werner, ed. 1989. *The Invention of Ethnicity.* New York: Oxford U P.

Sommers, Joseph. 1979. "Interpreting Tomás Rivera." In *Modern Chicano
Writers: A Collection of Critical Essays,* ed. Joseph Sommers and Tomás
Ybarra-Frausto, 94–107. Englewood Cliffs, N.J.: Prentice-Hall.

Spengemann, William. 1980. *The Forms of Autobiography: Episodes in the
History of a Literary Genre.* New Haven: Yale U P.

Spivak, Gayatri Chakravorty. 1983. "Displacement and the Discourse of
Woman." In *Displacement: Derrida and After,* ed. Mark Krupnick, 169–
95. Bloomington: Indiana U P.

Spivak, Gayatri Chakravorty. 1984. "Marx after Derrida." In *Philosophical*

Approaches to Literature, ed. William E. Cain, 227–46. Lewisburg, Pa.: Bucknell U P.

Spivak, Gayatri Chakravorty. 1987. "Feminism and Critical Theory." Also, "A Literary Representation of the Subaltern: A Woman's Text from the Third World." In *Other Worlds: Essays in Cultural Politics*, 77–92, 241–68. New York and London: Methuen.

Sweeney, Judith. 1977. "Chicana History: A Review of the Literature." In *Essays on La Mujer*, ed. Rosaura Sánchez and Rosa Martinez Cruz, 99–123. Los Angeles: Chicano Studies Center Publications, University of California.

Tatum, Charles. 1975. "Contemporary Chicano Prose Fiction: Its Ties to Mexican Literature." *Books Abroad* 49: 432–38.

Tatum, Charles. 1982. *Chicano Literature*. Boston: Twayne Publishers, 1982.

Taussig, Michael T. 1980. *The Devil and Commodity Fetishism in South America*. Chapel Hill: U of North Carolina P.

Testa, Daniel P. 1979. "Narrative Technique and Human Experience in Tomás Rivera." In *Modern Chicano Writers: A Collection of Critical Essays*, ed. Joseph Summers and Tomás Ybarro-Frausto, 86–93. Englewood Cliffs, N.J.: Prentice-Hall.

Therborn, Göran. 1980. *The Ideology of Power and the Power of Ideology*. London: NLB, Verso Editions.

Thompson, E. P. 1978. "Folklore, Anthropology, and Social History." *Indian Historical Review* 3, no. 2: 247–66.

Tucker, Robert C. 1978. "Introduction." *The Marx-Engels Reader*, 2d ed., ed. Robert C. Tucker, xix–xxxviii. New York: Norton.

√ Valenzuela, Liliana. 1986. " 'Nomás tres tiros le dió': Towards an Analysis of Women's Images in Greater Mexican Folksong and Folk Poetry." Paper, Department of Anthropology, University of Texas at Austin.

Valenzuela, Liliana. 1988. *Mexico's La Malinche: Mother or Whore, Creator or Traitor?*. M.A. thesis, the University of Texas at Austin.

Villanueva, Tino. 1980. "Sobre el término 'chicano.' " In *Chicanos: Antología histórica y literaria*, ed. Tino Villanueva, 7–34. Mexico: Fondo de Cultura Económica.

Villarreal, José Antonio. 1959. *Pocho*. Rpt. New York: Anchor Books, 1970.

Vogel, Lise. 1983. *Marxism and the Oppression of Women: Toward a Unitary Theory*. New Brunswick, N.J.: Rutgers U P.

Volosinov, V. N. [1929–30] 1973. *Marxism and the Philosophy of Language*, trans. Ladislav Matejka and I. R. Titunik. New York and London: Seminar Press.

Williams, Raymond. 1977. *Marxism and Literature*. Oxford: Oxford U P.

Williams, Raymond. 1981. *Culture*. Glasgow: Fontana P.

Williams, Raymond. 1983. *Keywords*. New York: Oxford U P.

Wolf, Eric R. 1958. "The Virgin of Guadalupe: A Mexican National Symbol." *American Journal of Folklore* 71: 34–39.

Yarbro-Bejarano, Yvonne. 1988. "Chicana Literature from a Chicana Feminist Perspective." In *Chicana Creativity and Criticism: Charting New Frontiers in American Literature*, ed. María Hererra-Sobek and Helena María Viramontes, 139–45. Houston: Arte Público Press.

Zavella, Patricia. 1987. *Women's Work & Chicano Families: Cannery Workers of the Santa Clara Valley*. Ithaca, N.Y.: Cornell U P.

Index

Acculturation, 54, 66, 164, 167–68
Acosta, Oscar Zeta, 6, 74, 90–98, 103, 106, 126, 128, 155, 218; as Buffalo Zeta Brown, 90–91, 98; critique of American hegemony, 92; historical place of, 74; and imaginary function, 98; and political action, 90; and satire, 90, 92; and social crises of 1960s, 95; and symbolic function, 98; and utopian vision, 98
—*Autobiography of a Brown Buffalo, The*, 90–95; altered consciousness in, 92; construction of self in, 92; East Los Angeles in, 92, 94; identity in, 92; political consciousness in, 97; and racism, 93; and women, 93
—*Revolt of the Cockroach People, The*, 95–98; and allegory, 96; Buffalo Zeta Brown in, 95–96; Catolicos Por La Raza in, 95; Chicano movement in, 95; class consciousness in, 96–97; construction of identity in, 96–97; differential structure in, 96–97; East Los Angeles in, 95; history in, 96; ideology in, 98; law in, 96–98; political consciousness in, 97; as satire, 95; social justice in, 95–96; truth in, 97;
Acuña, Rodolfo, 17, 28, 30–31, 51, 52n, 77n, 116–18
Adams, Henry, 164
Adams-Onís Treaty, 15
Adelitas, 189
Adorno, Theodor, 134–35, 154, 169, 173–74; on music, 57; *Negative Dialectics*, 173–74

African American, 4, 217; in the Southwest, 12; literature, 205, 215
Ahmad, Aijaz, 131
Alarcón, Norma, 172n, 198n
Allegory, 79, 84, 88, 106, 108, 130, 133, 157, 189, 206
Althusser, Louis, 76, 183, 210–13; on ideology, 167, 210–12; interpellation of subject, 68; on subject formation, 174
Alvarez, Rodolfo, 17
American Federation of Labor, 69
American history, 77
American literary history, 5, 7–8, 19, 204–5, 215–18; reconstruction of, 215–18
American literature, 3, 5, 8–9, 25, 76, 107, 126, 204–5, 214–18; and ethnic literature, 214; reification of, 205
American studies, 3
Anaya, Rudolfo A., 6, 103–26, 179; collective unconscious in, 103; and corrido, 103; and history, 104; political unconscious in, 103, 121; and precritical knowledge, 126; and representation of history, 118; and romance, 103
—*Bless Me, Ultima*, 104–26, 129–30; allegory in, 106, 108; and American literature, 107; apocalyptic imagery in, 105, 119–20, 122; aporia in, 124; Arcadia in, 112, 114; archetypes in, 107–8, 111n; binary structures in, 106, 110–11, 122–23; Catholicism in, 105, 114, 124; collective unconscious

Bless Me, Ultima (continued)
in, 103, 111, 120; consciousness in,
104, 108; construction of subject in,
103; critical reception of, 104, 106–
8; deconstruction in, 111; dialectics
of difference in, 108; division of labor
in, 111; fantasy in, 115; Garden of
Eden in, 104–6, 112, 115; Golden Age
in, 112–14, 117, 119, 122, 124; good
and evil in, 122; Guadalupe, Virgin
of in, 106, 110, 115, 124; history in,
105–6, 108–9, 113–15, 118, 122–23,
125–26; ideology in, 104, 106, 108,
122–23, 126; *la llorona* in, 107, 113–
14, 122, 125; manichean structure in,
124; messianic figure in, 113; mode
of production in, 111–12, 116; myth
in, 103–9, 112–16, 122, 124; narrative
structure of, 109, 122–23, 125; narrator in, 108–9, 113; patriarchy in, 112,
122; as phallocentric text, 122;
political unconscious in, 108, 130;
portrait of the artist in, 104; precritical knowledge in, 107, 126; realism
in, 106, 108, 111, 123, 125–26; representation of women in, 105, 122;
as romance, 104, 107, 111, 123, 126;
sexuality in, 120; structural model of,
111, 122; subtext of, 125; symbolic
function in, 104–5, 108, 110, 113,
115–16, 124–25; temporality of, 105,
109–10, 115, 126; thermonuclear war
in, 121–22, 125; Utopian vision in,
115, 118, 126; as wish-fulfillment,
108, 118, 125
Anderson, Benedict, 76
Anzaldúa, Gloria, 172n, 218
Aporia, 124, 213
Arias, Ron, 103, 126–31, 180; and fantasy, 103; and history, 103; realism in,
103
—*Road to Tamazunchale, The*, 126–30;
aesthetic base of, 129; consciousness
in, 129; dialectical method in, 129;
difference in, 129–30; East Los Angeles in, 127–28; fantasy in, 129, 131;
Faustian figure in, 128; history in,
129, 131; and Latin American novel,
126; magical realism in, 127; Quixote
figure in, 127–28; self-presence in,

128; song of life in, 127; symbolic
function in, 130; synthesis in, 128
Aristotle, 75
Arizona, 17, 19
Arkansas, 137
Asian-American literature, 205
Augustine, 154, 160–61, 192
Austin, J. L., 68
Authority, 76
Autobiography, 154–55, 157, 161–63,
167, 218; ethnic, 155; ideologies of,
155, 157; political, 155; rhetoric of,
155; women's 186, 188–98;

Bachelard, Gaston, 181n
Baker, Houston A., Jr., 63n, 157, 215,
217
Bakhtin, M. M., 37, 47, 75, 159–60, 169,
180, 206; on chronotope, 154, 165;
and dialogized heteroglossia, 192; on
heteroglossia, 168; and "internally
persuasive," word 196; and "word of
the fathers," 192, 197
Ballad and epic, 38
Barrera, Mario, 12n, 13, 17, 20
Baudrillard, Jean, 169, 180–81
Before Columbus Foundation American
Book Award, 181
Benjamin, Walter, 130, 154, 181
Bercovitch, Sacvan, 14n, 15, 209–10,
215–16; and dissensus, 215–16; and
ideological consensus, 209–10, 216,
218
Berg, Elizabeth, 179n
Bernstein, J. M., 36, 47–48
Beverly Hills, 160
Bloom, Harold, 73n
Booth, Wayne, 75
Border, 50–51, 75; conflict, 18, 26–
28, 30, 37, 133, 136; and corrido, 37;
culture, 17, 23, 25, 218; troubles,
50–52;
Border ballad, 6, 18, 19, 133, 135; heroic
epic, 35; ideological force of, 135
Brown Berets, 94–95
Brown, Claude, 154
Brownsville, Texas, 28–29, 50–51
Bruce-Novoa, 26n, 61n, 75, 77, 79, 111n
Bruss, Elizabeth W., 160

Calderón, Héctor, 96, 107–8, 111–12,
  118n, 121
Caliban, 155–57, 170
California, 17, 19, 26, 28, 61, 68, 92, 106,
  112, 137, 165, 180; agriculture in, 20;
  union organizing in, 19
Californios (native Mexicans of Califor-
  nia), 16
Cannery and Agricultural Workers
  Industrial Union (CAWIU), 69–70
Canon, 3, 204–5, 210, 218; formation,
  204–5
Cantú, Jovita, 38n
Cantú, Norma, 172n, 189n
Cantú, Roberto, 106, 110n
Capitalism, 17, 23, 82, 84–85, 90, 108,
  116, 119, 121, 124, 126, 134–37, 144;
  and family roles, 21; growth of Ameri-
  can, 18, 23; and patriarchy, 21, 183,
  187, 195, 197–98
Carby, Hazel, 197–98, 215
Carrasco, David, 107
Cartesian subject, 183, 185
Castillo, Adeliada del, 20n, 172n
Castillo, Ana, 199
Cervantes, Lorna Dee, 199
Chacón, Eusebio, 27n
Chavez, Denise, 199
Chicago, Illinois, 182
Chicana: and family roles, 19–21; femi-
  nism, 21, 171–99; in labor market,
  20–21; and union organizing, 21
Chicana authors, 71, 73, 171–99; binary
  oppositions in, 173; construction of
  identity in, 175; contra phallocentricism, 175; critique of patriarchy in,
  173, 180–81; dialectics in, 173, 175;
  ideology in, 173, 175; race and gender
  in, 173, 175, 180, 182; as resistance
  writers, 37, 173, 175; subject in, 181
Chicana narrative: metacritical function
  of, 173; as resistance, 173
Chicano: culture and patriarchy, 173,
  180; history, 4, 10–25; movement, 74,
  89, 92, 95; as self-identifying term, 12;
  and traditional family, 22
Chicano literature, 10, 135, 155, 205,
  212; literary history of, 7, 74, 171,
  204–5; semantic space of, 8; sexism
  in, 172

Chicano narrative, 47–50, 72–73, 171,
  204, 206, 211, 213–14, 217–18; and
  American literary history, 215–18;
  and aporia, 213; construction of
  identity in, 17, 62, 103, 173–74; and
  corrido, 32, 37, 39, 42, 47, 55, 103;
  and decentered subject, 174; dialectics
  of difference in, 173; and difference,
  173, 214; differential structure of,
  63, 72–73, 81, 218; folk base of, 42;
  history of, 47, 171, 217; identity in,
  211; and ideology, 4, 87, 104, 130–
  31, 206–215; imaginative geography
  of, 171; imaginative universe of, 26;
  interpretive model of, 10; literary history of, 70, 73; as oppositional form,
  210; origin of, 47–49; and patriarchal
  ideology, 59; paradigm of, 72–73; and
  phallocentric subject, 175; political
  function of, 25, 130; and realism, 126;
  representation of subject in, 175; as resistance literature, 4, 25, 50–51, 126,
  131, 213, 217–18; social context of,
  4, 136; subject position in, 218; and
  subjectivity, 173; symbolic function
  of, 25; theories of, 7; and Third World
  literature, 130; time and plot in, 37
Chicano National Moratoriums, 95
Chicano novel: and deconstruction,
  127; development of, 26–27; history
  and fiction in, 60; origin of, 60, 69;
  paradigm of, 72;
Choate, Boone, 32
Chronotope, 154, 164, 182, 218; defined,
  165
Cisneros, Sandra, 6, 175, 181–86, 199,
  213, 218; as winner of Before Columbus Foundation American Book
  Award, 181
—House on Mango Street, The, 181–
  6; "A House of My Own," 183–4;
  "Bums in the Attic," 183–4; chronotope in, 182; construction of gendered
  subject in, 181, 186; critique of patriarchy in, 181, 185–86; difference in,
  182, 184; domestic economy in, 183;
  gender and sexuality in, 182, 184;
  identity in, 183; ideology in, 181–82;
  "Mango Says Goodbye Sometimes,"
  184; metonymy in, 182; narrator in,

The House on Mango Street (continued)
181, 184; *oikonomia* in, 182, 184;
poetic self-creation in, 184; race in,
182, 186; "Red Clowns," 186; "Sally,"
185; sexual politics in, 182, 184–86;
subject position in, 182, 184; symbol
of house in, 184; "The Family of Little
Feet," 184; tropes in, 184; war of position in, 185; women's oppression in,
186
Cixous, Hélène, 179n
Class, 6, 22, 30, 35, 67–69, 79–80, 84,
115, 117, 131, 133, 211, 216; consciousness, 84, 89–90, 96, 137; and
corrido, 35, 40; and gender, 173, 180,
188, 193–99; struggle, 35, 42
Clément, Catherine, 179n
Collective unconscious, 103, 111, 120–
21
Colorado, 12, 17, 93
Colquitt, O. B., 33
Commodification, 49, 79, 85, 90, 134,
145
Commodity fetishism, 116
Conjunto music, 41; and social meaning, 41–42; as resistance form, 41
Consciousness, 104, 129–30, 190, 193–
95
Córdova, Teresa, 172n
Corrido, 27–42, 47–49, 59, 69, 71–72,
103, 108, 133, 136, 141, 146–47; authority in, 38, 48, 55, 58; and border
conflict, 28, 30, 37; and Chicano narrative, 18, 39; consciousness in, 136;
and epic, 47–48; as folk base of narrative, 73; as historicized life, 33; and
gender ideology, 38–40; hero, 18, 28,
35, 37, 136; heroic world view in, 38,
40; identity in, 36–37, 50, 62, 136; and
ideological analysis, 32; and ideology,
32, 38–40, 48; as male text, 38–39;
and narrative, 47–48, 55, 57, 59, 73,
77, 79–80; patriarchal ideology in,
38–39, 41, 59–60; performance of,
37–38; political imagination in, 37;
and political unconscious, 41; and
precapitalist forms, 37; race, class, and
gender in, 35, 40; as residual form,
39–42, 103; as resistance form, 31–42;
as socially symbolic act, 28, 32, 39;

stereotyped, 61, 71; subjectlessness in,
36; as subtext for narrative, 47; unity
of forms and themes, 37; and women,
38–39; world view in, 48, 58
"Corrido de General Cortina, El," 28
"Corrido de Gregorio Cortez, El," 26–28,
32, 35–37, 49, 133, 141, 147; text of,
34–35
"Corrido de José Mosqueda, El," 30
"Corrido de Kiansis, El," 28–29
"Corrido de los pronunciados, El,"
28–30
"Corrido de los sediciosos, El," 28, 31,
51
"Corrido de Rito Garcia, El," 28
Cortez, Gregorio, 26–42, 50, 136, 146;
and Rivera, 79
Cortina, Juan Nepomuceno, 28–29
Cotera, Marta, 172n
Crónicas diabólicas, 26
Crystal City, Texas, 77
Cultural productions, 73; use of, 134
Cultural studies, 3, 41, 132n, 154
Culture industry, 134–35

Dante, 160
Dasenbrock, Reed Way, 107
De la Rosa, Luis, 31
De Man, Paul, 63n; on autobiography,
161–63; on history, 164; on ideology,
212
De Tracy, Destutt, 208
Deconstruction, 3, 7, 82, 85, 111, 127,
173; political consequences of, 88
Derrida, Jacques, 63n, 64
Des Moines, Iowa, 86
Dialectic, 5, 7, 8, 10, 83–84, 164, 167–
69, 207; and gender, 173, 179–80; of
good and evil, 73, 83; and narrative,
206; of subject and object, 73, 84
Dialectics of difference, 4, 108, 129, 175,
217–18
Dialogism, 206, 215, 218
Dialogized heteroglossia, 192
Díaz, Porfirio, 29–30, 51n, 56n
Diegesis, 161, 176
Difference, 5, 7, 62, 67, 87, 96–97, 129–
30, 173, 175, 179, 190–91, 193, 214,
216–17; defined, 63; and identity, 179;
ideology of, 7, 8

Differential structure, 63, 66, 73, 81, 87, 96–97, 131, 173, 184, 192, 217–18; of Mexican American identity, 12–13

Dissensus, 214, 216–17

Division of labor, 144–45; in the home, 20; sexual, 20

Donnelley, Dyan, 105n

Douglass, Frederick, 154

Duban, James, 14n

Eagleton, Terry, 63n, 206, 210, 212

Eger, Ernestina, 49n

El Paso, Texas, 92–94

Emergent culture, 40, 42

Emerson, Ralph Waldo, 217

Entelechy, 180

Epic, 62; classical, 32, 36; and corrido, 32, 36, 47–48; and novel, 47–48

Escandón, José de, 17

Ethnic literature, 214, 216

Ethnicity, 134, 194; construction of, 216–17

False consciousness, 208–10, 212

Family, 20, 51; as site of political struggle, 21; social function of, 190–99

Fanon, Frantz, 23

Faulkner, William, 75

Feminism, 3, 4, 59, 175, 187, 193–99, 214–16; epistemology of, 193; politics of, 193; socialist, 21–22; Third World, 194–95, 198

Feuerbach, Ludwig, 67, 84

Fischer, Michael J., 155

Flores, Lauro, 80n, 89

Flores, Richard, 31

Florida, 15

Frankfurt School, 3, 133–35, 154

Franklin, Benjamin, 7

Freud, Sigmund, 179

Fuente, Pat de la, 80n

Fuentes, Carlos, 127

Fuss, Diana, 188n

Galarza, Ernesto, 6, 154–70, 182, 187, 218

—Barrio Boy, 155, 157, 163–70; acculturation in, 164, 167–68; binary opposition in, 168; chronotope in, 164–65; cogito in, 168; cognitive mapping in,

167; critical consciousness in, 170; critique of precritical ideologies, 169; dialectic in, 167–69; discursive mode of, 163; heteroglossia in, 168; historical self-explanation in, 168; history in, 163, 165, 168; identity in, 164, 167–69; ideology in, 165, 167, 169–70; as journey literature, 164; la raza in, 169; metaphor in, 167; narrative structure of, 163, 165; philosophical self-analysis in, 168; and picaresque novel, 164; poetic self-expression in, 168; private self in, 168–69; public self in, 168–69; representation in, 167; self-figuration in, 163; spatiality in, 167; subjectivity in, 168; symbolic function in, 164; temporality in, 164–65, 167; tropological structure of, 164

Galsworthy, John, 132

García, Catarino, 50

García, Margarito, 29

García, Mario T., 18–23

Garza, Catarino, 29

Gates, Henry Louis, Jr., 204–5, 215

Geertz, Clifford, 208–9, 212

Gender, 21–22, 173, 175, 179–82, 184, 188, 193–99, 208–9, 211, 212, 216; and corrido, 38; and gender politics, 175; and gendered subject, 194–99; social construction of, 22, 181, 193–99

Genette, Gérard, 176

Gilb, Dagoberto, 171

Glover, Robert, 33

Gómara, Francisco López de, 130

González-Berry, Erlinda, 80n

González, Genaro, 171

González, Rosalinda M., 20

Gorras Blancas, Las, 118

Goulden, Joseph C., 141n

Gramsci, Antonio, 24, 39–40, 133–34, 154; and autobiography, 155; on hegemony, 39; war of position, 133, 185, 187

Great Depression, 23–24, 42, 49, 118

Greimas, A. J., 123; and semiotic rectangle, 123

Griswold del Castillo, Richard A., 20n, 21n

Guadalupe, Virgin of, 106, 110, 115, 124–25, 189, 191

Guatemala, 94

Hagiography, 160, 168
Hall, Stuart, 3, 41, 134, 208–9
Harlow, Barbara, 172n
Hawthorne, Nathaniel, 217
Hebdige, Dick, 41
Hegel, G. W. F., 36, 126, 173–74
Hegemony, 4, 10, 17, 24, 38–40, 48, 85,
    103, 187–88, 214, 216; defined, 39;
    Gramsci on, 40
Heinzelman, Susan, 97n
Hernández, Guillermo E., 91n
Herrera-Sobek, María, 172n
Heteroglossia, 168
Higham, John, 209
Hinojosa, Rolando, 6, 26, 132–47,
    176, 218; allegory in, 133; "Belken
    County," 132, 137; Claros Varones de
    Belken (Fair Gentlemen of Belken),
    132; collective life in, 141, 145; con-
    sciousness in, 141; and corrido, 133;
    and folk art, 133, 135; and narrative
    verse, 136; history in 140–41, 145;
    Klail City y sus alrededores (Klail
    City), 132, 146; Klail City Death Trip
    Series, 132, 136, 140; Mi Querido Rafa
    (Dear Rafe), 132; narrative verse, 133;
    Partners in Crime, 132; representation
    of class and race in, 133; resistance in,
    133; Rites and Witnesses, 132
—Estampas del Valle (The Valley), 132,
    137–141; "Braulio Tapia," 139–40;
    genealogy in, 140; history in, 140–
    41; identity in, 140–41; ideology
    in, 137, 140; metaphor in, 139, 141;
    metonymy in, 139, 141; narrative
    structure, 137, 140–41; narrator in,
    140; realism in, 137; temporality in,
    137, 140–41
—Korean Love Songs, 132–37, 141–47
    and corrido, 133, 135–36, 141, 146–
    47; and folk art, 133; class and race
    in, 131; class consciousness in, 137;
    collective life in, 141, 145, 147; hero
    in, 141; history in, 145; identity in,
    136, 141, 143–44; ideology in, 133,
    147; and modernism, 133, 137; social
    justice in, 135, 146; subjectivity in,
    144; symbolic function in, 133, 135,
    147; utopian vision in, 143, 145

Hirst, Paul, 211–12
Hispano: as self-identifying term, 12
History, 5, 10–25, 48, 55, 60, 67–73, 77,
    84, 90, 103, 105, 106–9, 112, 114–15,
    117, 121, 125–26, 129, 133, 140–41,
    145, 154, 157, 160, 165, 168; and Chi-
    cano narrative, 19; and corrido, 33;
    devaluing of, 24; and difference, 64;
    and gender, 20; and ideology, 19, 207,
    209–12, 216–17; Mexican American,
    10–25; as subtext, 207; and women's
    oppression, 180–84, 189–99
Hobsbawm, Eric J., 30
Horkheimer, Max, 133–35

Idaho, 93
Identity, 18, 70–1, 77, 82, 85, 103, 117,
    136, 140–41, 143–44, 162, 164, 167–
    68; Chicano, 12; in corrido, 32; con-
    struction of, 68; decentered, 144; and
    ideology, 207, 209, 211; politics of,
    175–77; social construction of, 175;
    and women, 173–75, 177, 178–79,
    181, 190–91
Ideological analysis, 7, 32, 85, 87–88,
    207, 213–14
Ideological consensus, 209–10, 216, 218
Ideology, 5–7, 10, 15, 52, 70, 76, 90, 97–
    98, 104, 126, 129, 133, 135, 140, 147,
    154, 157–58, 165, 167, 169, 206–18;
    and aesthetics, 170; defined, 167, 210–
    15; and family, 21; function of, 39; and
    narrative, 206–18; production of, 8; of
    resistance, 30; of socially constructed
    sex-gender roles, 21; and subject, 104;
    and women's roles, 22, 178, 191–92,
    196–99
Illinois, 137
Imaginary function, 4, 6, 98, 167, 210,
    212–13
Imaginative geography, 4, 171
Imaginative universe, 25
Imagined communities, 76
Indiana, 137
Individualism: ideology of, 76, 90
Islas, Arturo, 171

Jalcocotán, México, 163, 165
Jameson, Fredric, 4, 37, 39, 63n, 83, 92,
    97–98, 103, 108, 134, 207–8, 211, 213,
    216; on cognitive mapping, 167,

183; and difference, 131; on expressive causality, 216; on history, 211; on ideology, 208; and ideological formations, 124; materiality of language, 129; metacommentary, 108; national allegory 131; and political unconscious, 108, 124n, 130, 211, 214, 216; on reification, 134; and semiotic rectangle, 123

JanMohamed, Abdul, 63n
Japan, 136–37, 141–44
Jay, Paul, 160
Jayawardena, Kumari, 195
Johnson, Barbara, 63n, 179n
Johnson, Elaine, 106
Juarez, Benito, 14
Juarez, México, 93
Jung, Carl, 111

Kahn, Coppelia, 179n
Kansas, 29
Kant, Immanuel, 134, 173
Kingston, Maxine Hong, 154
Knowledge, 6, 90; structures of, 7
Kolakowski, Leszek, 208
Korea, 79, 133, 135–37, 141, 144–46
Korean War, 23, 24, 48n, 133, 135, 146

La Llorona, 107, 113–14, 122, 125, 189
La Malinche, 189
La raza, 89–90, 95, 169
Labor, 85, 88, 111, 114, 118, 121, 134, 144–45; black slave, 17; early Chicano, 39; Mexican immigrant, 18, 23; Mexican wage, 17; market, 19; migratory, 20; struggles, 49–50, 70, 74, 77, 85, 88, 95; unions, 69–70
Lacan, Jacques, 212
Laredo, Texas, 33
Latin America, 4, 8, 25
Latino: as self-identifying term, 12
Lattin, Vernon E., 107
Lauter, Paul, 215
Leal, Luis, 49n
Leary, Timothy, 93
Lentricchia, Frank, 72, 169, 207, 212
Lesbian, 4, 188–89, 191–93, 195, 214, 216
Liga Femenil Mexicanista, 21
Limón, José E., 13n, 21n, 26–27, 32, 39–40, 59n, 72

Lipsitz, George, 39n
Literature, 7; English departments of, 3, 204–5; function of, 7; marginal, 6, 204; regional, 6; Spanish departments of, 3, 204–5
Lizárraga, Sylvia, 80n
Lomas, Clara, 171n
Lomelí, Francisco, 27n, 49n, 176n
Longoria de Flores, Petra, 38n
Los Alamos, 121
Los Angeles: colonial, 13; East Los Angeles, 92, 94–95, 127–28; Laguna Park demonstration, 95
Lukács, Georg, 42, 47, 194; and realism, 76; on reification, 89–90; Theory of the Novel, 58
Luna-Lawhn, Juanita, 172n

Macherey, Pierre, 214
MacKinnon, Katherine, 193–94, 197
Malcolm X, 154
Mallarmé, Stéphane, 98
Manifest destiny, 17
Marcuse, Herbert, 145n
Martin, Biddy, 198
Martínez, José Antonio E., 117, 127n
Martínez, Julio A., 49n
Martinez, Max, 171
Marvin, George, 52
Marx, Karl, 67, 134, 144, 145n, 174, 208
Marxist criticism, 3
Mass culture: theories of, 3
Matthiessen, F. O., 217
Mazatlán, México, 163, 165
McCracken, Ellen, 172n, 181n
McDowell, John Holmes, 27, 32, 38
McLemore, Dale S., 13–17, 23, 118
McMurtry, Larry, 75
McNeil, Norman Laird, 30
McWilliams, Carey, 13, 117
Meaning: construction of, 4, 7, 72–3
Mehlman, Jeffrey, 160
Melville, Margarita, 20n
Méndez, Miguel, 171
Mendoza, Lydia, 39n
Mestizo, 13, 116; society, 14
Metacommentary, 108
Metaphor, 139, 141, 167
Metonymy, 88, 139, 141, 182
Mexican American: representation of, 76

Mexican American women: in labor force, 20; in nineteenth century, 20; and traditional family structures, 20–21. See also Chicanas

Mexican Revolution, 24, 30, 35, 54, 60–62, 163, 189

Mexican-American War, 12, 17

Mexicano: as self-identifying term, 12

Michigan, 137

Minnesota, 86–87

Minneapolis, 86

Mirandé, Alfredo, 20–21

Misogyny, 197

Missouri, 137

Mode of production, 41, 112, 116

Modernism, 133, 137

Modleski, Tania, 59

Monleón, José A., 118

Monsiváis, Carlos, 127n

Montaigne, Michel de, 156

Montana, 93

Montejano, David, 12n, 16, 28, 32, 49–50, 51n

Monterrey, México, 31

Moquin, Wayne, 18

Moraga, Cherríe, 6, 172n, 175, 186–99, 213, 215, 218

—Loving in the War Years, 186–99; "A Long Line of Vendidas," 194–99; Adelitas in, 189; aesthetics of resistance in, 187, 193; allegory in, 189; authoritative discourses in, 193, 197; as autobiography, 186, 188–98; binarism in, 198; capitalism, 197–98; Catholicism in, 189, 191, 193, 197; Chicana feminism in, 195–99; class and gender in, 188, 193–94; class and race in, 188, 193–94; consciousness in, 190, 193–94; as critique of patriarchy, 187, 197–99; difference in, 190, 193; and ethnicity, 191–92, 194; feminism in, 187, 193–99; gender and race in, 188, 191–99; gender and consciousness in, 194; gender and construction of, 195; gender and politics of, 194; gendered "woman" in, 194; gendered subject in, 187, 193–95; Guadalupe, Virgin of in, 189, 191; on heterosexuality, 192, 197; history in, 189; history of oppression of Chicanas, 189; history of the

family, 195; and homophobia, 198; icons of Mexican womanhood in, 189; identity in, 191–99; identity politics in, 191; ideology in, 191, 196–99; internal dialogue in, 192; interpellation of subject in, 195–96; la Llorona in, 189; lesbianism in, 188–89, 191–93, 195–98; Malinche in, 189; on misogyny, 197; motherland of harmony in, 191, 195; mothers and daughters in, 190–91, 195; on objectification of women, 193–94; and phallocentricism, 191; policing of desire in, 195; politics of love in, 187, 193, 195–96; role of family in, 189, 197–99; role of father in, 192; sexual difference in, 197–99; subject-formation in, 187, 198; Third World feminism in, 191, 194–95, 198; as war of position, 187; word of the father in, 197; writing as politics in, 190, 199

Morales, Alejandro, 171

Morris, W. T. (Sheriff), 32

Morrison, Toni, 204–5, 215

Mosqueda, José, 30

Music, 58–59; industry, 40, 50, 59; popular, 50

Myth, 108–9, 112–16, 123, 125

Narrative, 5, 75–77, 80, 97–98, 104, 123; analysis of, 5, 10, 206; and dialectics, 205–8; and history, 25; and ideology, 208–15; as oppositional form, 6; as socially symbolic act, 70–72, 206; forms, 3, 5, 7; ideological function of, 4–6; master, 131; structure, 7, 205

Native American, 4, 12–13, 107, 118, 120, 126, 210, 217; literature, 205

Navarro, José Antonio, 16

Nelson, Cary, 215

Neruda, Pablo, 127

Nevada, 17

New Jerusalem, 210, 217

New Mexico, 12, 17, 19, 103–4, 106, 116–17; history of, 109, 115–18, 120, 125

Nieto, Eva Margarita, 129

Nietzsche, Friedrich, 8, 83

Nogales, Arizona, 163, 165

Norias, Texas: raid on, 31

Novel, 47, 69, 74–76, 130, 206; and
the real, 60, 69; and realism, 69; and
temporality, 69
Nuevo Santander, 17, 27

Oikonomia, 182, 184
Oklahoma, 137
Olivares, Julián, 80n, 181n
Olmito, Texas: train derailment in, 31,
53
Olney, James, 160
Oxnard, California, 176

Padilla, Genaro, 172n
Panama, 92
Paredes, Américo, 6, 11–12, 17–18, 47–
60, 70–73, 103, 105, 107n, 108, 117,
126, 135, 137, 213, 218; and Chicano
narrative, 74, 76, 79; and corrido, 26–
42, 32; and feminist consciousness,
59; George Washington Gomez, 48n;
"Hammon and the Beans, The," 48,
50–55; Jonesville-on-the-Grande, 51–
52; as organic intellectual, 72–73;
patriarchal values in, 59; political consciousness in, 72; portrait of the artist
in, 57; radical politics in, 55; resistance in, 55; and Rivera, 79; With His
Pistol in His Hand 26, 32–37, 47–60;
women's song in, 59
—"Over the Waves Is Out," 55–60;
fathers and sons in, 55, 57, 59; generational conflict in, 55; history in, 59;
narrator in, 50, 55; theme of music in,
56–60
Paredes, Raymond, 49n
Pastoral, 159, 161, 168
Patriarchy, 21, 38–39, 41, 59; and Chi-
cano culture, 175, 178–81, 185–87,
189–99; in colonial New Mexico, 117
Peña, Manuel, 50, 59n; and The Texas
Mexican Conjunto, 41
Peru, 127
Phallocentricism, 175, 191
Picaresque novel, 164
Pierce, Frank Cushman, 30
Pizaña, Aniceto, 31, 50–53
Plan de San Diego, 30
Political unconscious, 4, 41, 77, 108,
121, 130, 211. See also Jameson,
Fredric

Powell, Anthony, 132
Precapitalist modes of production:
aesthetic, 37, 41
Proust, Marcel, 132
Puritans, 210, 217; ideology of, 210

Quintana, Alvina, 172n
Quinto Sol Prize, 74, 104

Race, 22, 79, 133–34, 145–46, 211, 216;
and gender, 173, 180, 182, 186, 192–99
Radhakrishnan, R., 168
Raza Unida, La (political party), 77
Reagan, Ronald, 198
Real, 47, 127, 206, 210–12; narrativiza-
tion of, 131; structures of, 5, 6
Realism, 75–76, 88, 103, 106, 108, 126–
27; ideology of, 76; and Lukács, 76
Rebolledo, Tey Diana, 80n, 172n
Rechy, John, 171
Reification, 42, 134, 205, 207
Residual culture, 40–42, 47, 52
Resistance, 3, 5, 7, 19, 24, 27, 41–42,
49–52, 103; and corrido, 30–42, 48–
49; and narrative, 42, 79–80; in New
Mexico, 118; songs of cultural, 28,
30–42; symbolic, 41; women's, 175,
181–99
Resistance literature, 25, 217–18
Retamar, Roberto Fernández, 157
Rhetoric, 5, 205, 207
Ricouer, Paul, 84, 109n
Rio Grande Valley, Texas, 50, 132, 141
Ríos, Alberto, 171
Ríos, Isabella (Diane Lopez), 6, 155,
176–181, 199
—Victuum, 176–81; dialectics in, 179;
diegetic narrative in, 176; differential
structure in, 180; entelechy in, 180;
feminine voices in, 176–78; gender
formation in, 178–79; history in, 181,
190; identity in, 177–78; ideology
in, 178; mothers and daughters in,
179–80; narrative structure of, 176–
77; patriarchy in, 177–78; realism in,
176; role of family in, 177–79; role of
father in, 177, 179–80; role of mother
in, 178–80; subject position in, 178;
symbiosis in, 179; symbolic function
in, 180; utopian vision in, 178

Rivera, Tomás, 6, 26, 49, 74–90, 103, 105, 108, 126, 128, 132n, 176, 218; and corrido, 79–80; on history, 77, 79, 82–85, 90; interview with, 77, 79; and narrative experimentation, 75–6, 85; and Paredes, 79; and prose style, 74–76, 85–88; and realism, 75–76, 88, 90; and resistance, 77, 79

—Y no se lo trago la tierra, 74–90; alienation in, 85, 90; allegory in, 77, 79, 84, 88; alternative social formation in, 83; binary structures in, 81; capitalism in, 82, 84–85, 90; Cartesian cogito in, 79; Catholicism in, 81–82; class consciousness in, 80, 84, 89; commodification in, 79, 85, 90; consciousness in, 79, 82, 85; construction of meaning in, 83; construction of subject in, 82, 84–85, 89; critique of idealism in, 84; "Cuando lleguemos," 86–88; "Debajo de la casa," 88–90; deconstruction in, 82, 85, 88; dialectic in, 82–84, 88; dialectical analysis in, 89; difference in, 87; differential structure in, 81–82; existentialism in, 80, 83, 85; good and evil in, 83, 85; and hegemony, 85; hermeneutic circle in, 79; identity in, 77, 82, 85–90; ideological function of, 77, 80–81, 85, 87–88, 90; "La noche estaba plateada," 79–81; la raza in, 89–90; labor struggles in, 74, 77, 82; and literary history, 74; metonymy in, 88; narrator in, 75, 77, 79, 86, 89–90; and the political unconscious, 77; political struggles in, 77–78; reification in, 80, 90; representation of farmworker, 75, 87; self-determination in, 84; sexuality in, 79; social being in, 83; as socially symbolic act, 79; South Texas in, 75, 82, 89; stream-of-consciousness in, 75; subjectivity in, 82, 84–86, 88–90; under erasure, 89; unity of, 75, 89; utopian vision in, 74, 85–86, 88, 90; and will to power, 79, 83; working class in, 85, 89; "y no se lo trago la tierra," 82–85

Robinson, Cecil, 76n
Rodríguez, Juan, 26n, 49n, 80n

Rodriguez, Richard, 136, 155–70, 176, 187–89, 195

—Hunger of Memory, 155–63, 169–70; and affirmative action, 158–59; assimilation in, 168; on bilingual education, 158–59; Caliban in, 155–56, 160; Catholicism in, 157; as fiction, 162; as hagiography, 160; and history, 160; historical self-explanation in, 160–61; identity in, 158; ideology in, 7, 28, 157–58; modes of figuration in, 162–63; myth of individuality in, 169; narrative structure of, 158–60, 163–64; as pastoral, 159, 161; philosophical self-analysis in, 160; poetic self-expression in, 161; political consequences of, 159; private self in, 157–59, 161; public self in, 158–59, 161; race in, 160; subjectivity in, 160, 162; The Tempest in, 155–56; textual self in, 162

Rogers, Jane, 106–7
Rogin, Paul, 17
Romance genre, 104, 107–8, 111, 121, 123, 126, 131, 159
Romo, Ricardo, 13–17, 23, 118
Rosaldo, Renato, 71, 168
Rosas, Juventino, 56n
Rosenbaum, Robert J., 17
Rousseau, Jean-Jacques, 160–61
Ruiz, Vicki, 17, 20n
Rulfo, Juan, 75
Rushdie, Salman, 180
Ryan, Michael, 3, 63n, 161

Sacramento, California, 157, 165
Said, Edward W., 49n, 171
Saldívar, José D., 79, 80, 83n, 84, 129n, 132n, 172n
Saldívar, Ramón, 206
Saldívar-Hull, Sonia, 172n, 175
San Diego, Texas, 29, 31
San Francisco, 66
San Jose, California, 69
Sánchez, George, 13, 117
Sánchez, Rosaura, 20, 132–33, 172n
Sandinista revolution, 94
Santa Clara Valley, 62, 69
Schnabel, Henry, 33

Seguín, Juan, 16
Semiotic, 5; rectangle, 123
Sexism, 172, 198
Sexuality, 175, 184–99
Shakespeare, William: *The Tempest*,
  156–57
Slotkin, Richard, 14n
Socially symbolic acts, 2, 173, 206, 214;
  corrido as, 19, 28, 32
Sollors, Werner, 215–17
Sommers, Joseph, 90
Southwest, 3, 5, 11–12, 24, 60, 75, 217;
  American hegemony in, 69; capitalist
  development in, 18, 23, 19, 40, 42; as
  colonized land, 13; control of the, 39;
  corrido in the, 28; division of labor in,
  16; fight for civil rights in, 33; history
  of, 108, 126; ideological transformation of, 17; Mexican immigrants in,
  17–18, 168; racial and class differences
  in, 17–18; Republic of the, 31; resistance in, 29–42; slavery in, 17; U.S.
  expansion into, 15; violence in, 51
Southwest, colonial, 116, 126; Africans
  in, 12; American Indians in, 13; blacks
  in, 13; mulattoes in, 13; Sephardic
  Jews in, 13; Spanish in, 14
Spanish American, as self-identifying
  term, 12
Spengemann, William G., 160
Spivak, Gayatri Chakravorty, 63n, 179,
  182
Stendhal (Henri Beyle), 208
Structuralism, 3
Subject, 5, 67, 160–63, 168, 211–13,
  218; construction of, 50, 103, 211–13,
  218; construction of Chicana, 173–75,
  178–81, 182–86, 186–99; decentering
  of, 212
Sweeney, Judith, 21n
Symbolic function, 3–5, 25, 37–39, 48–
  50, 55, 67, 98, 103–4, 108, 120, 124,
  130, 133, 136, 164, 169, 211, 213–14;
  and forms of resistance, 30–31, 38;
  and oppositional discourse, 37; and
  women, 175, 183

Tamaulipas, México, 29
Taos, New Mexico, 117

Tatum, Charles, 49n, 126n
Taussig, Michael T., 116
Tejanos (Texas Mexicans), 15; as ethnic
  minority, 16
Texas, 18–19, 27, 30, 32, 75, 86–87,
  137, 141, 146; cotton cultivation in,
  20; fight for civil rights in, 33, 39;
  province of, 14–15; Republic of, 16
Texas, South, 12, 49–51, 75, 82, 89–90,
  132, 136, 143, 146–47; agriculture in,
  31; ranching economy in, 42; sedi-
  tion in, 31, 34, 39; train robbery in,
  30; U.S. annexation of, 15–16; union
  organizing in, 19; violence in, 42
Texas Rangers (*rinches*), 18, 30–31, 35,
  39, 51–53
Therborn, Göran, 212–13, 216
Third World, 4, 24, 157, 191, 218; litera-
  ture, 131; feminism, 194–95, 198
Thompson, E. P., 207
Thompson, Hunter, 90, 93
Thoreau, Henry David, 217
Treaty of Guadalupe Hidalgo, 16, 18
Trollope, Anthony, 132
Tropes, 182–84
Truth, 5, 8, 207, 210–11
Tucker, Robert C., 66n
Tucson, Arizona, 163, 165

Ulíca, Jorge, 26
Utah, 17
Utopian vision, 74, 85, 88, 90, 98, 115,
  118, 126, 143, 145, 213; women's, 174,
  178

Valdes, Gina, 199
Valenzuela, Liliana, 189n
VanSant, M. E., xii
Villa, Francisco, 54–55, 57, 61
Villarreal, José Antonio, 6, 47, 50, 60–
  72, 74, 76, 103, 105, 126, 155; and
  Chicano narrative, 64, 79; and corrido,
  60–61, 71; patriarchal ideology in,
  60–61, 70–72
—*Pocho*, 47, 50, 60–72; absolute value
  in, 60–72; Catholicism in, 62, 64–65;
  communist activism in, 64, 69–70;
  consciousness in, 72; construction
  of subject in, 67; death wish in, 67;

Villarreal, José Antonio *(continued)*
dialectic in, 66; difference in, 62–64,
67, 70, 72; differential structure in, 63,
66; family in, 62, 70–72; fathers and
sons in, 66; gender in, 62, 70–71; good
and evil in, 62–63; Great Depression
in, 68; history in, 64, 66, 72; homo-
sexuality in, 62; identity in, 61, 68,
71; individualism in, 66, 68; as model
text, 72; Mexican Revolution in, 61–
62; narrative stratagem, 61; politics of
change in, 62, 64, 70; political unconscious in, 61; and racism, 62; realism
in, 60, 65; portrait of the artist in, 62;
sexual identity in, 62, 71; symbolic
function in, 67; transformational criticism in, 66; utopian vision in, 69; will
to power in, 61; women in, 70–72
Viramontes, Helena María, 172n, 199
Vogel, Lise, 179
Volosinov, V. N., 197, 199, 209

War of 1812, 15

West, 12, 42, 75, 93; invention of Ameri-
can, 75–76
Whitman, Walt, 217
Will to power, 8, 61, 79, 83
Williams, Raymond, 10, 208, 216;
counterhegemony, 40; emergent cul-
ture, 40; hegemony, 40; *Marxism and
Literature*, 40; residual culture, 40–41
Wolf, Eric R., 189n
Working class, 216–17; and hegemony,
40; world view, 38
World War II, 23, 24, 42, 48n, 49, 68, 74–
75, 104, 106, 109, 111, 113–15, 118,
125, 133, 146

Xipetotec, 127

Yarbro-Bejarano, Yvonne, 172n

Zapata, Emiliano, 54–55, 61
Zavella Patricia, 20n, 21–2, 70

The Wisconsin Project on American Writers

A series edited by Frank Lentricchia

F. O. Matthiessen and the Politics of Criticism
William E. Cain

In Defense of Winters: The Poetry and Prose of Yvor Winters
Terry Comito

A Poetry of Presence: The Writing of William Carlos Williams
Bernard Duffey

Selves at Risk: Patterns of Quest in Contemporary American Letters
Ihab Hassan

Reading Faulkner
Wesley Morris with Barbara Alverson Morris

*Repression and Recovery: Modern American Poetry and the
Politics of Cultural Memory, 1910–1945*
Cary Nelson

Lionel Trilling: The Work of Liberation
Daniel T. O'Hara

*Visionary Compacts: American Renaissance Writings
in Cultural Context*
Donald E. Pease

"A White Heron" and the Question of Minor Literature
Louis A. Renza

The Theoretical Dimensions of Henry James
John Carlos Rowe

Chicano Narrative: The Dialectics of Difference
Ramón Saldívar

The Dickinson Sublime
Gary Lee Stonum

The American Evasion of Philosophy: A Genealogy of Pragmatism
Cornel West

Specifying: Black Women Writing the American Experience
Susan Willis